The Practice of
Musical Improvisation

The Practice of Musical Improvisation

Dialogues with Contemporary Musical Improvisers

Edited by Bertrand Denzler and Jean-Luc Guionnet

BLOOMSBURY ACADEMIC
NEW YORK • LONDON • OXFORD • NEW DELHI • SYDNEY

BLOOMSBURY ACADEMIC
Bloomsbury Publishing Inc
1385 Broadway, New York, NY 10018, USA
50 Bedford Square, London, WC1B 3DP, UK
29 Earlsfort Terrace, Dublin 2, Ireland

BLOOMSBURY, BLOOMSBURY ACADEMIC and the Diana logo
are trademarks of Bloomsbury Publishing Plc

First published in the United States of America 2020
Paperback edition first published 2021

Volume Editors' Part of the Work © Bertrand Denzler and Jean-Luc Guionnet, 2020
Each chapter © of Contributor

For legal purposes the Acknowledgments on p. vi constitute
an extension of this copyright page.

Cover design: Louise Dugdale
Cover image © age fotostock / Alamy Stock Photo

All rights reserved. No part of this publication may be reproduced or
transmitted in any form or by any means, electronic or mechanical,
including photocopying, recording, or any information storage or retrieval
system, without prior permission in writing from the publishers.

Bloomsbury Publishing Inc does not have any control over, or responsibility for,
any third-party websites referred to or in this book. All internet addresses given
in this book were correct at the time of going to press. The author and publisher
regret any inconvenience caused if addresses have changed or sites have
ceased to exist, but can accept no responsibility for any such changes.

Library of Congress Cataloging-in-Publication Data
Names: Denzler, Bertrand, editor. | Guionnet, Jean-Luc, 1966-editor.
Title: The practice of musical improvisation: dialogues with contemporary
musical improvisers / edited by Bertrand Denzler and Jean-Luc Guionnet.
Description: [1st.] | New York: Bloomsbury Academic, 2020. |
Includes bibliographical references and index. |
Summary: "A range of 50 musical improvisers discuss the complex processes
at work in their practice."–Provided by publisher.
Identifiers: LCCN 2019025890 (print) | LCCN 2019025891 (ebook) |
ISBN 9781501349768 (hardback) | ISBN 9781501349775 (epub) | ISBN 9781501349782 (pdf)
Subjects: LCSH: Improvisation (Music)–Psychological aspects. | Music–Performance–
Psychological aspects. | Improvisation (Music) | Musicians–Interviews.
Classification: LCC ML3838. P94 2020 (print) | LCC ML3838 (ebook) | DDC 781.3/6–dc23
LC record available at https://lccn.loc.gov/2019025890
LC ebook record available at https://lccn.loc.gov/2019025891

ISBN: HB: 978-1-5013-4976-8
PB: 978-1-5013-8465-3
ePDF: 978-1-5013-4978-2
eBook: 978-1-5013-4977-5

Typeset by Deanta Global Publishing Services, Chennai, India

To find out more about our authors and books visit
www.bloomsbury.com and sign up for our newsletters.

Contents

Acknowledgements	vi
Preface	vii

1	Starting an improvisation	1
2	The mental state during an improvisation	5
3	Listening to the other musicians, the human factor, the strategies	17
4	Memory and form	61
5	Process versus aesthetic result, improvisation as a tool to make music versus music as a tool to improvise, improvisation versus composition	77
6	Talking about improvisation and music in general	111
7	Non-idiomatic improvisation, experimental music, genre labels	115
8	Silence and dynamics	119
9	Sounds as material	123
10	Instrument and technique	131
11	Solo improvisation	147
12	The concert situation, the audience, the published recordings	151
13	Some political issues	163
14	How I came to play this music	169
15	How I listen to music, the music I listen to, some hidden gardens	177
16	Miscellaneous	191

List of the musicians interviewed	193
An ear for discord: Improvise, they say	195
Diagrams	208

Acknowledgements

Translation of the French interviews by Jack Sims.

The translation was made possible thanks to financial support from 'Musical Improvisation and Collective Action' (ANR-17-CE27-0021), an ANR JCJC project directed by Clément Canonne (CNRS-IRCAM-Sorbonne Université) and additional financial support from Babbel Productions (Paris), Jazz à Poitiers (Poitiers) and Muzzix (Lille).

The editors would like to thank Olivier Rodriguez, Adrien Chiquet, Erica Saïdah, Owen Martell, Will Guthrie, Nicolas Lefort, Jade McInally, Alex Savatovsky, Sarah Louise Phelan, Clémentine Blondeau, Sophie Agnel, Dan Warburton, Marc Baron, Nicolas Durand, Alister Keene Mew, Mathilde Coupeau, Clare Cooper, Louis Griffin Center, Jacques Oger, Pierre-Antoine Badaroux and Jean-Sébastien Mariage who helped transcribe the interviews; Christoph Cox, Clément Canonne, Matthieu Saladin, Philip Samartzis and Dan Warburton for their support; and all the musicians who participated in this project.

Preface

In music, improvisation has always played a central role. But as far as we know, terms such as 'free improvisation', 'free music' or 'improvised music' first appeared in the 1960s to designate a new musical movement whose actors did nothing other than improvise. The stated goal of these new improvisers was to invent their music at the very instant when it was heard, in real time and *in situ*.

Towards the end of the 1990s, especially in Europe, Japan and the United States, a new generation of musical improvisers emerged, which seemed to operate a break with the ones before. To reflect this development, new appellations such as 'lowercase improvisation', 'minimal improvisation' or 'electroacoustic improvisation (EAI)' began to spread.

However, these appellations are blurry and problematic. How can we know if an improvisation or even music itself is free or not? What exactly is freedom in music? Does total, absolute, pure improvisation exist? Is 'improvised music' always opposed to 'composed music'? When can music be considered minimal, and in comparison to what? Does the addition or the predominance of electric or electronic instruments justify the use of the word 'electroacoustic'? And so on.

In his book *Improvisation: Its Nature and Practice in Music*, Derek Bailey uses the term 'non-idiomatic improvisation', which adds clarity as it suggests that one of the specificities of this music is that it doesn't belong *a priori* to any particular musical idiom. The term allows a better understanding of an important issue of this practice, but is itself subject to multiple interpretations which would need to be differentiated from each other.

Therefore the problem remains unsolved. Attaching a label to music in order to reflect an affiliation to a style always raises many questions, especially concerning the boundaries of the genre in question. In the field we are interested in here, defining the mentioned styles and sub-genres is even more difficult, as this music is from the outset situated at the crossroads of countless ancient and recent musical aesthetics, traditions and cultures.

When talking about music, something always seems to elude us. And for the musical movement we are looking at here, the difficulty is even greater, as it seems impossible to name this movement satisfactorily – even though we know it exists. There is also another issue: in this case, the very notions of music and improvisation can be questioned. Is it still music? Or something else? Or a mere pretext for improvising? Is it truly improvised? Where does improvisation begin and end? Is improvisation a mere pretext for making music?

These terminological issues may reflect something else. Musicians often feel, especially when they improvise, that musical analysis doesn't possess an adequate set of tools to specify the processes at work in their music. When listening to an improvisation, it is obviously possible to describe the instruments and the techniques that are being used, or to analyse the sounds and the form of the piece. But how can one talk accurately about the space in which the music is solely produced by the relationships which develop, instantly and throughout the piece, between the sounds as well as between the people generating them? Here, the main problem seems to be that analysis always occurs *a posteriori* and from the outside, on the basis of the result, without telling us what is happening at the very instant this 'real-time music' is being created.

In order to find out more, we decided to meet the musicians themselves and to dialogue with improvisers from all generations and from various geographical and aesthetic backgrounds. We asked them to describe their praxis, to tell us what they think or believe they are doing when they play, to share their points of view, their opinions, their convictions. Located between an improbable experimental folklore of oral tradition and the erudite idiom of an idealized postmodern musician, the reality of improvised music is inhabited by a thicket of imprecise concepts. The goal therefore was to test the idea of musical improvisation and its multiple paradoxes in the field, and to see what could be said about it in the heat of the discussion. We wanted to address improvisation through its environment – almost in the mesological sense of the word: the habits and customs of a practice, as experienced by those who invent it on a daily basis.

We met around fifty musicians between 2003 and 2011. The body of the collected interviews can therefore be seen as a portrait of this period, a concentrate of what musical improvisers were able to say at that time about their praxis. But, for us, it also reveals some of the questions which have arisen since musical improvisation came into existence.

On transcribing the interviews, we noticed that in fact the collection of answers – as radically personal as they are – sketched the map of the territory of contemporary improvised music. This is why we chose to create a montage of excerpts from the interviews and to place them in dialogue with each other, in order to produce a sort of grand discussion – a form that, in our opinion, also reflects the way this musical practice works. At the end of each quotation, a number identifies the speaker, allowing two ways of reading the book: it is possible to reconstruct the discourse of one musician in particular, or to consider each quotation as a mere spot on the map. The list of musicians can be found at the end of the book.

B. Denzler & J.-L. Guionnet

1

Starting an improvisation

Often, I decide before a concert that I'm going to play this or that area of material at the beginning. But I bend how I play it depending on what the other musicians are doing. For example, today I decided to concentrate on noise. So no matter what you were doing, I was going to stick with my material but bend it so that hopefully it would work with what you were doing. I think I made that decision earlier because I don't like it when a group starts and there's one person who starts and you're thinking: 'What do I do with this?' It's an inevitable, slow process – the group getting into gear. In order to overcome that, I always have an idea of what I'm going to do. Sometimes though I change my mind completely … . [04B]

I think a crucial moment is the beginning of a piece. You don't know if and how the other musicians will start and how this will relate to how you start. You can either make a decision ('now I'm going to start') and then you'll see how it comes together with what the others do – maybe you're alone or somebody else starts at the same time and it's unpredictable how these two sounds come together – or wait until somebody else starts and you can connect to something that's already there. I try to vary it deliberately. Sometimes, a few minutes before the concert starts, I think: 'Tonight I should start with this', and sometimes I actually play that sound. But if I'm walking on stage and have had no thoughts about it a couple of minutes before, I try not to think about those things at that point. On stage, however, concentrating, just before starting, there are so many aspects of the actual situation that come to me that I might recognize that what I thought beforehand is not a good idea. So I skip the initial idea and start in another way. Or I alter my initial idea.

Quite often, during the day of the concert, I'm more or less already kind of working myself towards the moment of starting to play. Sometimes it's very conscious, sometimes it's rather subconscious. I'm already concentrating.

Thinking about the group we're going to play with in the evening, I try to make myself aware of the elements that are relevant in this group context and, even more, what is not relevant, what I should leave out or which preparations and objects I shouldn't bring with me. It's about coming to the concert with an awareness of what that group is for me or the fields we are working in, the sound of the group, the range of structures, the energy and so on. But if it becomes too specific, if you have too many clear elements, this can be a disadvantage for the concert. So I try not to do that too much. It's kind of unavoidable to think about these things but I don't force it. I don't want to anticipate the music too much. [44]

The first sound, of course, is important. And in a group situation, who makes that first sound is very important. What can that first sound be? It can be anything, of course. We're interested in the chance, the arbitrary, almost, because we feel confident that we can make sense of anything. And that's what we try to do. Sometimes it works, sometimes it doesn't. Sometimes it's a bit sticky – or you put your foot down and there's no solid ground there. You thought: 'At least we can make this step and we'll know where we are' but – no! The foot goes into a hole, puddle, mud – that wasn't a good idea. Those first decisions are almost a religious moment because they set such a train of events in motion – even if it goes wrong a little bit at the beginning it can still come right later. But it's much better if you get the understanding from the beginning. You could say it's like a serve in tennis or something: a nice return and then we have a rally. That's obviously a great way to start. But if I serve an ace, and then another ace, it's not great tennis to watch – even if it's great for the guy serving aces. But I don't plan my first sound hours in advance. [16]

Once, Derek Bailey was asked how he started an improvisation and he said: 'I usually start on a D.' So you can do that; you can just make any sound. I quite like that with groups I've worked on for a long time, where nobody plays a full idea at the beginning, somebody makes some suggestion and then you pick up on a suggestion and slowly the suggestions become a piece. [14]

During a soundcheck, it occurred to me to say to myself: 'Hey I wouldn't mind starting with that particular sound.' But once I'd done that once or twice, I came to realize that this was the worst thing to do, that it completely blocked me. So I never do that anymore. This means that at the beginning of a concert, things go very fast.

Starting an Improvisation

If I don't know the musician I'm going to play with, I'm interested in knowing who it is, so I'll try to listen to them beforehand. Out of curiosity, to find out something about what they do. To listen to them and choose what set-up I'm going to use. Especially if it's someone who also plays electronics. You can find yourself in some kind of ridiculous mirroring so it's good to have something that places you somewhere else. But I've also turned up saying to myself: 'I don't know who the person is but I'll see at the time.'

If I bring my Revox, that's a strategy in itself. Reworking things using another musician's sounds is a type of strategy. There's a strategy in how you build your set-up. Deciding how you're going to position yourself in relation to the speakers, in relation to the feedback, how you're going to do it, are strategies, but more of a technical nature.

At the same time, I often think many different things beforehand so that I can forget them afterwards. I come with lots of ideas that I have thought about, consciously or unconsciously, so that way I don't have to think while playing. I try to do the thinking beforehand. I prepare and then I forget. It's enough that you've thought about it. [36]

I don't know if what we call the first sound is really the first sound or if it hasn't actually started beforehand, in the period of concentration that there is between us when we're about to make it. That's what I like to believe: that the silence that precedes a concert is actually the first sound. [12]

I often start a concert saying to myself: 'I'm going to do something I've never done before', deliberately starting with a sound that I know almost never works, the riskiest sound possible, just to make sure that I'm attentive to what might happen right from the beginning. Sometimes this doesn't work, and if it doesn't work three times in a row, I end up falling back on things I've worked on. [13]

Once, I recorded a loop before the concert, but without listening to it. I asked someone to press play before the audience came in and I came in last. Then I discovered the loop myself. It was a way of planning without knowing. [02]

If I know the people I'm playing with, if I have an idea of what they are going to play, I could have a strategy before playing. [28]

I choose the first sound of the concert in the same way as the second, the seventh or the fifteenth: either arbitrarily, I look at my stopwatch and say: 'I'll play on minute X', or in a more felt way, because I feel that I'm relaxed enough physically and that in any case I'm going to have to start playing at some point. All the ceremony of the beginning of a concert often annoys me. [25]

I play different instruments. But I wouldn't decide which instrument I want to play five minutes before leaving the house, it would be a conscious choice. [06B]

The only real decision is about technical equipment. So, for instance, in the second concert the other night, I played amplified. That was my decision. For the first concert, I decided to play acoustically. Other concerts I decide to play with a computer. Things like that. What is decided is more or less the technical set-up, not the music. There are no musical decisions beforehand. Sometimes, of course, I have a 'pre-imagination' of how it will be, but things could turn out to be different too. And, in a way, I'm prepared for change, of course. [17]

Before playing, I think about lots of things, but I think less during and after. [41]

2

The mental state during an improvisation

I don't think things through at all while I'm playing. Somehow, I sort of short-circuit. If I do any reflecting, it happens beforehand, or afterwards, but not during. Sometimes, while I'm producing a sound, I hear another sound produced by another musician, and sometimes I can respond to that sound, find the same granulation. How does that happen? I can't say how. There's a kind of state, but I don't know how it happens, how the desire to make a sound, the desire to change sound, is born. Each sound has a beginning and an end, and sometimes I start a sound before abandoning it and making another one. Often, it's in the actual playing itself that this happens. I mean I make a sound and after a while I start thinking … not thinking but … my attention, my eyes focus on other objects I have brought with me with which I can make another sound. [02]

I don't know what is going on in my brain when I play. Very complex processes. I can tell you about my memories or my imaginings, what might happen. I kind of have a picture of the music. So in some ways it's visual but, in other ways, it isn't at all. It's a multidimensional picture. It wouldn't be possible to paint it but I can see it. It's like a space or something – I could conceive of a graphic approach but it would be very incomplete. For me, music is a very interesting way of being in time because nobody knows what time is. Music is a way to be in the present. So I'm completely in the present and I also have this picture, this image in my mind. Sometimes I have associations too. Like the associations you have when you listen to music. Sometimes it reminds me of a ventilation system or a fridge or insects – it could be any sound, a car … . Or I'm reminded of other music, from history. A history of music, which I have in my head, comes to the fore and my memories, all I know about music history, come into this … . Suddenly, if I lose my consciousness of the present and I drift away, I might think suddenly about washing the dishes but that rarely happens. It can happen if I find the concert uninteresting; then I fade away. But that rarely happens either.

There are a lot of different levels. What happens in the brain is very complex. There are so many different levels. Sometimes, because I never play with my eyes closed, I might see somebody coming into the room or somebody leaving, and I might become aware of it during the concert. Or somebody might be looking really intense, for example. My eyes are open but I'm not looking at anything in particular. I'm concentrating. I look to a certain point but not consciously. I fix my eyes on emptiness. It might happen that I'm suddenly looking around when something happens. It wasn't a decision I made, it just happened that way. I don't think I ever close my eyes to play. [17]

I don't know what's happening in my brain while I perform and that's what's really exciting. I think what goes on is outrageously complex, far more complex than we know. And improvisation has the possibility to access some of this complexity, beyond the current social, historical, scientific tools that exist for analysing how the brain works. I feel that some physical things happen as well. Sometimes it happens without me knowing.

When you're improvising and you hear something, depending on how you hear it and how that resonates with what you've heard before and what you think, it influences your decision-making process. But everything is going on very quickly.

I've always felt suspicious if I go into a trance while playing with musicians. On one level I really love it, it's beautiful to feel lost, but the critical part of me thinks: 'What are you doing, what's this about, was that predictable?'

The way you interpret or hear a sound is very ambiguous. When you improvise with 'noise', you become aware that what you listen to is quite subjective. You can listen to the timbre, the volume, the envelope and so on. It's actually getting to the roots of your listening systems and bending your notion of how you assume sounds to be or what you expect to hear. There is also some super-realist type of awareness of the physicality and the implication of what your fellow improvisers are doing. Because what you are doing will connote in a number of systems, it connotes simultaneously. It connotes in terms of your understanding of musical structures, real-time composition and the sonic potentials of a particular instrument. [21]

I trust sound. I go with the sound. Sounds feed vibrations back into the body, the vibrations of the instrument back to my ears or my body and the vibrations of the instrument back into my hand, something very primitive. When the sound is there, I'm confident. It's more difficult when the acoustics are dry because the sound isn't really there, and you really have to create the metaphor of resonance inside yourself.

Everything is constantly oscillating. We find ourselves in the oscillation and our sole job is to make sure we're right there in the place where it's oscillating. In the Western world, we're a bit binary and this artistic work makes it possible to see that there aren't only two poles, but a multitude of them. And that's what affords us the wonderful happiness of contradicting ourselves, in actions themselves, because they're something and its opposite, a variation and its opposite. It's an extraordinary journey. [15]

I'm interested in following sounds. Maybe you could liken it to when you repeat a word over and over. After a while it acquires a different meaning. It's the same with sound as well. If it's played long enough, it starts to be something different to what it was at the beginning. At the moment, I'm interested in finding another voice that comes in, to make the sound a bit more complex than it first appears to be, but in a subtle way, not in an obvious way. It sounds as if I only do 'long sounds' but I also work on how they exist in silence as well. Silence before, during or after has an effect on the whole thing as well. [10]

I certainly can't remove myself, but when I perform I consider myself to be more in the service of the sound, rather than the sound being in my service. [03]

Limitation is really important. Sometimes, though, you just do what you feel like doing. [04A]

Two recurrent images come to mind when I'm playing. In the first there's the feeling of really setting the piano in motion so that it becomes a sort of sound machine that I just stoke up. And I feel that there's a moment when the piano kind of takes off from the ground and exists on its own, without me doing anything. From the outside, it looks like I'm hyperactive, but from the inside I feel like I'm not doing anything and I'm just listening to this kind of brouhaha, this machine, and just adding a few bits inside it. Pushing a little in one direction, and then in the other, holding it but without really giving anything. I just give the initial impetus, but it happens on its own. The instrument and I vibrate together. The other image is that at some point, my body ... but in fact, it's related to listening. Listening is so much focused on space, that the piano extends to the whole space, to the room, to the air, and I feel as if I'm inflating. It feels as if the act of listening and my body encompass the whole room, people, everything. It feels as if everything is inside me, that I'm the room, that I'm vibrating with the space.

This trance state that I'm talking about is really very close to free speech in psychoanalysis, the link to the unconscious, which suddenly helps you to reveal truths. Suddenly, accepting that you're not in control, a kind of flow – when I say flow, I mean things that may be very deliberately positioned – can give birth to this free speech, a discourse that you accept without constant judgement, which is something that's very difficult to do and which is much more difficult for me to do with language, no doubt because in language, there's the problem of meaning. At those moments, there are a lot of things that emerge from very deep down and that really interest me.

The state of trance doesn't cut you off from the rest. It's really like a kind of awakening, a moment where you're ultra-available to everything around you, at least on the level of sound.

This trance is one of the reasons I play music. But is it essential to my survival? I'm not so sure. [38]

Sometimes you only need two seconds. It's not continuous ecstasy. It's often something very momentary. But once that state has been reached, that you're aware of being in a particular state, things go much better. What's strange with this 'state of grace' is that in those moments you're more precise … . To get there, you might have to go through a process of very attentive listening, before playing at all. But in general, it's when you're looking for it that you can't find it. It's probably something you can work on but I haven't worked out how yet. [13]

Improvisation works best for me when I lack consciousness. It's not the subconscious either, but it's when it goes beyond my consciousness. What I'm really interested in is not thinking any more at all, being in a context as neutral as possible where I use reflexes that are as neutral as possible. Then you're totally there, totally present. You're not manipulating. You don't have a goal. You're not really aware of what's happening. A bit like water flowing in a river that comes upon a rock and that doesn't decide to circumvent this rock but that, by the force of things, somehow does go around it – or not.

When I'm in a concert situation, I am absolutely not thinking about the result. When you think result, you think assessment, something that is finished, so the right term isn't 'result'. What I might call 'result' – but it's not the right term – is reaching a level of concentration that makes improvisation happen.

For me, the best state to be in is the absence of consciousness, that is, not making any decisions, not listening, not being involved in the sounds that I'm producing, the sounds that other musicians are producing – this is absence of consciousness.

It's the opposite of automatic action. It's like a dream. In fact, it's pretty close to sleep. It's like my body is doing what it needs to do to feel good.

There are situations where I suddenly wake up a little bit, open my eyes and say to myself: 'Hey, I'm making such-and-such a sound', 'Hey, so-and-so is making that sound', 'Ah, together it sounds like that' and so on. The times when I wake up are in fact the times when it doesn't work as well and where you have to work a bit harder, be a little more careful, be a little more aware. But the best state is the absence of consciousness, or a state that is beyond consciousness – but, and I insist on this point, it isn't unconsciousness either. To leave the realm of consciousness is to invent something.

Obviously sometimes you're not in an optimal situation and you can't fully get to that state. Then you don't just let it go, give up. You have to carry on – convincing yourself that you're in an optimal situation. Obviously, this is autosuggestion. If things aren't perfect and I focus on the imperfection, I get pulled in by it and things won't go well. I have to believe that the situation is optimal. This doesn't stop you from being aware of what has happened after the improvisation session, after you come down, but while you're doing it, you have to believe that you've reached that state. Even if there's a spot in my head, a little box, that knows this isn't really the case, I have to ignore this little box, because otherwise it will stop me from carrying on. I don't have a particular name for it, but it's definitely a deliberate state, an autosuggested state, a projected state … .

The times when I wake up are times when this state is no longer accessible or is no longer there. Quite simply, and I'm very pragmatic about this, these are times when I use my past experience. I remember similar contexts in which I've found myself – in which we've found ourselves (the musicians with whom I'm improvising at that moment) – in an impasse. What is very particular is that I'm the only one who believes that it's not working well enough, so of course it's rather tricky. But in any case, I use my experience, my memory of similar situations to find a solution, to get out of the situation and return to a state of nirvana. I cheat, but cheat so that I can get back to the state of extreme concentration. It's necessary cheating – we're only human after all. [46]

I need intense concentration when I play improvised music – but sometimes I can't concentrate. [08A]

I also believe that there's something about improvisation that is essentially related to a state of concentration. A state that, I think, you don't reach anywhere else. It's more or less the result of being very aware of what others are playing and how others may hear and receive what I am playing. [25]

Before, I wanted to have this sort of subject–object thing be meaningless, so it was a bit like meditation: I was aware of the whole and I was aware of my own actions and they were totally, totally the same. And I always found that successful improvisation of a certain type occurred when this thing happened. And I then tried to get to that place with something that could be developed – and you could get there quite easily if that was your goal. But I stopped doing that after a while because I thought that it was too serious and too dogmatic. I used to have a little rule that I would play like it was the last time I would ever play, and that I would die after I played because I thought it was very important. And then I added a new thing which was I would also play like it was the first time I'd ever played. I got that from Eddie Prévost and from AMM really. So grafted the two together. [05A]

I quite like not analysing improvised music. After working on analysing other music for years, I really try to regress intellectually and attach myself solely to what I'm feeling. At least that's what I aim for. But I still have ideas. Ideas of rather vague forms, or perhaps attitudes and tones, like when you talk about the tone of a piece of writing. You want to live through some experiences directly.

I don't remember self-censoring. I really let myself go. These days, I always make sure I let myself go, instinctively. [01]

We all fall, we all fail. And I think probably the best attitude to go into any performance is not to have any expectations at all, otherwise you're more likely to fail … . [07]

When I want something specific, it's not good for the music. Because it involves the slowest area of my brain. I often write the piece I want to play, but I let myself have a lot of freedom. So much so that sometimes I even lose track of the piece's theme. Then I do something else and I accept it. I'm not saying we shouldn't analyse what's happening, but we have to leave room for what's known as 'intuition', a sort of synthesis of everything I have learnt and listened to prior to that moment. When I improvise, I let myself be guided by what's happening and I feel that I am the music. I just need a space where there's silence and, after a few minutes, the ideas come of themselves. Some are conscious ideas and some come from who knows where. Sometimes ideas do whatever they want – like naughty kids! When I'm playing solo, this isn't a problem, because I'm used to it. But in a group, some musicians I play with don't like it.

When I'm improvising, I try not to think. I think you have to think beforehand. In fact, I like to be surprised, even if that can be difficult. I try not to judge, to disconnect the part of my brain that judges. I listen to the other musician and I know what I have to do. It's like a small nuclear reactor and, this goes without saying, it works by itself. I focus on listening and what I do just happens on its own. In any case, the reasoning never stops. I know this, so I don't need to worry about it. I have to forget myself, lose the consciousness I have of myself. Because I am in another part of myself. I can't understand, for example, that people might want to take pictures of a musician playing ... . The moment is what decides what I'm going to do. I know my material and all its variations, and I have the feeling decisions are made on their own. I am here and not anywhere else. There's no distance. [48]

I think a major element is that I don't like to repeat the same things. I like to surprise myself because that puts me in a state where the desire to play is stronger. Yes, that's the game: always bouncing off something, like a child who's in his own world, even though he's still playing cops and robbers. And this world changes, it varies. [02]

If I feel that I know something by heart, I sometimes decide not to do it because I want to remain in a state of necessity. Not follow convention, where there aren't any surprises anymore. What does 'there aren't any surprises anymore' mean? It means that everything's settled, that you're no longer on the edge of a cliff. What's interesting in improvisation is also that state in which you're bordering on rupture, which means that you remain in a state of necessity.

It's an emergency. It isn't uncomfortable. Is being surprised uncomfortable? In fact, it depends on how you take it. It can be uncomfortable, but in any case you don't suffer from the discomfort passively. You choose it, seek it out. [37]

What I like is to be surprised, to surprise myself. What's missing in the spectrum, and what's over the top? What can I add and what should I remove from the colour of the object that's forming? These are the questions I ask myself. Or perhaps, these are the words that I've found to talk about it. Maybe my body is stronger than my will and it does something else and I let myself be guided by it as if I'm a stranger to myself when I improvise, let myself be guided by who knows what.

I accept the fact that there are things that I can't control and maybe that's why I still like improvising, and that I think I'll never stop improvising.

I would say that, in terms of my physical sensations, the most beautiful improvisations I've done are when I was totally out of it. You no longer really exist. It's as if you're being guided. You're just the body of a higher thought, without it being mystical or anything, of a musical thought that passes through you and guides you.

I try to ask myself as many questions as I can about form, structure, dynamics, intensity, length, duration, pitch, all the parameters of music, the history of music.

But when I'm playing, it's pragmatic. When I take a cymbal in one hand and my bow in the other and I rub it like this, I don't really know what pitch it's going to produce, but I do know what colour it's going to give, so I tell myself, that's what's needed, at some point that's what's needed.

Maybe improvising is controlling and letting go. It's both at the same time. To improvise is to escape oneself and one's own limits. [42]

I'm trying to keep myself interested as well as the audience. [06A]

At home, I work on certain outlines, certain mechanisms, certain sound patterns. But when I play live, I move away from the sounds and things I'm used to working on. Essentially because it wouldn't help me progress to confine myself to what might be considered clichés. And also because in concerts, I try to achieve abstraction in terms of the sounds of the saxophone and my own personality as much as possible. I try to get as far away as possible from what I am and remove myself into what's going on. If, for example, I make a sound that I don't like but that fits in the context of the concert in progress and that takes me out of myself, it's not a problem. On the contrary, it's a nice surprise. When I'm involved in the process of listening, I'm in a state of tension and alert and I can fully open myself up to the outside, to others. So, it's a way of removing myself from myself, because I'm in a state of tension towards something. It's a kind of sensory acuity that 'takes me out' of myself at certain moments. But I quickly come back to myself, and I still think about something. This process of going back and forth very fast works like breath. While in a state of tension towards the sound, I retain a strong awareness of the form, of what's happening. I only ask myself questions about what's happening and how I'll contribute again after a series of sounds have been emitted, after a motif, a dynamic, an intention. It's often at the start and end of the sound, how I get in and how I get out. It's often in those moments that I come back to an awareness of myself. [45]

When I play improvised music, I put myself into a state of apnoea, immersion. I have to do this in order to be able to play, with 360° listening, all the aspects of sound, form, music – at least what I think all that consists of – and make conscious decisions about form and sounds, decisions in order to inscribe material within time. It's not like I'm thinking like I would if I were confronted with a maths problem. [37]

I haven't ever really put into words what I do, so it's quite difficult to pinpoint it and say: 'This is what I do', because every situation is different. Everybody that I play with is different, and I have different moods and attitudes and sometimes I'll say to myself that I'll do something but then I won't do it at all! Sometimes when I improvise I'm really not conscious of what I'm doing, it just happens. [10]

I think I would like to be able to use several musical languages and I can't. I always come back to the same ideas. Some days I feel really comfortable with this. Other days I'm going insane because I wish I could go on to something else. But when I try to do something else, I feel like I'm faking.

From one project to the other, there are different ways of dealing with the situation – but ultimately it's the same. [35A]

I wouldn't say that I have a particular attitude that I change for different groups. I know most of the people now. I would know the basic areas of their improvising – there are little schools now and I find that a little bit sad. I just like improvised music; I don't like the different genres. [18]

You don't have time to respond, to think about what you're playing.

I think that if you think about it too much, on a conscious level, you're probably not playing very well. To play, you have to feel rather than think.

It's just like a conversation really. It isn't that you've thought: 'It would be good if I did this and I hope he thinks the same thing.' It's a lot more natural than that.

Because we know the sort of sounds each person will be using. Even though there's a huge amount of variation within those sounds, we have all that in the backs of our minds before we start playing. It happens in a much more natural way than thinking about it consciously.

I think what we're trying to describe is that if you're thinking about it, it's not so successful. You should be feeling it, and perhaps what I mean by feeling it is non-verbal thought. Because that feeling is thought but if you're thinking of it in terms of words in your head, you're being so analytical that you're missing the moment. Some people say there's no such thing as non-verbal thought.

Anyone who plays music would probably accept that there is.

You're not analysing it in that verbal form. All of these things are factors which our brains analyse – and again it's non-verbal thought and that's precisely why it's interesting. It might be that it's in this area of non-verbal thought that you find these group minds emerging.

The way we sound, like it or not, is not a result of analysis by us. It's a result of us playing whatever comes naturally to us. [11]

While I'm playing, I think of nothing. Your mind has to be a clean sheet of paper, sensitive enough so that no matter what someone does it makes a mark on there. You can be playing something and someone does something and that becomes a part of what you're doing. You become like a sponge. If someone drops something on you, you absorb it. There are lots of things that happen that you have to make use of, unless you're playing in a space capsule. If you're recording during a war, you can't tell them to hold that bomb they're going to throw because there's a silence in your music. You isolate yourself from the things that are unimportant but the world doesn't stop. The creative thing, if there is such a thing, is of such magnitude that no matter what happens it manages to get through – if it's strong enough. When you get ready to do the thing that you want to do, nothing else matters. Because this is the thing that takes all of your attention. It's a highly selfish endeavour out of which this world has been made.

The best players, the most effective ones, have all gone through the same process. But when they play something, you never have the feeling that they learnt it somewhere. When it comes out of them, it seems like originated with them. But nothing originates with anyone; it all comes from the outside. It goes in and it's processed with everything else, it's moved around and when it comes out you have no awareness that it originally went in. [34]

During a concert I might think about anything. Sometimes it even surprises me. I can be completely engaged with what I'm doing and be thinking that I need to book a train ticket. Playing the drums, I can reach a kind of ecstatic state, physically, where I'm so overwhelmed, there's so much going on, and I do really love that. It's a bit like a drug. That's where music can really change me. And it's the same with the music I'm really affected by as a listener – it's always very emotional music. It could be flamenco or free jazz or a beautiful singer, often it's singers or very romantic stuff. It could also be a very bad ballad on the radio. [35A]

I perceive the sounds that other musicians make as part of what I am producing. Everything that is produced is immediately integrated into my imagination and feeds it. At some point, I feel that the sounds produced by others are part of my organism, my gestures and, I would almost say, the same brain. I sometimes feel like I'm dreaming about the music I hear and everyone is participating in this dream. But there's still this strange feeling that this dream is produced by my mind, by me myself. [38]

Do you ever really know where you are? There are always more unanswered questions about this kind of music and this way of making music than there are questions with answers. [06B]

I think it would be more problematic if I thought I knew what I was doing all the time. [06A]

3

Listening to the other musicians, the human factor, the strategies

Obviously we make music. And yes, for me, making music in real time and the interaction with other musicians are important. You're trying to find new ways; you're forced to interact with other musicians, with your instrument. And there's no time to consolidate your approach. It's like building up a relationship with the others. You have to discover how they interact and your own way to interact, so it's extremely interesting.

With another person, there's a different understanding of the context, of the place where you are and other people's responses to it; it's very direct and confrontational. When I play solo, it's not as direct. There is the audience and the space in which you're playing, but it's easier to bring forth your own ideas of how to react, because you don't have anything to counter them with – except for the audience, which is much more subtle. I definitely think that it's stronger with other people. [09B]

Things happen with others that no one of us individually could ever think of. [11]

What I can say is that, at heart, when I improvise all I'm trying to do is play with other people. Now I'm probably bringing along quite a lot of baggage in terms of the way I want to play with them, but I don't want to import one way of playing into every situation. I want each situation to bring something a little different out of me. [14]

When I'm playing with someone I don't know, I ask myself questions like: 'What are their strategies? How do they think? What do they expect? How do they make their choices?' [37]

Things have changed for me. I've changed in the way I view things. I'm always very self-aware about what I'm doing and why I'm doing it. But the 'why' has changed overtime. I try to push others. And I still do that frequently, but I stay in my own little zone as well nowadays.

The first thing is, you've got to be hearing everything and not be thinking about yourself. And then, second of all, you've got to make other people play well. These are the two things for me. I don't even think about my own playing really apart from in the sense of: 'I must keep myself interested.' My intellectual interest, or my emotional interest, my own interest, in any case, in what I'm doing is important. So my sounds need to be interesting to me, in the context of the history of sound making. It's a certain level of care, a certain level of energy that I'm putting into making sounds that are still interesting. [05A]

When I play with other musicians, lots of barriers fall. It's no longer me and them, but rather a kind of unity that forms, that's part of the listening. In general, I know what sound I'm making and what sound they're producing – even if sometimes you don't really know who is doing what. But how do I know if I'm actually playing with them? I don't know and I don't care, because sometimes I really want to play with them, to follow them, almost like a dialogue, while at other times, I feel as if there's a freedom that means that I'm completely indifferent to what can happen. I can let go of them completely – even if they haven't actually been fully let go of: I can still hear them. But I don't want to react to what they're doing, so I carry on with what I'm doing. Anyway, my ears are still working. Therefore, the question that arises is rather whether I'm playing with them, against them or without them. But I think these are also impulses. … I don't know how it works and I don't want to know how it works. [02]

I try to create as much space and balance as possible in what's going on. I'm interested in kind of really spreading things out. It's listening but it's also trying to generate as much space as possible in the music. I might decide to do something which I know is going to take a minute and I'm going to do it anyway because I made that decision based on what happened just before or maybe on what's happened over the last two minutes or what I think is about to happen. So it's not necessarily about continual instant response. But I am still listening. And I could also change my mind. Just because you start something doesn't mean you have to complete it. A lot of the things I do are kind of procedural. Even if I'm not sure how exactly I'm going to do them. For me, it's still improvisation because

I wouldn't think about those things before it started. When I talk about space, I suppose I'm talking about a kind of sound or textural or sonic territory. It doesn't preclude the call and response; it's just one way of dealing with it. It's the idea of things happening at once independently and together. Part of the point of having all this space is to have the freedom that I think this music requires. I think improvised music should be fundamentally free music and about having different possibilities – and I think you start with the space. I want to create as much place and as much freedom as possible. I'm not interested in developing things for the sake of development, but I'm interested in making a musical space as rich as possible. But, depending on who I'm playing with, that's more or less easy to do. So the decisions I make are very much informed by the people I'm playing with – if I'm playing with people who I know very well there's much more that I can do and I can stretch it further. [05B]

I don't think there's one way of listening. It's not fixed. When you're listening to something you haven't heard before ... I can't fix it or give it a formula and say: 'This is the way I listen.' I try to be as aware as possible of the situation and to respond according to that situation, not according to a formula in my mind. I try to respond to other people's playing more than to my own. I have my own way of playing, which you might say has its own characteristics, but I hope that it changes somehow each time. If you're asking me what I like, I like 'chock-a-blocks', on-off, clear contrasts, so that each sound becomes a statement. I'm more interested in the structural side, perhaps, than in the actual quality of the sounds. Obviously I have an awareness of the quality of sounds, and of the sounds that I find more interesting than others but, for me, it's much more about the relationship that occurs, how it occurs and how you discover it and push it forward. And about trying to deal with it. If you try to see improvisation as a result or listen to a CD, you're really missing what the potential of this music is. I think this music is much more about producing than making a product. [09B]

What do you decide to listen to? The rhythm, the notes, the pitch, the volume? These are rather simple notions, and then there's the rest: such-and-such a musician plays a harmony in a slightly strange way, another plays an attack; what's in this particular attack? Here, I'm being displaced, it's unusual.

The difficulty, I think, that I often feel, is: 'Am I hearing the same thing as the other musicians? Are we hearing the same thing?' [19]

Everybody hears what they want to hear, and what they're able to hear. [27]

We're beginning to stumble into some of the major items of philosophical debate down the centuries: How does anybody know that they perceive the same thing as someone else, and what grounds do we have for saying that our perceptions are shared?

Sometimes I have difficulty knowing who's doing what even at the time. I'm sitting there myself making sounds and thinking: 'Is that me? I want that noise to stop but I'm not sure if it's me doing it!'

But what about those areas where sounds are similar? Bowed cymbals can sound similar to some other bowed metallic thing or a synthesizer growling noise can sound like a bowed cardboard box. We deliberately head into those kinds of areas sometimes.

Those are my favourite bits – when I'm not sure what's happening. There's a good chance I'll like that quite a lot. Often my favourite moments are those lost moments, which carry on as they are, when you're not sure what your contribution is or why it's working, but it's just this lovely, bizarre thing which you couldn't think of putting together unless it was ... random. [11]

I wish I could listen to others in the same way that I listen to 'the world'. That would be an interesting operation. It would make us play differently. Except that it doesn't quite work in the same way.

There's not only one way of listening, but a multitude of ways of listening. Listening, it seems to me, works rather like a stack of different layers, something thick. When we listen, we constantly move from one layer to another, deliberately or not. For me, this is also what improvising is somehow, choosing how or what to listen to. The sound that you produce only comes afterwards, as a consequence. I think that each sound can be listened to in different ways, and that ways of listening are not to do with the sound itself. That is, a sound does not suggest how it should be listened to. When this is the case, it's because someone overinvests or forcefully implies a particular way of listening in what they're playing, and in this case produces, I feel, closed music. So that means that even if, in itself, a sound does not dictate how it should be listened to, a musician nevertheless has the power to direct others' listening, obviously without any certainty as to the nature of how this is received. For sure, however, background noise does not have this virtue. This is, for me, the main difference between solo and group work.

I believe that my way of listening is loaded with other musicians' ways of listening and vice versa. So yes, you do influence each other. This is one of the interesting things about concerts. But I like that influence to be secret. I feel that if I haven't played for three minutes, I'm expected to play – and the other musician communicates that to me. ... When I'm at home, there's nothing like that going on. In fact, then, there are no expectations at all. The issue no longer exists. But it isn't necessarily heard, because such an influence does not necessarily produce what could be described as a reflex. The meandering can be quite complicated.

I wish that listening always came first and that sound took on its shape, that what I played was the trace, imperfect of course, of what I am listening to or rather how I'm listening. But that the form taken by this trace remained as open as possible. So as not to fall into what I was talking about, that is, a sound that's a sign saying, 'listen to me like that' ... I don't assume that what I'm playing is interesting in terms of sound. What interests me more is the relationship of this sound with 'the world': sound as the relationship between the individual and the world, the expression of my way of listening to the world.

You could approach it in another way by saying that I'm not interested in the material in itself ... primarily. It's not just the material itself that creates the shape. It's time. It's a way of listening permitted by this material ... .

My way of listening doesn't always result from choice. Sometimes my way of listening is orientated by the outside. ... But listening is always a production I think. I try to listen to what's going on as fully as possible, knowing that I won't be able to succeed fully. Then there's a second filter, because the first applies to all listening, and this second filter has its locus within the decision of what I play. I choose, if I choose, to listen to this or that, in this or that way, and then the sound that I play depends on this filtering.

I choose the sound I play beforehand and I don't question myself about it again. It's that sound and that's it. Not constantly updating your choices is a way of going against your interests ... .

I always try to use the same sound material whatever the degree of subjectivity or arbitrariness of my way of listening. I don't want to 'select' my material based on what I am listening to or how I'm listening.

I always use the same sounds, either two or three held notes, or more rarely impacts. I try to sort out the issue of what sounds to choose in advance and shift the issue of variation elsewhere, onto the duration of these sounds, the amount of sound, the moment when they're emitted. The last concert I did I played 90 per cent of the time. Sometimes I play 5 per cent of the time.

I'd sometimes like my way of listening to be entirely dispassionate, with all the magic taken out of it, a way of listening in which none of the events are any more influential than the others, a way of listening in which everything is potentially 'loaded' equally, which doesn't mean that everything is loaded in the same way. A way of listening in which there's no such thing as a venue that has a particularly good sound, nothing that has to be reacted to, no background and no foreground, in other words that everything is material to be listened to and therefore used.

I'm absolutely not trying to get the audience to listen to the world! I try to experience listening in a certain situation, and to produce a form in return, as the residue of this listening. This is one way of doing things. My sounds don't have the virtue of making people listen to an environment in a 'better' way! People don't need me in order to listen to birds! What really interests me is the form generated in return, the superposition. [25]

In the trio r.mutt with Sébastien Beliah and Antonin Gerbal, I function within a restricted sound field trying to see what's happening at a given moment: I try to erase what came before. But I think this is a fantasy, an illusion. I feel like I manage it, but I'm sure it's not possible to forget. It's very dense music, and so there's a kind of permanent remanence. There isn't a single section of silence to give us the opportunity to erase it. That's also what I like about this group: trying to be in the moment as much as possible and not thinking that the music has a beginning and an end.

I don't see it as a freedom, but as a constraint that I impose on myself. It's not something I believe I'm liberated from. It's not for the purpose of giving free rein to ... actually I don't even know to what!

It may be to open up another form of 'interaction', reactivity, another form of playing as a trio. Yet from the beginning, we imposed a certain approach on ourselves: we do our best to imagine we're separated or disconnected from each other.

We listen to each other, we definitely listen to each other, but it's the way we listen that's different. I would say that it's listening to each other listening to each other. Listening to the others listening to each other. Listening to the others listening to each other listening to the others listening to each other.

It seems more interesting to me to make the project live, to be surprised by trying to position oneself all the time in relation to someone else, rather than trying to produce a new sound or an incredible phrase. ... In my opinion, when you work regularly with the same people, that's where improvisation happens. [47]

If Elvin Jones got into a situation with Derek Bailey – which isn't such a far-flung idea, it could have happened – they both would have gone and played like Elvin Jones and Derek Bailey. It probably would have been fantastic, both of them playing their improvised styles. I've never worked that way myself. I would never think: 'I'm just going to do my improvisation'. I always relate to people, try and get inspiration from people. I suppose if it were Elvin and Derek Bailey, they too, subconsciously, would be listening to each other. But I've heard some improvising that consisted of two very strong people that don't seem to be having any relationship at all. [18]

I also play rock music, using an electric violin with effects, e-bow, delay, filters and distortion sometimes. For me, rock music and improvised music are quite different. It's a different approach. In rock music, it's very important to communicate with the other members of the group, with their sounds. In improvised music, communication with other musicians, other sounds, is not very important: listening is important, listening to the whole sound. So, when I improvise, I play my music, I play my sound. If all musicians play their own music at the same time, some interesting sound is going to happen. I don't intentionally communicate with the others' sounds, the others' music, but finally, the influence of my sound on the whole is there. When it sounds like interaction, it happens accidentally. For example, I wanted to make a sudden percussive sound just before you played yours. In a good improvisation, I can play what I decided before I started to play without thinking about the others. The result is another problem. [08A]

If I don't feel comfortable with what the other musicians are playing, one possibility is just not to react and to follow my own track. But, usually, I am quite reactive. [32]

I had one bad experience. We played with a group and the first time was really horrible. There were two people doing their sounds and the other three were confronted with this mass of sounds, and there was no interaction. And we did it again, it was really bad once again – I didn't find any productive aspect in it. I felt bad, completely disrespected and I don't want to be confronted with this kind of situation in which … it doesn't matter what I'm doing. These two musicians with whom I was playing, it really didn't matter to them what I did. It really was a bad experience. It really took away my whole inspiration and appreciation for the music. These people were supposed to care about the music, but when you play with them and they don't give a fuck about what you do … . It wasn't that I was being confronted with something that I could maybe do something with; it was like I wasn't there. It didn't matter if I played or not. It was a bad experience. Either I do something with an idea in mind of creating something or … I don't do something just for the sake of doing it. I'd rather do something else. [09B]

One of the things I like about improvisation is that, ideally, you can react to what's happening. What I don't like about improvisation is when it becomes just habit, playing basically the same piece over and over and over again. If I know exactly what's going to happen, I don't really see the point. [28]

It all depends on what I'm hearing from other people. Sometimes there's no point in me continuing to manipulate something just for the sake of it. I try to make it fit with whatever I am hearing. Or other times I might just do that and see what happens; see how other people react to the sound.

I can't help but be influenced by what I hear so in a way I'm just reacting to what I hear musically and that's the main thing. I'm just able to listen and react. [10]

The choices I make are actually counter-intuitive to traditional modes of music-making; they're not radical or anything like that. I favour this notion of parallel musical events in the specific case of the trio with Jean-Luc Guionnet and Eric La Casa. It's like three voices sounding simultaneously, but I don't actually want to converse with them whatsoever. I don't want it to be that when someone does this, I have to do that, that kind of thing. So I like to have something that coexists with the sounds that they're making but retains a certain independent quality as well and sometimes that creates a synergy with what's going on. Sometimes, though, it might feel out of place or not quite right or raise questions about what I'm actually doing or contributing – but I kind of like that notion. I've got nothing much to say in terms of conversation so I'm just making sounds as a kind of provocative action.

My job is not to contribute to the form but to somehow be outside its development. Sonically I might not be able to do that as brutally or as forcefully as some musicians might be able to but, intellectually, my choices, which are related to my materials, are always about going a little bit against what's going on. [22]

I have several different theories. Sometimes, I just play to the stopwatch, even if I'm playing with someone. Of course, I listen to the other's sound, but I only play to the stopwatch. But as it's still improvised, I decide to stop after one minute or after thirty seconds. It's improvised, so I make these decisions during the performance. Watching the stopwatch is a way of avoiding reacting to the others. I use this technique sometimes but not all the time.

Sometimes, I play with a very simple rule. For example, I handclap soon after some sound from the other players is finished. Not like a machine though. I decide if I want to follow the rule or not. And actually these rules are not set beforehand. [23]

What makes it interesting is trying not to react to what can happen. Then, rather, my reactions are longer-lasting reactions. Perhaps this is a way of integrating sounds, continuous playing modes, whether repetitive or not, and perhaps this can itself become a bit systematic. In the end, you realize that in the greater scheme of things, there's still a kind of personal tempo … . [13]

Do you think that second-by-second group interaction is important or not? Maybe not. It's not like we go to sleep for thirty seconds, we're just not jumping on it. [04A]

My background is in a very reactive improvisation. I still enjoy working that way, and a lot of musicians I really like hearing also work that way. But when something's been around for thirty years, clearly, very strong clichés develop. I think it's like almost any kind of music. [14]

To a certain extent with this music, it's about not reacting. [04B]

Even if you don't react, whatever you do is going to be related; you're always going to be there. [04A]

Even in groups where you don't react obviously, you are working reactively because you're listening and you're making decisions. But there's no gesture in the reaction.

If you have one person playing Ligeti and one person playing Beethoven, it might be possible to have two people working independently, playing somebody else's composed music, but in improvisation it seems to be almost impossible. There's always some connection to do with a sense of what the rhythm of the music is. It's uncanny how hard it is not to play with someone. [14]

I try to avoid whatever's being produced in a logical way or is too obvious, according almost to a principle of questions and answers. For me, the improvisational relationship mustn't work like that. What I mean is that when I send out a signal, I do everything I can to do so in such a way that it doesn't ask for a response.

It's a signifier – in any case it's clearly a message – but I don't think the message should have a deterministic implication. I don't have that relationship to choice at all. I don't say to myself: 'If I do that, I do it to get that, so that the other person hears it in that way.' Basically for me, it's an open angle. It's not a straight line at all.

I think I have no connection to sociology when I play, or to anthropology, to tension or even communication. I don't treat it like a human relationship. What I mean is that when a guy is making sounds, I receive his message. I don't ask what relationship I have with the guy. I don't care about that at all.

Sometimes, you feel that there's something going on and you know why but I don't give a damn about that.

When I'm experiencing something, even if I think that the other person is in an emotional state, I don't listen to their emotional state. I listen to the sounds they're making. I mean, I separate their emotional state from what they're proposing, even though there have been instances when I've felt another musician is feeling fragile, and I feel that this fragility is going to make things complicated.

When that happens it's usually over. When I hear that, it's over. I think that the concert won't be any good.

Once again, what I might call really detailed listening is a kind of breaking free from the psychology of the person's character.

In psychoanalysis, you call it the unconscious. What I mean is that I take my psychology into account. There are things that come out that I don't control.

I'd like to have optimal listening capabilities and be able to function like a mixing desk. [39]

I hate reaction. I prefer indirect reaction. In improvisation, what matters to me is trying to come up with something together. Sometimes, at the same time, we make sounds together. That's not a reaction. Or perhaps it's an indirect reaction, with reference to the future. Though for me reaction is something that's part of the past. That's my impression. [41]

I think, to a certain extent, I always have something premeditated. It depends what you mean by premeditated, of course. I don't think I do anything that is an automatic reaction. It might be due to a thought-out process or decision, or it might just be a decision based on an intuition … . [04A]

When you improvise in a group, there's necessarily a reaction. Because reacting does not necessarily mean going in the direction of the other musician, it can be against him/her, it can take things somewhere else. Maybe there actually are people who are strong enough to be truly autistic? [36]

It's reaction. I think the only thing you really ought to be asking, on a conscious level, is: 'Is what I'm going to do going to improve what's already there or will it make it worse?' You shouldn't play anything if what's there is good already, unless you think you can improve it. [11]

It's psychological when you try to influence the other person by some action. There's nothing psychological in actually making choices. There's no message that you're sending to the other person.
I think reacting is also not reacting. [37]

The biggest reaction altogether lies in trying to never react. In my opinion, you have to work on minimizing reaction times. You may react quickly to an event but in an awkward way. And the other way round is to do something fantastic, but too late. The two must be combined into one, so it's a question of reacting as quickly as possible, even if the reaction is a silence, so that you can call up all your technique, everything you've heard in your life since you've been a musician and everything you've seen. That's what you have to do, go back and forth between consciousness and projection. That's what I feel when I'm making music in general, not just in improvised music.

For me, an improviser is a transceiver. I would say that whatever the musical proposal you offer in the moment, it always comes too late, because it has just been changed by what has been proposed alongside it. In fact, you're always late to the party when you're improvising. But you have to make do with that. [42]

Whether you're in reactive mode or out of a desire to impose something, it's always relative to the other musicians. I can't be indifferent to what's being played next to me. In principle, I don't want to hear two separate discourses. And if they seem compatible, that's proof enough that they're connected. As far as I'm concerned, then, there's necessarily some sort of coherence.

If I'm in a different timescale, it's always by reaction. It's a difference, a determinant relationship. I'm in a perceptual space that I'm part of and that the other musician is also part of. Listening is the basis of this music. I'm in a state of listening. All the intentions I may have come out of the situation, the space, out of what's happening at that moment. But I don't make an irremediable, definitive decision for a predetermined length of time: changes in the situation will make me change my mind. [45]

What you learn, while playing, about how the musicians in the group react to each other can influence your input into the process. If you feel that everything is forced or, the other way round, if you feel that everyone is just following each other, you can try to stir it up by bringing in some irritation or by making some strong decision. But if you come up with strategies, you should still stay open to what's emerging from the group. If something unexpected emerges, you have to re-examine your anticipation of what the piece might become. Sometimes, all of a sudden, there is a moment where it's going over the edge and falls into something totally different, and you need to be ready to go with that. [44]

Nearly all of the kind of sound areas I've been interested in looking at with the saxophone came through playing with other people, they didn't come through sitting at home thinking about it. It was being in a situation and that would spark my imagination. In the early days, it was with string players and all the incredible things they can do with overtones and bows. That's a great stimulus, inspiration for trying to do it on a wind instrument. I'm a big believer in the fact that the work that's done in improvised music benefits a lot from coming into contact with playing situations – and not from abstract concepts about it. Because the sounds, their uses, come from practical situations you can use them. [14]

In the quintet Hubbub, it's extremely controlled. There's less loss of control. There's a strong desire to build collective music. For me, playing collectively is the other aspect of improvisation, which kind of counterbalances trance. It can open doors and paths for the construction of elements that I wouldn't be able to find on my own. Different universes meet and give birth to an even wider universe, an even wider playing space. The willingness to work with these elements, compose collectively, permanently counterbalances trance. It's a more controlled trance. [38]

I may not feel particularly comfortable with everybody, but I think it's really important to play with very different musicians because it opens up a completely different language of possibilities and ways of thinking that you would never think of yourself. It would be interesting to be involved in a more stable group, but, then again, it opens up more possibilities playing with different groups. [10]

I'm interested in engagement with human beings that I like and respect. One of my motivations for playing music is that I love the people that play music and I love the act of engagement outside of social engagement. It's a driving thing for me. The basic act of improvising is about finding relationships with the people I'm with at that time. So it's the same thing regardless of what music I'm playing, provided it's not about composition.

Maybe you could say that music is only made up of a few basic, fundamental areas.

The act of improvising is, in part, looking for someone else to help you open doors. [35B]

I could very well play with someone who fascinates me musically and who I hate. Well, I don't know, that's never happened to me. What's important is the music. [37]

I really have to respect the person I am playing with, or like the person I am playing with. And I really can't work with people that I don't like, even if their music is brilliant. [06A]

A lot of the people I'm involved with have great command of their instruments and very singular voices, recognizable anywhere, and they can play completely differently from one day to the next. I really value that. They have a voice that you can recognize but still they have that incredible diversity and variation. That's amazing. And that's something that I never really thought was possible because you tend to narrow things down and become very singular. But it is possible to do things this other way as well. [05A]

Because I see improvisation as some sort of interrelation with other people, I change my approach radically depending on what other people want to explore. So, for example, recently what I've done is adapt my material to noise material and minimal material. Because if the other musicians are using noise material for a fifty-minute block and the idea is to create a listening space where you're not necessarily aware of the sound source – it's about ambiguity, it's about a sort of mesmeric fragility of listening – and if I was to include the material that I do in a textual context, it would demolish the fragility of the structures that they're setting up. It would be overbearing, rude, and would destroy the listening field they're trying to develop. So, for me, working with other improvisers is about … not doing what they want, but trying to understand the philosophical and sonic area they're coming from. And if I don't respect it, of course, I'm not going to work with them. But if I do respect it, then I want to develop a shared ethos. It could be a perverse ethos, but – even if it sounds like such a cliché – the social implications of the activity are important. [21]

I like to modify my language in accordance with who I'm playing with. Of course, it should sound like me. But in a situation with a pianist playing a certain kind of recognizable harmonic structure, that's one situation; in a situation with somebody playing percussion – no fixed reference – that's another. I like to be able to, in a way, find the middle way in the languages – my language, your language – where we can speak. We have to find a place in the middle. And if you're not very happy to move, then I have to come more towards you. Another mix of personalities can also produce interesting possibilities – but my approach is always to ask where these two fields of music overlap, where the common ground is. [16]

I have to play what I think is best. I have to make the best musical decisions I can and, often, the decision is to stay where I think is the best place for me to play. In a way, I decide to 'play myself'. In my pre-imagination I always trust my spontaneous reactions or decisions. I never make decisions before listening to what the other players do. I would never do that. 'Being myself' is a basic decision of my music. I think it's more musical if I'm myself than if I follow some other musician and try to be like him. If I tried to do that, and to be something I'm not, the musical qualities, from my point of view, would be less than if I'm being myself. So it's a musical decision to be myself. It wouldn't be honest to try and be like the other person. I'm not able to go into his world. It might be technically possible for me to do so – but not mentally. It's just not possible. [17]

It does sometimes happen that I do the same thing in different groups. But every time I play with someone, I try to find something different. If I'm playing with a string quartet, it'll be different than if I'm playing with a saxophonist or a tape. So when it comes to different groups, I think more about the orchestration, the instruments that are there. And I think that where I'm concerned this induces some kind of behaviour. [02]

I play in different ways in different groups. Consciously and unconsciously I think we're playing in different ways.

Within a performance, within this sitting down and playing with people or within a slightly longer timeframe or within a much longer time frame, I think that's always the way I'll play for ever. Because that's what I do and I don't think that will change. Everything else will change but that will remain constant, that working out of things with other people. Because it's how you kind of live your life as well. You sort of just work stuff out. You do it with the people you meet and trust and with the people you meet but don't necessarily trust. There are some people you want to see; there are some people you might not want to see, or people you don't know you're going to see. Then you have to work it out and think about it and come up with ways of working it out in the longer term or in the moment. [05B]

Sometimes, when you play in a group, you suffer, because you can find yourself in a system of constraints that you don't have when you're playing on your own. When it's a solo, you decide on the constraints. When I'm playing by myself, constraints open up onto a field, a space, whereas in a group, constraints can lead you not to play, or to stop playing. It might be interesting if there were a group where individuality takes precedence over the collective, where individual interests take precedence but give something collective. However, I think that would be difficult to achieve.

I'm interested in shared space. I find it interesting to work with a dancer doing oriental dance, for example, because although their space is different from mine, we try to build a shared space, but a space within which I exist. My journey to experimental music came about as part of my search to find my place in the public space. Solos are very comfortable because there aren't any disruptive elements, that is, other musicians. Other musicians are an issue for me in the group. The solo is an affirmation of something very individualistic.

That's something, an apprenticeship, that good groups give you: they help you understand how you can exist yourself inside the group by being strong. Experiencing the group means being able to stop leaning on other people, in this interplay of memory, finding the security of being in a group but without trying to subscribe to a particular group identity. I think, when you manage to do that, you get a group with extremely independent individuals, who respect the group and who bring out the identity of others. For me the idea of a symbiotic music in improvisation is outdated. As far I'm concerned, the idea of collective trance is outdated.

Improvised music is special because it's music where you experience relationship. There are times when I don't want to play solo, where it bores me. I want to bring myself face to face with others.

It's sociological, a group portrait as a collective. I have the same problem in life – if I were in a restaurant talking with people, I would end up with the same problems: not wanting to play or to express myself, or being doubtful about what to say, or talking too much … . I find myself with the same questions, the same communication issues. I like the saxophone quartet I play in with Marc Baron, Bertrand Denzler and Jean-Luc Guionnet because I find that I can use it to experiment with different communication combinations that go through the sound. For me it's an interesting metaphor for human relationships in a group.

I'm not judging, but I can see what people have been trying to do for nearly sixty years to question the field of social relationships within music or visual art. I think that the field of social relationships has been reinjected into art and that, as improvisers, that's what we do. Even just taking the space in which we're playing, calling the face-to-face musician/audience relationship into question, all the questions we ask ourselves about why we break open performance spaces, why we do electronic music instead of acoustic music. In fact we displace spaces; we try to change relationships within social spaces, mental spaces and cultural spaces. Because it's not so much the style that matters any more, but rather the space or the field. [26]

What we are dealing with, our music, is a very direct form of interaction. We can't look at the score and say: 'That's a terrible piece of music.' We've made the music and it's our responsibility, and it's very direct. I am saying to you, and you to me: 'This is who I am.' So what we are is sound – it's quite an exposed position. [07]

The human factor is very important and then we add … the music. I feel like the relationship I have with people and music is quite physical, and it's true that it doesn't work with some people: being in the same room at the same time doesn't work even if they play well. First of all, there has to be some sort of atomic compatibility and then, following on from that, the feeling that some kind of possible future exists musically speaking. You could say that, in human relationships, you improvise every second that goes by as well. We're atoms on a planet and whatever we do, we always do the same thing. I have the impression that I always feel the human factor, but through the aesthetics. Actually, I don't know. … For me, it's not possible not to care about the music. I mean if we're friends, but the music we do together isn't any good, we may as well just go and have a drink! [01]

When you're playing, you're fine-tuning all the time, you're constantly adapting to different factors which more or less generate the content. The human factors are just part of the process. I don't know how I connect these human factors to the musical form but I do, and this also inputs into my compositions and by its very nature is often the hardest aspect to communicate in the score – so I try to inform my composing with this dynamic evolution of form even though it can only really exist in improvisation. [40]

It's not only the sound. There's also the presence, the state of mind of the person, things that essentially you discover before playing, in a discussion, in a social relationship with the person. So it's a whole. In the end what I'm looking for isn't music, but rather a particular space for exchange. It just so happens that this takes place with sound, so I have to take sound into account since that's the locus of the action. But music remains a tool. It's not my goal.

It's the human being behind the music that I'm interested in. Whether this human being is playing the washing machine, the violin or something else doesn't matter. It's the human being that I'm interested in.

For me, improvisation is a means to living experiences collectively. As a listener, in improvisation, you witness the fabrication of this human experience in real time. [46]

I think a lot of improvising is like speaking to someone because when you're talking to someone, you kind of behave in the same way as the person talking to you. It's a kind of respect for the way people address you. [10]

Improvisation is a story of moments of life shared with people. I do think that improvisation is more enjoyable shared than alone, although it's an interesting exercise when you're on your own. Besides, you never do it on your own, except when you're working at home. You're with a space, with someone who's listening, someone who's watching …. In improvisation, not pure but total improvisation, there's this additional parameter that also exists in graphic performance, for example, but not when you're painting a painting. When you write a score, you write down a multitude of moments that are very much your inner moments and you transcribe them as part of a discourse. The only difference with improvisation is that, in improvisation, these moments are shared between people.

I think I started improvising in order to share moments with other people, and when I saw what happened, very quickly, I thought: 'Well, I would've spent six months writing this and I would never have written anything as good as what we've just done.' So of course I said to myself that this was an interesting tool to use in order to get this kind of result.

But when you improvise with other people, it's not like a discussion: in improvisation you're always trying to make music, whereas when you're in a discussion, you're not trying to create literature.

At certain moments you feel like you're sharing love with the people you're playing with. At others you feel humble. At others you feel violent towards them … .

Rather than a human relationship, it's a moment of humanity.

What is commonly known as the paranoid gaze is a smile, a way of checking behind you while you're being told something. And if you pay attention to such things, it changes your perception of what the person is telling you. People can be more or less sensitive to that. You can lie to some people without them seeing it. But how do you know if someone's lying to you? Not because they tell you. It's because you feel it in the detail. … When you're playing, the process is to some extent the same except that in this music, you try to make something of this sensibility instead of experiencing it passively and being suspicious of other people. [12]

Improvising has always been something serious for me. This doesn't mean that it's not joyful, but there's a solemnity to this work. The joyful part lies in the human relationships, in the fact that nobody is telling you what to do.

I'm really not interested in music in itself, as an object. What I'm really interested in are the people, because they can go places. Contexts and environments are important circumstances but they're only the circumstances of the here and now, of social life, political life, human life, human relations, a certain history of the West, North/South relations, whatever. States and circumstances, or aesthetics are born and die – and there are fantastic people around who go through all this, who are able to go from one thing to another while remaining themselves. That's what reassures me and means that I know what I need to work on: to be that thing, someone who manages to go through all kinds of situations and come out the other side. Maybe that's the goal ... .

I'm much more interested in playing with other people than playing alone. Playing with others is eminently complex. It's amazing how many interactions per second there are, and for me it's also a political project, a political poetic or a poetic politics. All this is interrelated. When you're playing with other people, suddenly, sometimes, you realize that you're living in the same house. However, even with other people, you're always confronted with yourself and sometimes it's incredibly lonely. Loneliness isn't necessarily painful. I love loneliness. I love being alone. I don't mind, I'm inhabited by so many things. But the fact of being so much 'with other people' only to find yourself alone is a little odd, right?

There's nevertheless, implicitly, something fundamentally social in this practice. It's even perhaps a utopia created in the here and now, in the instant in which you're playing. But in the end, despite this extraordinarily social aspect which seems to me as horizontal as you can get and which is connected, at least in my personal history, to an ideology that very quickly attracted me almost religiously actually, despite this extraordinarily social aspect and these social experiences which I find very powerful, you find yourself alone. [15]

Music gives you a happiness that you feel all over your body or at least a satisfaction that is still very ... sensory. I think what really matters is the people, their presence, not what they play. It's not the style of music that makes the difference. [01]

Improvising with other people is a sort of supportive, agitated, trusting, perverse or whatever group game. It works something like a small society: people who get organized, who gang up together, who abandon each other and so on.

There's always a kind of movement back and forth between different ways of functioning: arbitrariness, reaction, everything in between of course, everything that I imagine doing beforehand or on the spot in order to introduce something to the group or to let the others know that I'm there. ... More often than not I invent simple or more complex playing rules that are obvious or concealed. For example, every time a particular person plays, I play a specific sound. Or each time a particular person stops, I play something of an equivalent duration to what they've played, sometimes mixing things up, confusing them, sometimes even confusing myself all on my own.

A sound plays a double role. It's a sound object within the overall form, but it's also a vector for information that I send to the group. And then if I take any preliminary decisions, I leave space to respond to any intimidation sent my way, to any solidarity I receive from others, or to non-awareness.

You start with music, musical material, an instrument and so on, but I think that you can't really avoid extra-musical, strategic, anthropological digressions ... before, in the end, returning to the music ... if you're going to succeed in making music effectively. I honestly believe that when I play in a group I don't think much about music while I'm playing. However, I honestly feel that you need these digressions for it to work, as music.

Even where there's a group musical project at the beginning, when you're actually playing you probably ought to be more interested in other stuff than in the result. That's the big difference with composition as far as I'm concerned. In my opinion, a musical project consists in agreeing on what you want to do together, then using the right tool, improvisation for example, to serve this common desire, and trying to leave yourselves open, at the time, to the possibility of destroying your presumptions. But it only works if there's a lot of trust and an underlying understanding between people. [25]

Music is a social activity; it's not completely cut off from social things. I try not to play in order to show that I can play, in order to be impressive, but it can happen, of course. If there is a silence, there's a temptation to play something impressive, and I think most of us are probably not completely free of this, especially if we try to live from this music and want to be invited back. But this is something I try to avoid. Because this seems to me a very sad reason to make music.

A very long silence can be very impressive too, or very boring, it depends on its quality. And that depends on what happened before or what happens afterwards. When a lot of people use long silences, it becomes less interesting. That is maybe an ego thing as well: you want to be a bit different.

I am interested in the social aspect of music, not only in the musical result. But I think they are related. If the music doesn't work, it's also a social thing that isn't working. And if the music is working then usually the social thing also does. Not always, of course. You can get situations of conflict – but in a sense that's 'working together' as well. When everybody is just being polite in their playing, and after the concert, that can lead to a stifling of honest criticism. There's a social set-up, the fact that we are playing together. I probably wouldn't choose to play with somebody whose music I didn't like, so it shows that there is some social and musical connection already, before we even play together. While playing, I sometimes do something that's not obvious, like play a loud note, for example. But for musical reasons, not social reasons, unless it's in the sense that I want to place us all in a more difficult situation, in order for us to get out of our habits. I think that's a strategy that I use quite a lot. And you can do that through silence as well, actually, except when everybody uses silence a lot. It's not that I want to make someone angry, it seems like it can make the music more interesting, make the music more edgy. Because improvised music can get to be safe, quite quickly. In composition, I find it a bit easier to bypass my habits. It's possible also in improvisation, but you have to keep working on strategies, putting a spanner in the works, making disturbances or being critical. One strategy is also who I choose to play or not to play with. [28]

With those people that I play with most of the time, one of the reasons I choose to play with them is because they surprise me. If I start to play with people and the same things happen all the time, or I know that A is going to happen before B and then C, I think I'd get bored of it or I'd have to figure out some kind of pre-composed structure that means we can't actually predict the result, or a structure that highlights or messes with this assumption. [30]

The first thing is whom I'm playing with. More than in early music and composed music, which are the other areas I'm involved in, the choice of players defines the music. Therefore, to a certain extent, a lot will already be pre-decided (composed), although it's improvised. That is the most important aspect; from there I will probably decide which instrument I play: electronics, the hurdy-gurdy or the violin. Recently I have been playing with youth refugees who are incredibly musical, with not much in common we just play (I give them donated violins) and by imitating them they then zone into my sound and imitate that and start to develop a technique, and we really produce something worth listening to almost from the beginning, whereas I do not hear this level of musical richness from others around me who teach a (their) song, or go in with preset music. This is only possible with improvisation and seems like a gift. [40]

Nowadays I tend to choose the players I play with. Basically, I choose to play with people who don't try to take control of the music or others. I tend to choose musicians who play independently, in their own way. [08B]

I'm open to playing with anybody, but if I play with someone and I feel that it doesn't fit, then I'll never play with that person again. [08A]

When playing with someone for the first time, you can actually read a lot from so many signals even before anybody makes a sound. You can read things about their personality. You just look at the instrument, you look at how they look on stage and you can get some idea of what to expect if you don't know them. In a way, it's not a hard thing as an improviser to be in that situation. Clearly you may find someone you don't want to play with – often I've noticed it only takes one person to ruin an improvisation. Have you ever played with people really throwing different samples at you, stuff that can change idiom and sound, moment by moment? It's a bit of a nightmare for a saxophone player, but it's kind of an interesting technical exercise. In a way you throw your own aesthetics out the window and just try to keep up this barrage of ever-changing stuff, and you can apply that, hopefully, on a more musical level to any situation. [14]

With my projects, the more the project and what we're trying to do is defined, the more I feel like I am really improvising, the more I feel a real sense of freedom, where I can really do anything. Whereas in a much more problematic situation, where it's not working at all, I would be more inclined to throw out some completely unmusical solutions to try to force the situation, or to force myself, into a different direction. And maybe that's real improvising. [35A]

I think that musicians make too many sounds and that they have an innate need to make sounds all the time without always thinking about why they're making that sound or its role, particularly in a collaborative kind of context. These questions are always in my mind because I've always stated categorically that I'm not a musician and I've never wanted to be a musician, even if I've found myself in musical contexts more and more and I certainly enjoy working with people. There's a big difference between working solo and working collaboratively and there's a social dimension about collaborations, which I enjoy more and more.

I've been reconsidering why I make music and what I want to do with it and started to collaborate with other musicians who I admired more or less as a fan, whose instrumental techniques or concepts appealed to me. I'm not a performer who plays with lots of people. I work very specifically with people – a certain idea that I'd like to develop with another musician, for example – so there are a couple of musicians that I work with quite regularly and the advantage of that is the social dimension. We can sit down and talk about different ideas and how different ideas might work with or against each other. Playing with other musicians brings another level of knowledge, sophistication and expertise to your own work. Having someone interact with what you do broadens what you can do. That was a very profound experience for me, to hear my music, to play my music with someone else. And then to hear something I could never do by myself was wonderful. [22]

I'm more interested in the stability of a kind of group of people who play together and inform each other a lot and are very critical as well – self-critical, constructively critical. I play with people who are really good friends. There's little distinction between playing and not. We could just as easily go to the museum, or go into town to have a look at pictures together. I think that they're very much the same thing to me. We sit around together, listening to whatever we're listening to at that moment, talking about whatever we're talking about, and this informs the music we made the day before or the music we'll make the day after. But then we might listen to it again, a couple of months down the line, and things will have changed really quite a lot. It will be the same but things will have moved on and there'll be new things and it almost has an endless life. I think it's very important to talk about our music and also to talk about other music. Because through talking about other music you're ultimately talking about the music you're making yourself. Broadly speaking, all I really talk about is music, or an extension of it. [05B]

What's most wonderful for me is playing with a musician I've known for a long time and continuing to be surprised by what we do together. I don't think you can really work on this. But I'm not sure either.

With Olivier Benoit, I have the impression (unique by the way) that I'm not doing anything, that it's our sounds that make the music. I feel as if I'm a machine, a tool that gives access to sound. And I think he shares this feeling too. It's very satisfying. [43]

My whole focus really is on regular groups. Personally I think that, as improvisers, it's the easiest thing in the world to meet somebody and just play for the first time, I don't find that hard at all. What I find more difficult and ultimately more interesting is the challenge of playing within the context of regular groups, or long-standing collaborations, and working in the context of your group sound – taking it in new directions, to progress. But that progression doesn't have to be from concert to concert, it might be a slow progression: you could look back over six months, or twelve months, or three years and see that you have moved, that you have gone somewhere with that group, and things haven't stayed still and got boring and that's why I've begun to really focus on that over the last three years. But that's not to say that I don't enjoy ad hoc meetings. [06B]

I think I find it more of a challenge when there's a group history. [06A]

Of course, when I play with a group with a history – when we've learnt to play this music together, from the beginning – the mode of listening is predetermined because of the history, gestures, people and so on. You develop your little rituals, of course. Things move faster if you set up the way you listen in advance one way or another, but you can give yourself a fright or surprise yourself by reversing the phases, by changing the way you listen.

I've done this many times in the trio with John Butcher and Axel Dörner: I don't listen to myself at all. I don't listen to what I'm playing. I don't give it any importance. I just analyse what's going on with them, for them very very quickly. It's actually a kind of ping-pong listening between the two other instruments, super-fast, as fast as I can. [19]

I think in terms of improvising, you should always be trying to seek out some freshness in the relationship with the materials, with the things you're playing and, often, the information and the stimulus come from what you're hearing, from the 'other ingredient', the other people you're playing with. So it should always be the same, in a sense, whether you've been playing with somebody for a long time, or whether you're playing together for the first time. I guess with a longer relationship like AMM I'm obviously more familiar with what comes up, but I also hope, and I feel it is the case, that Keith Rowe and John Tilbury have always been pretty creative people; therefore, they're always pushing me and pushing themselves. So although I am familiar with their language, they sometimes say things in a new poetic way that I've not heard before, and that's what one likes.

Playing with somebody for the first time is always fresh poetry, and you cherish that, that is a nice thing to happen. I know some musicians feel that they need constant refreshment from other new relationships, and I understand that, but I think there's also something quite interesting in dealing with a relationship, and even the sound of relationships over a long period of time because you mature, and the whole relationship with those things matures, rather than you going off for a fresh thing here and a fresh thing there. You come up against the same kind of textual and musical problems and you see them in a deeper way, I think. It's worth spending time doing it, rather than saying: 'I've had enough of that' and then moving on. Sometimes it's at that very point where you feel you have no more to find out, or no more to give, that it opens up a new vista. So it's worth persevering, I think. [07]

There are exceptions. Sometimes there are new encounters where this happens too, but for me you have to continue working together for a long time, because in ten years it'll be insane. Some improvisers love to change partners or instrument all the time, and I'm not criticizing them because that's also a valid approach, but personally I've never been able to work like that. [15]

My main interest has been in longer term collaborations with regular groups. I think, for me, there's always this interest in building up some shared musical language and, again, finding an area where we can build something in such a way that you're not quite sure who's making which sound all the time. In order to play just once with someone, it would seem to me that you'd have to have a very fixed idea about what do to, which contradicts my ethos in improvising – you'd just be repeating yourself with different people.

What I would say about that is when we used to get together most frequently, maybe not quite as often as once a week, I think there were times when it felt like a bit of a habit. I actually thought to myself, I don't know if the others did too: 'Are those two improvisations really different pieces of music or are they in effect two different realizations of the same score?' I think there have been times when I've felt that we've got into a habit of playing.

For the first seven years or so of the group's history we used to play every week, week in week out and, of course, in the end that did get a bit much, I think. We're all quite happy now to meet less regularly, but perhaps each occasion is a bit more unique because of that. [11]

I guess the pattern of work for somebody like me is to hit and split. It's always: you're there, you play, you're gone. You don't always get the chance to work like a real fine artist would, thinking about every specific. But in a way, we celebrate that, we like that. We like that rough approximation. And it's got this kind of rough and ready quality to it. That's what it is. [16]

In music, and more precisely with the musicians I've chosen, I'm not nice and I'm not mean. That's exactly what I'm interested in, establishing other types of relationship. Not playing too loudly with a violinist isn't a question of kindness or politeness; it's just consideration of what's possible. I want the violinist to be able to offer me something. [46]

I want to experience something. If I know that the musicians I'm playing with won't feel comfortable if I play very loud, I don't do it because I won't feel comfortable either. There are some things I know before the concert starts. I can't forget them. But the idea of surprise is still there, maybe on another level of perception. [32]

If I play with someone for the first time and he plays very loud, for example, and I don't like it, I play very quietly and wait. In such cases, it's as if my role is not to play good music but to show that we don't like each other. I try to follow my own way but sometimes it's difficult to survive.

If a musician decides beforehand to have a strategy to play with me, I don't like it. But I'm not against it.

Music is something like a fight. But the good thing is that no one really dies because of the music. This kind of fight allows us to find a lot of ideas. [33]

If, for example, I make a percussive sound while the other musicians are playing a continuous sound, I give them the freedom to choose whether they want to ignore it and continue what they're doing or use it as a means to change what they're doing. And I accept their decision, whatever it may be. I never play something to get something specific from the musicians I'm playing with. I don't do anything to provoke them. I don't feel the need to help them either. I figure that their music is as it should be. In the same way, when someone makes a sound, changes something, I can use it or not. For this to work everyone has to have a certain self-confidence. And it can even become a kind of game. But I always play what I want to hear. When I force myself to play something because my reason tells me it's what I should play, it doesn't work. I really want to see what I'm doing gives, so I do it and let the other musicians decide if they want to do something with it or not, if they want to react or not. And I expect the same from other musicians. I like playing with other musicians but remaining entirely myself at the same time. I also like everyone to have the freedom to stop playing if they want. Even if that may seem risky. I really like accidents. [48]

It's very intuitive ... but it's not intuition. I have a whole lot of rules inside me. Sometimes there's imitation, sometimes counterpoint or something really different, short structures, long ones ... or there's doing something in parallel, ignoring without ignoring.

Sometimes, you're playing in a vocabulary everyone knows and then suddenly you do something unexpected, which isn't part of that language. I don't do that very much. Sometimes I don't dare ... because I'm afraid of having everyone against me. It's a social thing, it's not musical. It's easier when there are two of you, because you can count on each other to spring surprises, and vice versa. When you're playing in a group, it's much more difficult. It's as if you had to jump. First you check that everything is ready and then you go for it. I really like that feeling, but it's a bit like a physical assault. It's a bit violent.

With some musicians, you get the feeling right away that they're going to make clear decisions, always go against, and that isn't very interesting. The problem comes when things are no longer alive. And if the musicians who are improvising are sure of themselves and always do the same thing, the playing becomes a style and that's not what I'm after.

Sometimes someone makes quick movements and everyone starts to follow them. That's a road to nowhere, not really worth bothering with. If there's a structure and everyone's doing different stuff, that's fine, but if you're handing out roles, it's not good. [29]

For me, to adapt is negative. I want to be at a distance from the others. I don't want to fit in with the other musicians. But I think it's a kind of communication. In the end, I can say that I do communicate with the other musicians. It depends on the situation but basically my decision depends on the other sounds. For example, if there are some sounds, I want to play as if there is no relationship with those sounds but, of course, it is a kind of relationship. If a sound is in a certain place, I want to put my sound in another. Somewhere else. I don't want to imitate but maybe it happens sometimes. Sometimes, this is a problem – I'm waiting for silence, for the moment the sound stops, but if I play like that, it becomes like tennis. I don't like that but it happens. I'm a bit cynical: if there is good music I want to create a storm or break it, in a subjective way, keep my distance from the others. It's like drawing. If there's a round spot and I draw a square of the same colour, there will be some kind of relationship. So if there's a blue round spot, I want to draw an umbrella. I want to create a distance between other sounds and my own. Also, I want to put distance between my previous sound and the next one. And the result is what it is. If there's a kind of drawing and I put something in, it's like a ship in the river. So there are layers. Actually, I've only started improvising like that recently. Before, it was more like baseball. [08B]

I love that feeling of 'being played' by somebody else. It doesn't mean that it's a literal thing, because you can go against the grain and use all sorts of compositional strategic decisions. But when we are making music together – even if this sounds like a cliché about improvisation – there is something that unfolds which reveals so much about the persons, their politics and so on. I do love that. [21]

It's a strategy, but not with the intent of winning, not like a military strategy. It's more a question of being aware of the circumstances, the situation that makes things possible. Because every gig is a very privileged moment. [16]

The decision lies in the choice of materials, timbres … . And then there are strategies, choices that are made to guide the form. [37]

I don't decide, and this can raise problems that have to be solved. Problems to do with the situation and environment: I'm in a forest and I have to find my way. But I don't decide whether to go right or left. … I know a lot of improvisers talk about decisions. Steve Lacy spoke about that a lot, but for me things have never presented themselves like that: the path unfolds as I move forward, a bit like Victor Fleming's *The Wizard of Oz* really. I have to make myself fluid in order to accept the fluidity of that path. Sometimes I no longer feel any apprehension, and it's like a moment of grace. That's where things happen of themselves and I'm almost a spectator of what's going on. It's quite rare, but when it happens it's thrilling because you don't even have to concern yourself with your body, like in metempsychosis. We're back to the idea of harmony as spoken of by the mystics. Perhaps this is the state of grace that you seek. This almost mystical state, this state of suspension, during which the soul is traversed, in which you don't even have to think, don't even have to put your confidence in the body or its muscles to play your instrument. Things just happen. You're inhabited. You're possessed. [15]

What matters is how I listen, the listening situation I put myself into when I work with people on sound. And it's that particular situation – which can change and fluctuate, sometimes very quickly – that makes me take decisions.

Listening to the Other Musicians, the Human Factor, the Strategies   45

In fact, I think I don't make decisions anymore. I just try to be ears, breath, fingers. I try to eliminate the reflective part of the brain as much as possible, really to abandon myself within this state. ... What bothers me about deciding is the judgement. You have to judge the situation and sometimes that's very disturbing. And I realized that judging what's going on completely obstructs the rest of the work, whereas in those moments you need to listen and work.

When I play with a musician and feel that they have made a lot of decisions before playing, it gets very difficult for me. [19]

You do have strategies, but they necessarily depend on the particular moment, the context. These aren't things that I prepare in advance, but rather react to in the moment, during the process of interaction. If someone wants to take me somewhere else, I may, for example, not go. Or pretend to take someone somewhere and once the person sets themselves in that direction, change direction abruptly. This is about – and strangely, this contradicts what I said about the state that I put myself into when I'm improvising – taking the other musician out of their state and bringing about a little awakening of consciousness so that they realize where they are and that I'm there too. ... It may also mean stopping playing, stopping making sound. Or taking a path that's completely independent of the other musician's path.

Sometimes I anticipate. I tell myself: 'I have to make that particular sound.' But it's instantaneous. I mean, it comes to me when a sound ends. It's extremely rapid. There's time for reflection, but it's so short that reflection can't actually take place. In fact, there's a relationship to time. There's a present that's quite broad and perhaps a short period of anticipation. But how to put into words, explain, that this isn't 'manipulation', that this isn't the same as deciding? [46]

My decisions are more about my attitude than the musical result. For example, I can decide – or want to decide – to play more soberly, calmly with one musician, while at other times I say to myself: 'Here, it's going to be chaotic.' Yes, it's more about the attitude than the musical result. Even if it's unspoken, in most things I do, there's always an idea, an idea that emerges as a line or framework and it's almost as if taking things outside it would be a mistake – or there must be some meaning in relation to this framework, because at the same time, you always allow yourself a great deal of freedom. This is the kind of attitude I'm talking about. I don't worry about the result. ... You give yourselves a framework and the result doesn't really matter. ... It follows on from the framework. When I play with someone for the first time, I'm pretty polite. ... But basically, it's the same. Depending on the instrument and what I can feel from the person – indications that may, moreover, be totally at odds with the music – a certain idea emerges. In such cases, as soon as I hear the first sound, I start and then ... . Anyway, you have to give yourself something to work on so that there's at least some sort of analysis. ... Of course, this contradicts what I said about not reflecting. In fact, it's not that I don't reflect on this stuff, it's that there's a kind of reflection that takes place in a domain other than the usual domain of thought and analysis, but which means that when I meet someone, some kind of intelligence is established. For me, some kind of intelligence of the music forms as part of the encounter. What I mean is that if the other musician plays in certain a way, a certain musical attitude results. And vice versa. [02]

How do you know what the music needs? I'm thinking of this thing which is called 'genius loci'. It's a label for things that you cannot describe. I'm happy not to label it. [05A]

When you improvise, if you have to make a decision, you are already late. You don't make decisions. The problem doesn't lie there. You should be able to look into the future. There is a very interesting album by Thelonious Monk – an amazing one – in which you can hear that when the rest of the musicians play their solos, he can anticipate everything they play. It's like magic. To improvise means to look into the future: in one millisecond you know what's best to do. You know it, you don't decide. You have this ability to look into the future. Then you know immediately what to do – no questions. It's not that you don't think, but you don't speculate: 'Shall I stop now? Shall I play this note like this?' That is not useful. You'd better don't make decisions when you play. [31]

It's not possible to describe how I make decisions while playing. I think about it before and after but while I'm doing it, I can't think like that otherwise it'll be too late. Somebody plays a certain sound, somebody else plays a certain sound, they come together in my mind and the aesthetic system that I follow tells me what to do. I can't think before it happens. I can't say: 'In about ten seconds I'll make this sound' because by then the situation might be completely different. When I stop during a piece, if there's no reason to play again, I don't play. If there's a reason to play, I play. It's like walking on the street: your relationship to the environment and what you have to do within it. If there's a glass wall and you walk through it, you're likely to hurt yourself. [17]

I don't really have the impression of choosing to make one particular sound rather than another. When I improvise, that's the sound that comes out. When I start choosing, I might as well stop playing – I mean, I'm no longer really in the music. Or rather: I think it's a conscious choice, but not a deliberate choice. It's not: 'I've decided to make this sound', it's: 'I have to make this particular sound.'

Making the deliberate decision to play very aggressive sounds very much louder than everyone else when they're all playing pianissimo is still improvisation as far as I'm concerned. I said it was reactive, but sometimes you throw things in anyway, whether that means putting a cat among the pigeons or starting down a path that others follow, there's still a moment when you throw things in.

When I said: 'I don't really have the impression of choosing to make one particular sound rather than another', that's a kind of ideal. The first sound of a concert, for example, will necessarily be much more deliberate than the second. … In fact, we shouldn't confuse 'deliberate' with what is 'eventful in terms of the music'. Something can be eventful in terms of the music and just as unintentional as the rest, just as it can be very deliberate and less significant in musical terms. [12]

In the best moments, when I feel good, I know what I want to play. I feel it inside myself. I want something, something weak or strong, short or long … . I have an idea of the sound. It's not a matter of technique or how I'm going to make that sound. It's rather the appearance of the sound. Then I look at how to get there. [29]

How do I choose the sounds? Not through reasoning, I don't think. It's not a rational choice. I don't weigh the pros and cons while I'm playing. The choice is made in relation to a vocabulary that we have chosen and that has been put into place over time and in relation to the idea of avoiding instrumental reflexes. There's reflection but not reasoning. In fact, I don't know what's going on. I think my actions also have a relationship to the listening postures everyone else adopts; I try to focus on the ways of listening of everyone around, at the same time as trying to carry on. When I say that it's not through reasoning, I mean there's no musical reason that motivates a change or what will happen next; it may have more to do with the psychological or physiological realm. [47]

You're making these sorts of decision, it can almost be second-by-second in a group, and I think some of these decisions are being made subconsciously. You're not thinking: 'I'll go with, I'll go against that.' It doesn't work on that kind of level. [14]

If I trust the musicians I'm playing with, I know that, within that context, my decision is going to be right. [06B]

Ideally, I don't think much while playing. But in a situation that I feel is problematic, I do. In situations where I'm thinking a lot, I would imagine I don't make such interesting improvised music, and I would say that I probably don't make much improvised music then. If you make a lot of decisions, that's probably like saying: 'Here is a solution that I understand, let's see what it does.' And maybe this will provoke improvisation, when you aren't really in it, to really conceive of where you will go. That's where improvised music really is, at that point where you're actually having to learn as you go.

I feel that I have an ideal, imagined playing state. But I don't think that state has a particular sound.

I think musical decisions and decisions based on the relationship with the other musicians are very related – perhaps unfortunately.

Every point where you make a decision is hopefully going to open up an avenue where the music pulls you forward without you having to make too many decisions.

When I make the decision to change from one sound to another, I am probably very influenced by emotion and circumstances and my own sense of the power of the sound and the sense of how the room is responding, how I'm experiencing that sound in the room with the audience. Sometimes you're in a situation where you think: 'Playing this sound was a waste of time, how do I get out of that situation?' The failure of a compositional choice and the failure of an emotional state become connected.

I would say that in situations where you're more conscious, where you're making more decisions that are about problem-solving, or about your sense of sonic need, you're more able to start making choices about form. And the performances where this happens can be very interesting to listen to. But I'm still looking for that state where things happen that aren't part of your psychological make-up, where events that surprise you occur. [35B]

Actually, decisions are made, but it's not easy to think them through. Because I would like it if these decisions were taken by good old music itself. … If, for example, I take the decision to stop something and inject a very different element, do I take a decision to create a contrast or is the decision taken?

Fortunately, during a concert, there's no time for self-reflection or analysis on why, otherwise I think we would fall into a process that is no longer live improvisation, but that would already be composition. Decisions would be taken in the name of the goddess Music … .

During concerts, you're in the vein of time and you don't stop to analyse. You don't listen to what has been played, see if you could cut earlier and so on. Therefore, you have to negotiate your decisions in real time, the moments you take responsibility, in the name of a … in the name of what? In the name of definitions, presuppositions, intentions, norms therefore …. So, you're actually still composing, but in the moment, without any time for reflection, analysis, choice. This probably means that certain small sections, small cells of ideology are produced in relation to the music, and, why not, in relation to the state of the world … .

You'd need to spend a century archiving, ranking all the types of decisions and their consequences because there are harsh decisions, gentle decisions, wiles and so on.

Personally, I'm conscious of taking a lot of decisions. And I already see a relationship in that with what I could call the political realm because to make a decision is already to impose, to constrain. … Why do I approach this with such precaution and mistrust? Because already it's almost in the realm of power play.

At the same time, someone who thinks that they make a decision for each of their musical acts is very strange.

That's something that's very strange to imagine happening. And if everyone is always master of their own decisions, then does that mean we're promoting some supreme fascism or more moderately total anarchism? It's very strange.

My background is one of democratic idealism, which isn't really credible – it's sweet but full of leaks. It's at least as moribund as jazz and maybe European improvised music. … Personally, I'm going to wait and see … .

On the spot, I try to eliminate asking myself why I'm doing one thing or another. What's disturbing is that if I listen to the recording of a concert, I very quickly understand why I made a particular decision at a particular time. [20]

In a group, there's a to-ing and fro-ing of decisions and generation. I listen and I decide to do this or that.

I don't calculate anything at all, I don't calculate silences. It's a relationship to time and space. It's sentient, but very intellectual. It's a group decision. If I feel that I shouldn't play, I don't play. If I feel that I want to play something, I do so. It's a relationship with the whole.

But I don't approach it as a musician. I approach it as a visual artist. There are lines. There's a surface and I draw lines.

I decide at the very moment of playing. Actually I decide just before. I feel and I play. They're just ideas of how you occupy densities.

It's not logical, it's more physical than logical, it's more related to space, a mass relationship. It's more like this: I add more darkness, more lightness, more density. I create more space. It's malleable. I see it more in terms of balance, volume, shaping things in a space. That's what I'm most interested in. [26]

More and more, I don't disconnect the brain from my whole self, particularly when I'm improvising and when I'm very involved. The action doesn't happen in my brain ... it comes more from a physical impulse. I enjoy it when I'm really thinking about things and making very conscious decisions to do things – 'There's been enough space. ... I have an interesting idea, I'm going to put it here ...' – but that's not what seems to happen most of the time. This situation isn't necessarily the ideal. Most of the time a sound feels as though it needs to happen, not that I've decided that it will.

I'll often have either the bow or the drumsticks in my hand, or the bells ... and of course there is quite a lot of preparation time required to make a particular sound with the *guzheng* as opposed to a saxophonist or a singer.

So if you were to zoom into my brain, or zoom into me anywhere, you would feel, for example, a rush of adrenaline, then an attempt to grab the most appropriate tool to create the sound that needed to happen – and I guess I would feel that sound before it happened.

There is a preview of the feeling of the sound, perhaps not the actual tone or timbre. With the *guzheng*, I often have it set up so that I don't know which note is going to come out or how textured the sound of the bow is going to be. So if I've just put a bridge up and haven't tested the tuning, if I hit a particular string with the drumsticks or the bow, at a particular point, I have to approximate what the sound is going to be – so there's that element of chance also. I do this on purpose, I like this element of chance – it excites me. For example, when I sit at the harp I know that the red strings will give me a C. With the *guzheng*, I can't preview the whole sound, but I know what the feeling of it will be – how hard I hit it, or how much tension I apply, perhaps. In my mind, I don't think I'm consciously thinking: 'I'm going to make this sound now to alter the music in this way.' It's very much like a rush of blood rather than a mathematical decision.

Preview? For me, it's less than a second a lot of the time. The human brain, and emotion, everything happens so quickly ... .

There are times when I'm improvising when I feel like I'm made up of millions of needles and options, and it's at those times when I feel like I don't choose – that's what I find the most exciting.

This moment for me is like an electrical impulse and it is one of the reasons why I continue to play music: it's almost like a high – a drug high – a moment of ecstasy almost ... but maybe that's too extreme. It doesn't happen so often. I continue to be addicted to this, or I continue to pursue this because of that potential.

You can't compose those moments. I think you can compose situations where those moments can occur more often perhaps. [30]

With instruments like the hurdy-gurdy, it's similar to electronics in that you have to set things up in advance as you do with presets on a computer. It's not like the violin or the harp, where all the strings and sound potentials are available as a given. On the hurdy-gurdy, I decide which strings can touch the wheel and which strings don't – like the computer you can trigger sounds on and off very fast but in general one does not have all the sound potentials available at the same time because there are so many and they depend on how the instrument is preset. So I could narrow it down by deciding to use just bass strings for a while, or I might even have composed some musical figurations or Foley sounds in advance. Or feel my way back into baroque and earlier music, where you have the *basso continuo* with its harmonic structure given as a numerical shorthand, but how you join up all the parts is improvised. I really like that type of thing. If I'm really on top of the material with a huge amount of time to practise, then I might decide to improvise completely freely. [40]

Sometimes I would like to choose a frequency randomly, which is of course not possible because I have to click somewhere on my screen. And I never made a random generator, which would be easy to do, of course. There are situations where I don't care which frequency I play, I pick up one and I listen to it and after that I can find the next one.

Sometimes I want to get something that I know is possible to do together and so I kind of offer a frequency to somebody, so that we can play together. It can also be that I play with the audience, with their perception, for example, playing a frequency at a very low volume, which will take them some time to hear. But, consciously at least, I don't want to force the other musicians to do things.

I know that some of my sounds work well together. There are some known patterns that I use. On the other hand I want to surprise myself. But it's very difficult to forget that I already know these sounds. In a concert situation, I have to forget. So I try to listen to it as if I was hearing them for the first time.

I have a vision of the sounds I can make, but I don't know what will happen next. With my instrument, I'm pretty slow, for example, if I want to change something. When I decide that I want to do something, I often have to prepare it. So it's not very spontaneous. It's hard 'not to think'. But I really try to be driven by my listening.

We often make some decisions before the concert starts – for example, whether it's going to be a loud or a soft set. It depends mostly on the situation, the space where we play, the audience and sometimes, depending on whom I'm playing with, if it's going to be static or not. If there is a second set, or maybe another group on the same bill, we talk about what we could do to play something different – or not. But I can't make decisions about the form of the piece. It can happen that I take some very simple decisions concerning the form, like starting very quietly and then getting very loud. Quite often, though, we decide on the length of the piece. But while playing, I don't decide beforehand that a sound will last for two minutes or so. I just decide which sound to play. [32]

I think you have to be concise. Only make a sound if it's 'necessary', not let yourself be drawn into the energy, channel it better. How do I position myself within a temporality affected by urgency – but which isn't anecdotal – and remain true to an intention, an energy that aims to be concise? It's like an organism whose whole entity is changed each time someone plays something. Suddenly, a certain space-time opens up and I feel I have to produce a particular type of sound in order to contribute. It goes very fast. It can happen in fractions of a second. [45]

I think I've got pretty quick on the instrument now, the voice. I used to improvise with the trumpet but I can't do that anymore, because the trumpet is a whole machine to run! With the voice, the message from head to machine is quicker! Compared to laptops, for example. Some electronic players I know are so fucking slow! The only safe thing they can do is set off a sound layer. Before starting a sound, though, I have to make a placement with my larynx to get that sound, physically, make a little adjustment. I couldn't do that without thinking about it – but hopefully it's all very quick. I often stop because I need a rest. There are quite physical reasons for stopping. Other than that, I start singing again when I think I can add something to what's there already – that's what I would think. There are times when nothing comes, for a while, and you enjoy listening. Then, hopefully, something comes. But if nothing does you just sit there, all night! [18]

Your mental process, especially in a group situation, sometimes runs in sync with the other players and sometimes it runs out of sync. So you have the idea that this and this will fit really well, but if somebody else is moving in a different direction, you can't count on what they're doing anymore so suddenly you're in a new situation. There are, of course, chance elements in improvised music but it's not chance in the way John Cage works with chance. We also work with intuition and telepathy, something like telepathy, and look for an understanding which is different from celebrating the notion of the arbitrary nature of chance. Certain kinds of decisions are very fast – it's also true if, say, somebody's playing Chopin or something; they're not thinking about every note, they're playing groups of notes, patterns, shapes, forms, dynamics, everything is in long lines, which aren't the consequence of adding together single intellectual decisions.

Very often we talk about left brain and right brain – some of it is left brain, some of it is right brain. I know with solo playing, for example, that, in order to do certain things, I have to get myself into right brain dominance before things really start to happen. This really means that I'm not making decisions in that sense about anything. I'm simply there and something is happening. And I'm sort of in control and sort of not in control. It's like the feedback between what's happening and what I'm trying to make happen. So, of course, you need that kind of pragmatism. It's a kind of pragmatism in a way; you accept that what's happening is happening. You don't say: 'Something else should be happening.' Or you can say that too! Another analogy: it's like steering those big oil tankers; they have to decide to turn left about two hours before they want to turn, they have to start thinking about turning left. ... Maybe with some kinds of improvisation it's similar; you have to start the turn a long time before it happens. But with other kinds, it turns on a sixpence, the changes and decisions are very rapid. [16]

Things can move very quickly, or they can take a long time. The pace thing is interesting. Derek Bailey used to say that there were two types of improvisations, the fast and the slow, and he would try to play at a middle pace. But I think it's interesting to explore them all, trying as many possibilities as you can. [06A]

I think five years ago I was more spontaneous. [23]

How do I make decisions while playing? First of all, I would say there are no rules. Sometimes it's very spontaneous – whatever that means, because I don't really believe in spontaneity. … To me, 'spontaneous' is planned as well. The period of deciding – 'I'm going to do this' and 'I'm doing that' – is very short. But it's not at the same time. Because that isn't the way our brain works. I just read about a very interesting discovery: our brain actually decides upwards of seven seconds before we do something. The decision is made in the brain. Like if I say, I consciously, deliberately raise my arm – I'm doing it but in my brain the stimulus was there maybe seven seconds before I did it! Which is frightening in a way but fantastic. It's very long. The research done was this: they injected an electrical impulse into the brain, into the area which controls the right arm. That part of the brain was stimulated and the person raised the arm and was asked: 'Did you decide to do that?' and the person said: 'Yes, it was me, I wanted to do that.' That's beside the point, but I find it very interesting. Actually, it has something to do with your question, because I might think I'm doing something very consciously, but then, was it that? There's a certain pool of information, of knowledge, which I carry around with me. And this pool is the result of millions and millions of pieces of information. I react, I don't really act consciously. I react to my own understanding. Of what? Now it's very complicated: of my knowledge, of my consciousness, of my brain. So then there are decisions … they are planned, but a long time ago. It could be a day before, or it could be a month before or a couple of hours before. In improvised music, for instance – we're not talking about composition – if I make a decision that I don't want to react to what's going on, that is actually a reaction to what will happen.

It's an old idea, maybe you could call it a Cagean idea: 'Everybody should play for himself and not react.' There was a certain time in improvised music when everybody was really free – but a lot of things were not allowed, a lot of things were forbidden. … That was about thirty years ago. It's a very reactionary state and I don't care much for that. Today, I react, quite often. I hear something, a sound I like, and I decide I want to go into that sound, maybe in, unison, go into it and play with it. Which was forbidden in free music – but as I said, that was a long time ago and that's a very old-fashioned way of playing music. And then of course there is the question of composition. That changes things as well. At a certain point I was trying to compose – but I would like to say 'write' rather than 'compose' – and that was a similar situation. The musician should play for himself what is written down and try not to react to others. But then again, that was a long time ago. The compositions I'm doing now are the exact opposite: if we're going to play a piece together, I'd like us to play it together.

Sometimes I say to myself: 'I'm going to start after seven minutes and play my first note, regardless of what happens.' And sometimes I do it, sometimes I don't, because there's something very interesting happening and I want to talk with it. I can't shut up. Or, there is something I dislike so I break my own rule and start later. That's playing around a little bit. [27]

In general, if I know why I'm playing a particular sound, that means it's going badly. ... When I say to myself: 'I'm going to make this particular sound because we're playing this particular music' and I play sounds while reflecting on the music, it's because I'm trying to put something right. ... But in general, I don't really know why I'm playing one particular sound rather than another. The decision that I take may come from what I have in my hands, objects that I'm using. It may also come from what happens to be easy for me to pick up. It may come from focusing on a frequency, a texture or an attack. Sometimes I try to play the sounds that I've worked on and integrate them into what's happening in the group's play. Sometimes I give myself a kind of score, a little bit in advance. That happens. But these are things that can also be done while playing. For example, I say to myself: 'I'll count to forty, I'll make that sound, I'll count to forty and I'll stop.' Sometimes I do that. Especially during passages where the music is settled, steady. I do this more often with bands I play with regularly, when I'm more familiar with the sounds that are played. [13]

You're being influenced by what's happening so sometimes I might decide, let's say, to play a long sound. Other sounds I start and I don't know how long they're going to be. It depends on who I'm playing with. Sometimes I know that the other musician is going to play one sound for quite a long time. But within that there is a lot of room for exploration, lots of ways to make decisions. [04A]

There are times when I find myself making longer sounds, doing more static stuff, which settle, which are all the more interesting because they take time to develop, with stratifications, which wouldn't be anything if I only played them for two seconds. So, there's a temporality that's spread out over five, ten or twelve minutes. In that case there's a kind of base, a foundation that's laid, on which I insist. And if I'm not on my own, it's up to others to follow, or to place themselves on top of it. Some decisions are made like that. [36]

In some projects, I also like to tell myself that I'm going to work for a quarter of an hour on certain material and develop it as much as possible with those musicians. I limit myself a lot in terms of the tools and try to explore an idea, try to make it grow, pay attention to all the attacks.

When there's too much politeness, too much waiting, no one daring, the music turns into soft dough with nothing happening. Then, yes, I may try to kick it about a bit to see if I can shake the tree a bit. [38]

Once, I was almost consciously trying not to let the piece sound like what it was going to sound like. And as soon as it started to sound like something, I was trying to redirect it. That's another way of approaching playing, another way of making choices. As soon as anything starts, just change it and always try to change it, quite consciously. As a procedure, it's just as valid as balancing something on there and waiting until it falls off. And that happens on almost every level. You choose your space, you chose your people, you choose … . For example, today we plan to play within certain parameters: you're only here till five o'clock, we're going to do it here – that's no different to saying: 'I'm going to do such-and-such for a minute.' It's the same thing, just on a smaller or larger scale. [05B]

When, for me, something is too clear, too well defined, it may well be that I really make decisions with the aim of creating something which has a bit of an indefinite character, so that the musical framework can offer that indefiniteness, something not nameable, music that aims to be indeterminate. As soon as clarity becomes more definite, a logic such as 'that leads to playing that, I absolutely have to do that', I do it with a minute's delay; that is, 'It's there, but I'm not playing it there and it's better somewhere else.' [39]

I don't think that everything in a so-called improvised form is improvised. Certain things are necessarily sorted out beforehand. Actually, I choose to improvise with certain parameters.

Sometimes I vary sounds just because I can't hold on anymore. Other times it's completely arbitrary decisions, such as count to 100 before the next sound or wait for the next external event before stopping. … There are a lot of strategies, counting is one, not being able to hold on is another. I don't think this means that it's not related to listening. … Sometimes I can't stand being there without playing, so I just play. The opposite also happens, no longer standing playing and stopping. Because I like the complexity and tenseness that's established in the relationship between listening and the sound produced. This zone of tension is a richness for me. I'm constantly stretching and releasing a rubber band: what I'm listening to, what I'm playing out of what I'm listening to, what I'm listening to out of what I'm playing while listening and so on. [25]

I like this idea of camouflage, of using the other instruments to instigate change in what I'm doing. I don't like audiences to hear how I'm shaping my music, so for me it's about waiting for something to happen and using that as a moment to my advantage. I don't like the obvious gesture, I don't like people hearing me do crazy stuff, that's the last thing I want to do. [22]

During a piece, I sometimes say to myself: 'I've already played that, I don't want to do it again, but I'm doing it again.' I say to myself that if I'm saying to myself that I don't want to do it again, then I shouldn't be doing it again and therefore that actually I can do it again! [47]

When there is a silence, if I have an idea, which I think would be interesting in the specific situation and lead to other things, which are interesting too in terms of the musical result, I might play. But if I think it might be interesting not to play or to let someone else play, and if generally I have the feeling people are playing too much, then my tendency would be not to play. I once – just once – did a gig where I didn't play the whole evening, not because I didn't want to, but because every time there was a silence, somebody else played, and I didn't see the point of playing. But I know I sometimes make the wrong decision. [28]

I think it's more about deciding not to do certain things really. I think, within a performance too, you adopt different roles. I might think of myself as bringing two different things together, or I might think: 'It's about time we move away from this', and you make some definite moves to get away from what's happening. [07]

From time to time, I take purely formal decisions in relation to the form that I've played and the memory that I have of it. I reckon that in this or that place, there should be a long silence, for example. I feel that I need to establish something. Silence is always orientated to either the following or the prior event.

It's never silence for silence's sake. Moreover, as we know, silence does not exist, it's a function. This does not mean that all silences have the same quality. Some are fuller than others and how the quality of the 'silence' is dealt with also falls within the set of improvisational choices. I may tell myself, 'the next event has to occur in 200 seconds', but I don't stop myself from playing a sound in the middle of this period of time if this is not simply due to the fact that I've given in. Sometimes it's obvious what you have to do so I ride with it: a huge external cause that I don't want to watch slip past, or simply the obvious fact that the decision I've made isn't going in the right direction.

I tend to think that making decisions helps to counter something, either in yourself or in others, calls into question where things are going spontaneously and musically this can turn into something that offers a lot to the group. [25]

The beginning of a concert is a contingent situation created by people's unpredictable decisions. That's why from this moment on, the whole thing is immediately more limited in the options you have, although they are still quite broad, because even if the situation is really asking for something particular, you can still do the opposite or deliberately work against it or not choose an obvious solution. But from then on, it's about making connections to the situation and the options you have. Within the process, there are two possible levels: you can try to be 'in the moment' as much as possible and, at the same time, remembering what happened and to anticipate an overall form. In addition to your awareness of the situation, you can also anticipate where it might lead to or where you might wish that it leads to and your decisions can become influenced by that too, although it's not given that it will work out because of the other players' decisions, which will be based upon their own interpretation of the situation. But you still have an influence. So it's a mixture of anticipation and of revising your plans when recognizing what is actually happening. And you have to do these two things at the same time – and not hesitate. Because if you wait until you have analysed the situation to its full extend before you act, then you're building up a distance to the actual process. It's like tightrope walking. If you reflect too much, you fall. You might just act without thinking – and sometimes it's great to do that – but if you really try to do everything at the same time – being 'in the moment', being aware of the situation, analyse, plan, revise your plans, act and so on – it can be so overwhelming that you reach a point where it all falls together, in the same moment. For example, you think of something to do and you notice that you're already doing it. So you lose the distance between reflection and action and this is an ideal state. This does happen in groups, but sometimes, though, if it doesn't work like this, it can become a real struggle. This can be intense as well, and the music won't necessarily be less interesting, from the outside view. Struggling intensely is also a way of making music. In these situations, it's just that you become very much aware of the ambiguity of the process. I'm talking of the inside perspective, how it is for me as the performing musician. But it's good to realize that there are also endless outside perspectives. After the music has been played and you look back on it, or if you listen to recordings, your perspective on it changes and if you get feedback from the audience, that can change your perspective as well. There might be good reasons why people perceived it differently to how you thought it was. [44]

I think that improvisation should not be reduced to 'you are an arrow going from A to B, and you listen, and then you receive and you make choices'. Personally, I determine all kinds of things. There are things that I do not want to do and actually I think that what I propose is very minimal indeed. It can even be very narrow, which can be very problematic. I'm aware of this. But I don't see it as more limited than what someone else may be offering, because there's always a limit somewhere. [39]

4

Memory and form

I've noticed that it's not a good thing when I have a fairly clear memory of everything that has happened or when I have some sort of position on what we're doing. It's not a good thing if I'm outside what's going on. I don't get a good feeling for it. [36]

The concerts that seem the most intense to me are often the concerts I can't remember anything about. This is something I get quite often. It's not because I have a bad memory, it's because I'm not any longer thinking during those moments. If I have to think during a concert, I don't like it. [43]

Sometimes I can remember different episodes of the twenty minutes we just played, but I wouldn't say that always happens because the way I really like to improvise is to get into deep concentration and follow that to its completion. [10]

Do I keep in mind what has happened before? I don't know how conscious I am of this. I try not to have a vision of the end. I try to see the next movement only. But I do have a memory of what has happened. [09B]

When I'm playing the drums, when it's loud and highly energetic, it can be a purely physical thing, where everything is going at once and it's a physical state where I'm not really thinking. I'm still thinking about the form but it's completely instinctive. The physical thing takes over and I'm just doing it. Most of the time though, I still remember how the piece started, for example. I can collect some reference points along the way, things to come back to. But I don't really have any projection of what is going to happen next. [35A]

I don't want to remember – but I do sometimes. In a way I do remember. But actually, it's the short-term memory, which I don't stress. It's there and the short-term memory says, 'You just did this.' But I don't try to push this into long-term memory in order to remember an hour of material or how it started. It isn't a problem. [27]

I try to eliminate memory from my solos, but in a group it's impossible. You can't ignore what others have done, and what you've done. You can't forget it. I don't work at it – it is what it is. It's a safety net: when you feel lost you can call on this memory. When you have no perspective, you turn to what has happened and you draw on it again. It's a game of glances. [26]

I can remember what happened before, during the first part of the piece. If there's something that worked, I sometimes say to myself: 'There's something interesting there. Might as well develop it or bring it out, so as to take a proper look at it and really see what it means. We'll see afterwards if we carry on with it.' When that happens, I try to return to the same modes of playing or at least the same impression, the same idea. [02]

I think sometimes I try to make something end the way it began. And getting towards that deliberately. I'll try and remember what the start was like – quiet sounds that built up, for example – and bring it back at the end. But maybe nobody except me notices it! [11]

Something else I use is memory. I try to memorize what's happening, store it somewhere and use it or not. This helps me to feed the rest, to go back to the beginning, to keep the beginning in mind all the time. For all that, I don't think about form because this memory may be accurate regarding just one piece of sound material that was pretty successful or pretty amazing, and you memorize that little fragment. [19]

I use the term 'aural notation'. In a way, memory structures, the way we categorize aural sounds coming from the voice, are more fixed than written notation. There is this idea that written notation is fixed and that there is no such thing as 'aural notation', that aurality just disappears – but no, it doesn't, it's all stored in our memories and, in many ways, it's more fixed than written notation. I'm not interested in notating the aural complexity of my writing; I'm interested in the disjunction between aural and written systems in language.

If we speak language and if I'm language-based, I've internalized all those codes, they are fixed, they are only being recombined. So is that improvisation? I don't know. [21]

For me, with patches, I can't remember where I've come from. I just don't know – either where I've come from or where I've gone to. It's horribly random sometimes. Sometimes I get stuck and have to begin again because I've lost what I'm doing. [11]

I think with improvised music, these questions of form are, in critical terms, taken over from notated music, where you can look at the notation and say: 'Ah, I see the form here.' Form in music is a different thing to form in architecture. I agree that there must be a sense of narrative, of beginning, journey, completion, end – that's maybe a form. But it's not a form in the sense of an architecture. It's a sequence and that's all we're dealing with. After all, if you can turn music into a voltage and send it down a wire, you're not really talking about architecture; you're talking about something sequential, something narrative. And, of course, in the course of a narrative you have the possibility of evoking the future or evoking the past. You have memory, you have imagination. So the idea of being in the moment can be, like Ornette Coleman says: 'Playing without memory.' I don't believe in that. I don't believe Ornette Coleman plays without memory; I don't believe anybody plays without memory. But I believe in the idea of the moment, the preciousness of the moment, the Zen kind of being; these are great things. But there's also memory and anticipation and these are great things as well – and we have to work with all of that.

For me, the great thing about music is that it's an art that unfolds in time. The notion of form and something that unfolds in time – those two notions don't fit together. It's much more to do with process or morphogenesis – the evolution of forms, not a static form but the time-based evolution of forms. It has much more to do with biology, say, than architecture. That's the thing with music. It should be refreshing itself all the time, not repeating. The idea that it repeats and that you play the same piece note for note and that, somehow, you have a formula for a perfect composition – this doesn't interest me at all. I'm interested in a new version of that piece. Doing it and seeing where the new stuff is and where it's going. [16]

Some concerts I can't remember how they started or how they ended, and others I remember very well. Most of the time, people don't believe me, but I'm being sincere: I have no concern for form in improvisation. As much as I'm fascinated by form in writing, in improvised music, I don't take form into account at all. On the other hand, I don't refuse to forget or harbour a desire for amnesia. When listening to someone else, especially an improviser, I don't pay attention to form. [15]

I don't think I really ask the question of form.

If you really listen to the sound material, if you dive into the microscopic detail of what's going on, I think that form disappears. The consciousness of form may disappear, but you know that that fact will induce a form.

It's blatantly obvious. There's no such thing as a standard fugue in Bach. You play form. Form is just a presupposition, a small basic postulate that you use in order to take one path or another, to underline the discourse a bit, in order to be more effective, more relevant. Often, it's just a tool. We do improvisation, which means that, theoretically, it's not prepared, it's not necessarily predetermined.

In solos, for example, I've decided not to think about form. I play a sound and when I'm fed up of it, I stop and play another one. It's just a bag full of ammo, and you take the ammo out piece by piece. And then when you want to develop a piece of sound material, you develop it and that's it. [19]

There's no deliberate decision to think about form. There's no desire to do so. Whether you're on your own or in a group of 200 musicians, it doesn't matter: in any case, some form will exist, because the concert or the piece is part of space-time, at a precise moment. Any concert, whether it lasts five seconds or one hour secretes its form. Some form will in any case exist, so I don't have to worry about it. It's not something I'm interested in at all – but you do feel something.

Before, I thought that I did not have this problem, as I was illiterate, self-taught and had gone into music by imitating and looting music played by former black slaves. Unlike people who had learnt music, mainly academic music, and who were forced to consider improvisation from the point of view of the diktats of obligatory form. There was the pure act of being in the sound, in the energy, and I wasn't ready to confront myself with the problems of the white bourgeoisie because those problems were the problems of contemporary, classical music. [20]

I have never had the sort of grand arc or grand structure thinking beyond the sound that I'm making just before or just after or during what I'm playing. I've always thought that the structure comes from the improvisation. I often find myself in very different places from where I started. Listening back, I can find all sorts of connections with the first sound or the section at the beginning, but I'm not aware of them at all when I play. [06A]

While playing, I am not that conscious of where we come from or where we're going, but I think I try to have a sense of the progression. ... But for the most part – virtually identical to theatrical improvisation – I just try to be in the moment and react. [03]

I'm not so concerned with form. Sorry, that's a ridiculous statement! But every set of vibrational activity in a space has maybe some six billion options form-wise and some of them are going to be awesome and some of them are going to be boring as hell and I can't define what works and what doesn't, as far as form goes. When I play solo, the language elements that I'm interested in exploring have their own inherent logic, in terms of duration and dynamic. [35B]

During a concert, I don't think. I don't wonder about what I'm going to play. Of course, I may have sensations, let's call them memories, of what I have already played but that doesn't determine what I'm going to do next. Nevertheless, I may, for example, take up an idea again that has already been expressed previously. But for me this 'mastery' of structure, of the process under way does not consist of analytical thinking based on questions but rather sensory thinking. I 'feel' that I've done something before and it might be good to do it again now. This is not analytical thinking.

A priori, if I really thought, I would tell myself not to replay what I've just played. For fear of ending up with a piece that's too gift wrapped, that looks too pretty and so on. I tend rather to move forward, including when reacting to 'accidents', but without really being aware of them.

I feel as if my body is playing. Energies, gestures, sounds. I feel I do very little thinking, that I don't analyse during a concert. I may tell myself: 'Well, such-and-such a thing is going on and I'm going to try to do something with it ... '.

What I probably think most about when I'm playing is time, the progression, the length of time already spent and what has happened within this time frame (and that I may have memory of), and I 'manage things' according to time. I won't play in the same way if I'm asked to play for thirty minutes compared to an hour and a half. So, yes, in this case I play according to time and a certain memory that I may constantly hold in mind of what has already happened. Calling that a formal musical thought doesn't bother me. That's part of my work. There was a (recent) period where I could play for hours without stopping, without any preoccupations in terms of form, at the same time as retaining an awareness of time. The piece could have gone on forever, and when I stopped it became a slice of a continuous stream.

For a long time, I believed that consciousness of time in a concert depended above all on experience. But there are a lot of counterexamples. ... I don't understand where this acute consciousness of time comes from. I sometimes lose it and then find it again. All this remains a mystery to me. But when I have it, I'm fine. I don't feel lost. Even though I like to lose myself in the moment. In fact, there's a place of reflection in me that places itself in time. I have a consciousness of time rather than structure, although they're linked. It suits me that it's there, in a corner of my thoughts, without me having to reflect on it too much.

I dream of playing songs, pop songs. I like square stuff, temporal structures, twelve-bar blues, thirty-two-bar standards. And when I improvise, I may also feel like I'm playing internally on four-beat bars. ... I also play with this. It's fundamental to me. It's deeply embedded in me. I don't need to think about it, it's always there. [43]

I don't think I've really found a solution to the question of form. It's not the big thing in my music. I'm not really able to do logical stuff! I believe that where I am now, if I want a form that suits me, I have to prepare it in advance. In improvised music, I haven't found a solution yet.

It only works when people significantly pare back their material and it stays alive. I decided very recently not to change ideas too quickly, but to keep to one direction, even if it's boring, and to look for different ways to look at the material.

Sometimes I don't know what to do. I can't hear anything. But you know you have to play and you tell yourself you have to do something. You're under pressure, and reflexes take over. I feel paralysed in those moments because I don't like doing just anything just in order to do something.

While I'm playing, I have a vision of the form, but I have ideas with respect to the next ten or twenty seconds, no more. When you're too involved in what has happened and you have ideas for how to continue it, you can become paralysed. [29]

Let's say that, when I'm improvising, there's not too much mental projection going on. But I'm not saying that I deny or refuse form in improvisation. Just that it doesn't have the same objective as in composition.

When I say form, it's the idea of having a form from A to Z. However, in improvisation, there comes a moment when that's no longer possible, and in any case that's not what improvisation is about. But then, organizing things that are repeated, kind of microcells that are repeated, is exciting.

I do not have an active enough brain in order to be able to have a projection of form from A to Z while I'm improvising. But the listener is able to create form. [36]

You're not shaping the performance, thinking: 'It will start this way, continue in this way and end this way.' If you do that, it will be very mechanical. But you can still have an aesthetic appraisal of what you're going to decide to do yourself, what materials you're going to use and how they're going to relate to the other materials you hear around you. I think the shape has got to come out of the moment, I mean, if you're not in that one moment, the now, when you're playing, you're nowhere. We all have a memory of what just happened, we all have maybe half an anticipation of what's coming next – we're human beings, we're bound to think this way – but if you're not focused primarily on the moment then you're lost, I think. [07]

Basically, I think about the moment but, of course, time is running. Both are important, the moment and the whole. It's impossible to think only about the moment because the moment is in a relationship with the previous moment and the future moment maybe as well. [08B]

Sometimes I really care about the form, sometimes I really don't. If I play a four-hour concert, for example, I just can't remember the time structure. If I play for ten or twenty minutes, I try to forget it but I never succeed, it's too difficult. I try to forget because otherwise I'm going to play like a composition. And, as I'm unable to forget, I'm never satisfied. It's like life itself. It's really impossible to forget. And when I think about trying to forget or not, something is wrong. [33]

I would like not to give a damn about form, but that's not possible. [26]

When I improvise I try to have some kind of form in mind. It doesn't always happen. I guess that comes from my classical training. I'd like to think that I have an idea of the form of the whole piece, but it's impossible because I don't know where that piece is going to go. No one really knows exactly where the piece is going to go. I just try and form something in between, as it's going, and bring the piece to some kind of completion. I hear something and I think that this sound might make sense, to make the music go in a particular direction (or not), or to take it in a different direction to where it's heading. [10]

You know that the piece has got to be resolved. It's got to end. It's got to come to a conclusion so everything is on its way towards something. ... I would like to work in one of those situations that just goes on. But for me, there are physical limitations. It can start to get physically hard after about forty minutes. [18]

If you are clear about what you're doing and make the right decisions, the overall form will take care of itself. When I improvise, I don't really plan things, I only know what's happened. I sometimes try to make the form go in a more interesting direction if it seems like it's too predictable. At the end of a piece, I don't think about the form of it. I don't judge it the same way I would judge a composition anyway. I'm concerned about the overall form of an improvisation, but I don't think about it consciously in terms of planning.

One thing I do miss a lot when I listen to improvisation is structure. [28]

In the trio r.mutt, the form is defined by the way of functioning. We don't try to start, end or tell a story. ... But this is a type of form. I think that from the moment that someone is listening, or if a trace is left, there is necessarily a form. [47]

In the end, by improvising, form takes shape like a landscape, like a kind of territory that comes into being. The trance, then, is just a walk inside this territory. When I pay attention to form, I have the feeling of being aware that there's a coherence to this landscape. There's no sudden jump into the universe, from one environment to another. What I mean is that there may be some fairly brutal passages in this territory, from one part of it to another, but there will still be a consistency to it. For example, I'm not going to move suddenly from a world of the order of forests and streams – I often see something that looks like a forest or a slightly delirious scene from nature – I'm not going to go suddenly into the metro, or something industrial. In general, there's a kind of coherence in the way things fit together, a kind of displacement. It's within this that this sort of imaginary form takes shape. It isn't a structure in the sense of a pre-established thought. There's an almost sensory logic between the different materials, in the environment in which they coexist. And the trance doesn't stop me from walking within this landscape.

The landscape I'm talking about isn't something you look at and observe; it's something you build, that you generate constantly. It is not something contemplative.

What I'm interested in is when there's a kind of link between the initial sounds, the initial material, the initial ideas for the beginning of the concert and the end. That is, when there's a kind of path. Form isn't positioned like a structure that tries to articulate different ideas. For me, the idea of form comes from the coherence between the succession of different ideas.

It's a kind of development, but a development that can contain fractures. Rather it's a way of managing to assemble ideas in a certain form of overall logic. [38]

I think another important point to make is that other considerations have influenced how we sound. Developments in technology, for example. I mean, I don't know the exact dates that particular things emerged, but when we first started, we used to record onto C90 tape. The first thirty or forty improvisations were onto C90s. Obviously, a C90 tape has two forty-five-minute sides, so we had some improvisations that lasted forty-five minutes. And after that we thought about it, and thought about perhaps being a bit more concise. We were also thinking about ending one improvisation and psychologically starting another, thinking of other ideas to use – so the pieces became shorter, in a way. We discovered other ways, we discovered C60s!

We'll often say, if we have a certain amount of time, like fifty minutes, for example: 'OK, let's do twenty and then thirty minutes.' That's a kind of minimum structure – deciding how long you're going to play for. Before we start we'll say: 'OK, let's do two sets, about twenty minutes and about thirty minutes long respectively.'

Sometimes, adding to that basic structure, we'll say something about trying to give the pieces a particular shape. But more often than not, we don't say anything about that. The best pieces of music, I think, have come when we didn't have any particular plan and we just improvised. But the worst pieces we've done have also come out of that too. So you can kind of prevent the worst pieces by saying: 'It'll have this shape, it'll last twenty minutes, it'll start with quiet sounds, build up in the middle and finish with a big loud noise' or something like that. But by imposing a structure, you're also constraining the possibilities and maybe stopping something from happening which might otherwise have happened. It might be that you prevent some disasters too.

I mean, sometimes we think about structure and sometimes we don't.
There's a danger in being too logical about these things.
It's always been based on intuition and telepathy and things that you can't nail down in such a way. [11]

I try and wait for the other musicians to start before I decide how I'm going to contribute to the session. And within the first five minutes, I think, it's pretty clear in which direction the piece is likely to go, if everyone is – well, there are many factors to a performance, but if the performers are in sync with a certain feeling or mentality then it's going to create a predictable outcome and you can actually chart where the piece of music is going to go in the space of thirty minutes. This is the music that's least interesting to me, when you know what's going to happen in thirty minutes time before you even get there. It's not a very populist idea, but I'm actually looking for a music that's awkward, that lacks fluidity or has a lot of ruptures or some disintegration to it. And there are obviously other musicians that explore these ideas as well.

I look back at the avant-garde music and other types of music that were produced in the post-war period, at least, and I think: 'What can I contribute? What kind of experience do I want to have as a musician and also as an audience member?' The extremes of sound have well and truly been explored, from silence to noise. It seems, though, that temporal rupture is one area that offers new possibilities, at least. Not John Zorn-type thirty-second passages of Napalm Death but within compositions and within performances where, after five minutes, no one knows where you're going to be going. I think that's an intellectual process that requires a lot of discipline. [22]

If I make a sound that melts too much into the surrounding sound, it may quite quickly lose its relevance. I prefer dynamic music, which 'moves' in time, in form, like moving matter. So, I prefer to think in terms of transitions, articulation and form.

Form is transitions, articulation, sound masses that move, volume effects in what we might call the 'microform', such as for example going from touching your instrument lightly to fully affirming its sound. Often, for me, form is something that only comes to mind after the event. My vision of form is somewhat *a posteriori*. Form rather thinks me. ... If I think about form, it's during the moments of transition. And that influences my intentions further on. For example, if the form has been too 'languid', I will want to propose something clearer, more assertive, or to change the timescale, looking to faster and more concise sequences for example, after slow, long passages. This may be more microform than general form. Nevertheless, I retain a fairly precise memory of what has happened. Knowing what has already happened helps my concentration, my precision, helps me maintain my listening. But my decision-making will be more a function of what has just happened at a specific moment, or over a rather short period of time, never since the very beginning of the concert: I cannot imagine remembering anything that had happened during the previous forty-five minutes, for example. [45]

I don't care about the shape of the piece – the form though, yes. [27]

While I'm playing, 'form' is more like a sense for the balance of the piece. I'm aware of it, but I don't necessarily put it into words. I would still call it a reflection on form, because through this sense of balance, I become aware of what might be still needed and this influences my further input. [44]

When I speak about form, I'm in the realm of utopias to some extent.
I think I hear what I want to do before I do it: there's an intention, I do it and either it works or it doesn't.
I project a form in my mind, in the instant, I imagine a form for the music to come. I have a desire, a desire for what might transpire.
I make a choice in relation to this desire, while fully accepting that it will not transpire, while accepting that I will be surprised by what does come and isn't planned, because that's also what improvisation is about.
Besides projection of form, there's also what has happened. It's constantly there in my memory. And the beginning influences the end.
The problem of form is fundamental in improvised music, and it's constantly called into question. Constructing form is one of the goals. [37]

I'm always aware of an overall shape in the music – but I'm also aware that I can't control this if I'm not the only person making the music. As a soloist, this is something that I have much more control over.
I like to return to actions and events, to recontextualize them within an improvisation. ... The character of the sound changes, the role of the sound changes. [30]

The form of the piece is a conscious thing for me. I remember what happened at the beginning of a piece or a concert. I have a vision of what might happen and move from past to present to future.

In the trio with John Butcher and Xavier Charles, we say beforehand how long we want to play for. For me, that's important. When we play a concert we decide how long the concert is going to last and how the concert might be divided into pieces. Sometimes we define it closely – longer pieces, shorter pieces or endings. We decide together. Forty minutes is the usual length. I would very much enjoy doing different lengths – three hours or five or ten minutes. I would like more diversity in that sense. [17]

There must be people who care less about the temporal aspect of improvisation. But for me, the temporal aspect is quite important: the durations, the moments … the form – although the form is not chosen deliberately. The form I perceive influences what I play. In the same way as the sounds others play do. The duration of each sound, of each sequence is as important for me as each sound, each sequence. I cannot not think about form. I'm not saying that thinking about the form that has just transpired makes me want to devise a particular form for what's coming next, but it does influence me as much as the sound at a given moment. I have the impression that the same process happens in everyone, but that some musicians are more aware of it than others. [12]

In each project, I feel like I'm trying to do similar things but more clearly each time I do them. I'm working on the same ideas that I've been working on for a really long time, ideas that are flexible enough to work with in all the different projects that I do. And the approach is becoming narrower and narrower. In musical terms, these ideas could be about repetition, about form, how to construct form in an improvised setting, really thinking about the form the whole time, about systems of phrases … . [35A]

Being aware of the overall form of the piece you're playing is a bit of a responsibility really. The brain stores what's happened in the last five or twenty or thirty minutes, even though you're not conscious of it. The brain is so incredibly complex that you can have multiple memory structures simultaneously. And they are far more profound than we are able to be aware of. You might not be conscious of it but you are simultaneously storing everything.

I am quite concerned about form. But the idea of abandoning form is quite an interesting thing. [21]

What I liked was improvisation as a material: the terrain, the formal framework, the relationship, the form, everything in relation to the sound, to the way of listening. All that is a truly mad, extremely complex material and that wasn't something I wanted to do without. It intrigued me a lot.

At first, what interested me were all the processes, improvisation procedures, the relationship to sound … . I spent a lot of time on these questions. I thought a lot about the sounds I was making. It changed everything: the duration of my sounds, my way of playing nuances, listening to others. But today, that's something that interests me much less than form. Indeed, in this second phase, what has really motivated me and interested me the most are the formal results that can be obtained using improvised material.

I do not necessarily see form as my goal, but what I'm interested in is the final appearance of the music, that is, its formal aspect. I think it's a dead end, that there's a bit of an issue in using improvisation for the purpose of obtaining formal results, but I think it would be a real shame not to try. What I mean is that what I believe improvisation consists of is not at all what I'm doing when I improvise. … I'm not an improviser in complete terms.

What I mean by the final appearance is the form that all this takes. A drawing in other words. There are two drawings: the drawing you are currently working on and the drawing *a posteriori*. The first drawing is something you're doing and you do not have the same relationship with that drawing as with the one you have already finished. For me, we're talking about these two drawings.

I don't consider the drawing that I am drawing *a priori* as a drawing. Because in improvisation, if you think of a drawing, that drawing will not be what transpires; the drawing that transpires is not the one you're thinking about. This is where it gets interesting. This is where the formal superiority of improvised music over written music can come about. Writing is superior elsewhere. Formally, it goes further than improvisation elsewhere. [39]

Form is crucial in music, in all music and especially when the musical language is complex and defies notation. Often improvisation is a 'stream of consciousness' and can be rather linear. We go from one idea, we develop it, we take it as far as we can and then we go on to the next. So while improvising, I sense form and structure at least in my own part, and in teaching and where possible (but all too rarely) in starting a new composition, I use this to sculpt the music, but avoiding trying to put this into words or notation (at least until afterwards). Improvisation is a bit niche in terms of audience, venue and so on. As with contemporary music in general I hope also to reach a broader place, building on historical models, the ideas of things coming back, things repeating, things like sonata form, or using word-based (classical) forms when I work with Alice Oswald (to give a poetic example).

Sometimes what I do, especially in solo concerts, is play in quite a strict form but nevertheless with improvised content. This is quite demanding, and I have to practise much more than if I am playing a composition in the same form such as a medieval *estampie* or one of my own which may be noise-based so not at all medieval but still has this form (one of my favourites). I have learnt a lot from conversation and jamming with Paula Chateauneuf, as seriously brilliant lute and theorbo players can do this – listening to it you would think it was all written down but in fact they are improvising it all within one of their Renaissance forms. The further we go back from the baroque the more composition is improvisation anyway. Sometimes I might write a note to help me to memorize the form – I often use techniques picked up from seeing how medieval music scribes compressed musical information onto a tiny piece of parchment in a non-linear design based upon a shared knowledge of form.

A good improvising ensemble, working together over a longer period of time, will create its own architecture anyway (if they want to). Often improvisers play as this 'stream of consciousness', and I try to add more to this linear process, to add polyphony, or some structures, to take the risk of attempting to listen, play, think about what's gone and what's coming and where you are now, in the act of performance. Perhaps this is why I also compose, even though I find it far more difficult and time-consuming. Nevertheless I don't want to lose this 'stream of consciousness' feeling of spontaneity.

I'll often think about what has already occurred in a concert and what I want to occur that hasn't yet happened. So if, for example, a musician suddenly stops and makes an unexpected silence or, another extreme, if he suddenly plays very loudly, I might go to glissando clusters (of harmonics), if there hasn't been much so far in the concert. Or, formally speaking, if I felt there was bass at the beginning and I wanted to bring it back for the overall form of the sound architecture being created, then I might go back to my idea of improvised form. Having notated a few improvisations, I see that it's easy to make things quite complex very quickly in improvisation. It's often easier to do lots of things very quickly than to actually be committed to one idea. So I would probably move into what might be a difficult area by thinking of form because I think form will slow down the busyness. I always remember what happened before. I don't try to remember, I just do. And this influences my playing. That's why I tend to play in small groups and with musicians that I know and understand very well. [40]

I like to think about the whole ... the overall sound ... the sound result. I need a path, a continuum. In fact, I have the impression that that's the only thing I experience. I don't think it's form. It's about time and that that's the only thing I experience. [41]

Sometimes the form may be overtaken by something ... happening in the playing or truly in the concrete substance of the music. [02]

5

Process versus aesthetic result, improvisation as a tool to make music versus music as a tool to improvise, improvisation versus composition

You can't anticipate. You have to keep focused on what you're doing and not worry about the result at all. If you're in that position, it's more likely to be a satisfying performance for the audience. That's how it seems to work. [07]

I don't have any aesthetic foundation. When I say, for example, that some musicians hold back too much, it's because I see that their bodies aren't adapted to what they're doing. They tremble, and then everything is almost a series of disasters. At the same time, I know that by the force of things, their bodies may also be transformed, due perhaps to their own volition. But I do not particularly like willpower in music or art in general. When I see people like the drummer Hamid Drake, I am always amazed. In my opinion, there is no volition in what he does. He is what he is. He has poise. It's fluid and I do not think he is at all costs trying to produce what he's producing: it's just what he is.

Musicians are probably people who have chosen an instrument in order to try to discover what they are through that particular medium.

When it comes down to it, the only remaining religion has never been the religion of an aesthetic or a way of doing things. [15]

When you improvise, attempts that both fail and succeed are included in the result. Improvisation is the only musical practice that allows for that.

What interests me is being in the moment, being aware of all that I have experienced. No matter the result. [42]

In Eddie Prévost's workshop, there is no kind of aesthetic continuity because first of all we never know who is going to be there anyway and it really can sound like anything. But I think the way that people approach it is the one thing that, on a broader level, binds that group of people together. [05B]

I don't look for results. I'm not religious! I look more for propositions. A result for me is: 'Eureka, I've found it!' That would be a result. And if somebody says, 'I've found it', that's the beginning of stagnation. I look for propositions. I'm very interested in this. Other people's propositions too. You think: 'Ah, that's interesting.' Results, not really. [27]

I find that the most interesting aspect of improvisation is 'means without an end'. Improvising is about trying to communicate without making a final statement. There is no goal, it's not about a result, it's about doing it; what Giorgio Agamben calls 'means without ends' which, for me, can be applied to improvisation. [09B]

There are lots of different types of improvising. And again it goes back to who I'm playing with. I think I'd be the last person to say that I have a definite aesthetic because I'm still exploring and finding my voice, or finding a way because I've only really concentrated on improvising intensely for the last year and a half. I'm in no position really to be able to give a definite answer. [10]

What's important to me is that when I imagine something, I do it with conviction and not by searching for it. And if the sound isn't what I wanted, it doesn't matter. It's something else and I accept it. What I have learnt from experience is that you have to say 'yes'. That's what I like in improvisation: you have to say 'yes' because if you say 'no' to yourself or the sounds of others, it doesn't work. It's a bit of a lifestyle too, take what comes. And then you continue with that. And if it leads you in another direction than the one you had intended, that's good too! [29]

On my journey, I find myself facing real problems today, in the playing itself, which has never happened to me before. Until now, it was not at all easy, but there was no element of doubt. I was really in the action. There was a movement and I just had to dive into the flow and things happened. And then, suddenly, some time ago, there was a sudden loss of innocence in relation to that, a total loss of innocence. And I asked myself: 'What am I doing, what am I doing with that?' There was a kind of distance, and all of a sudden, rather difficult issues started coming up. I was confronted with a sort of 'disacceptance' of what I had accepted de facto and which was for me the very heart of improvisation: accepting everything that came, including stuff you'd rather be inclined to push away, accepting everything and letting many different states flow through you. It was for me the foundation, not necessarily an explicit one, but the foundation of a kind of philosophy of this work: accept everything, things that happen have to happen, these states must be experienced, without judgement – you just have to do it. There was a kind of tacit duty of solidarity with the moment. Now there's more restraint, and sometimes I say to myself: 'No, I do not want that, no I really do not want that.' Sometimes, because of this loss of innocence, things don't go as smoothly as before, and I even have a phrasing problem, that is, things continue to sing out but the body no longer follows suit, and it's difficult. Fear has always been present, but it's growing and I feel I'm losing touch with what I call my personal poetry, everything and nothing, that which allows me to stay in touch with the flow of the action. It's more abrupt, there are more barriers inside the work, more walls to bang up against, more stones on the path.

Before, I never spoke about music with my fellow players, never. No one ever uttered a word about what we were doing. Now sometimes we do and that's where there's a loss of innocence.

I want to carry on giving out, because for me life is that, nothing else. It's a constant giving out, the act of playing is a constant giving out. Things happen. They flow through you and you disintegrate.

I remain attracted by the practice of improvisation that takes us to places we don't know, not necessarily producing a beautiful improvisation that works. This may be a metaphor for the human condition: we have to go through what we are carrying with us, what we are carting around, using the tools we have chosen, knowing that no doubt by steadying ourselves in these places we may fall down holes. I don't know why but that's the image that always comes to mind, falling into holes that I'll be able to explore, holes that I do not know, or rather falling into the same hole and apprehending it with a new perspective. The moments that I like most, and which are rare, are those moments where there is real novelty, in the sense that that which has appeared is really original, not in terms of the effect of the result but in the perception we have and the position that we take up inside it. [15]

I use improvisation as a tool to achieve things that touch me, concern me, interest me. I don't give a damn about improvisation in itself. I don't go on marches for improvisation. There are situations in which I like to plan everything in advance because this constraint enables something, a state that serves a desire, a direction, work that I need to do. Even when I decide everything in advance, this does not prevent me from experiencing things related to everything that surrounds me. I experience things even if what I'm playing in real time does not really render this experience. If what I want to do takes place by listening in the moment, then I use improvisation because it allows me to do it effectively, because it allows flexibility and reveals something. But there is really no value hierarchy between deciding everything in advance, applying a protocol and leaving a lot unplanned in order to decide in the moment. What matters to me is what it produces. [25]

As an improviser, I don't see why you would have to reinvent yourself, or reinvent the way you play or your aesthetic or your settings on a daily basis. It's impossible. You can't do that. [06B]

There's the way you make music and there's the result. I think what initially interested me in music in general was the result. I told myself that I heard things that I did not hear elsewhere and that these things had to be done. When you spend six months on a score and it is played, you absolutely do not get the same result as when you spend six months rehearsing with improvisers. And I think that's the only difference. It's a difference in terms of result, acoustic space that will be more related to one practice than another. [12]

I'd like there to be some sort of musical result at the end. Not just the social idea of being with people. [18]

Sorting out the mediocre is so important. Making sure you can judge the quality. It's a very hard thing in improvised music. But there is a standard, a quality standard. It's very hard to describe it but it is there. It's the most important thing really. Being able to understand that. [05A]

I am not good at improvising if I can't see the sense of what's happening around me. At those times, I just want to stop. [28]

When I play solo, I'm much more in my own world and I can construct my music without any disturbances. But when I play with others, everything I play is in relation to what the other person does. So I have to keep an eye on the complete musical picture – the musicians and their instruments and sounds, both affecting the result. So I try to ensure the best possible musical result, overall. And the best musical result is often a conflict – the conflict entailed in trying to be myself and losing myself. It's problematic.

I always think about the result, the complete picture. On a certain level. I don't know what forgetting is. It might be more subconscious sometimes but it's always there. [17]

Increasingly, I want to work on written music. With improvisation, I often feel like I'm going around in circles. This is probably more related to the result than to improvising itself. [43]

I think the meta-structure is the most important thing to me. Whether I contribute 1 per cent of the sound or 90 per cent of the sound doesn't matter to me whatsoever – it's the structure itself, the end result and that the external experience is worthwhile. I'm looking for a minimal kind of structure with which we can make maximal impact. I think in some ways that the collaborations I'm looking for allow me to explore these ideas. The collaborations that I forge are either with musicians who have a certain sensibility or with musical vocabulary that I find complementary but it's always at the service of a concept or idea and that's the most important thing.

When I compose, I develop a structure, which is then refined over time. But, in performance, I actually want the refined structure to be there during the performance itself. I have a memory or an idea of what I would like ideally, and the kind of music that I'd like to hear from this particular group. Whether we ever get there or not is another thing. [22]

I'm interested in both things: the improvising and the result. I'm not so desperately interested in improvising that I don't care what it sounds like! [16]

I don't mind presenting music that doesn't have a clear statement behind it. I mean, I don't usually like complete 'stream of consciousness' improvisation but, on the other hand, I don't like it when you hear the first few seconds and you have an idea of the whole performance. I can enjoy a lot of music that's produced like that but I'm not sure I enjoy it because of any connection I have to improvisation. [14]

Of course, I also think in musical terms, but I want to experience something. And to achieve that you can use any physical laws. [32]

When I improvise, I try to make music. There's a journey, that I try to experience every moment of, and there's a result, that I hear. I don't know about the audience. But I don't want to make banal music, so I try to make sure that the music doesn't come to an end easily. … It's about producing something unpredictable, alive. You can bring things to an end in an easy way. You can start in an easy way. But that's not what I want. [41]

All the same, the result is what you share most. And despite everything, you also see the person's qualities in the result. You see if they're delicate. You see their brutality if they're brutal. You see their qualities and above all you see how they position themselves physically when playing. The music isn't important as an object. What's important is the tension with which it's done. It's not the music itself. Everything is intertwined, but it seems to me that we know that aesthetics carry values, benevolent or malicious, generous or stingy or whatever. They may also be social values. Beyond all aesthetics, I am more attracted to honesty. Ultimately that's the most important value. But I do not think this is a judgement on my part. It's really purely felt. It's absolutely animal. [15]

We were talking about process and results and assessing the result. Well, the two things are interconnected. And I think my conception is a mixed one really. I'm not very pure in terms of process. I'm interested in all aspects and I'm constantly amazed by the results. The unexpected result in improvised music. And the unexpected beauty. It feeds my mind and my emotions. It affects me physically as well because I have quite a physical approach. My awareness of my body when I'm playing is really important. I don't come from a very doctrinaire or dogmatic viewpoint. I need to be aware of everything. [05A]

For a very long time, in so-called free music, in free improvisation situations, I tried to operate the belief – even if it was an illusion – that I wasn't taking any decisions (musical, aesthetic, instrumental, etc.), that I was allowing a process to take place in which I was only the instrument, the receiver. And for a long time, to get to this state quickly, I used certain substances that help you, a kind of elevator to speed things up, mainly things that you smoke. It passed through me, and I was a kind of witness, an instrument, an assistant to a process that traversed me, operated through me. In this type of process, some semi-conscious decisions, or even small conscious decisions, did possibly take place, for example at the beginning of a concert. Within that, it was easy. I didn't have to take care of anything. It worked by itself, at least more or less. … Accidents did of course happen: a reed splitting, a pad sticking and so on. There was a feeling of duration, then a sensation that told me: 'Here, let's stop here, that must be it.'

When I picked up the baritone saxophone, at first I very much played it as a dilettante because the alto remained my main instrument, and for a year, a year and a half, I spent a bit of time practising the baritone like that, casually, secretly, like having a mistress, but I must have felt that it wasn't coming. Then, at that moment, there must have been a period of crisis. I spent a lot of time searching on the baritone, for a few years. Things didn't move quickly. First the circular breathing came and then something in terms of the timbre, the sound; I felt something being fashioned that I began to hear. That was my path, my area of work. In fact, it gave me a huge desire to really get to work and build everything up. I call it a new grammar that I devised for myself through work, through discipline on the baritone while forgetting the alto. I had started with the alto in an imitation of jazz players, especially American jazz of course, and then I began to feel at home with the baritone, as if I were starting a new chapter, a chapter that was truly my own … still with lots of influences but influences that were at a greater distance and no longer operating by means of imitation. I was at least sure that I was no longer imitating and looting from jazz. But suddenly innocence went out the window, and I felt an ever-increasing responsibility for the musical result. Music was no longer a flow within which I just had to get myself into the right state in order to receive.

That's where I am now, and I think that this situation has brought balance between improvising alone and improvising with other musicians because when you're improvising you meet people who, if not creators of their own grammar, are at least responsible for the slightest emission of sound. [20]

I have a desire to start from a position of consensus, and to explore this consensus beyond known limits … .

Concerts, for example – even when you're face to face with an audience, even with a sound system, the truly classic set-up – can lead to completely abstract moments that totally deconstruct the context. This is my way of doing things: I accept the initial consensus.

I am not looking for a particular context. The context is the one in which I find myself. What interests me is the perception I have of where I am, with what surrounds me, whether it's people, walls, trees, whatever. It's my relationship to my surroundings. What excites me is feeling the place where I am at, and that's what I use to improvise with. This brings constraints – but I don't experience them as constraints, rather as data. This isn't annoying. It doesn't take anything away. It forces me to prioritize some things over others.

I try to exist in the middle of what already exists. In a concert context, I don't have the impression I'm imposing anything – me and the musicians I play with. I just feel as if I'm looking for a space in the middle of what already exists. [46]

In general terms, you want to produce something meaningful, communicate and create space. You're not thinking that all the time but whatever you do is sort of based on questions such as 'What's best for the situation? What's necessary?' As an improviser, it feels like I'm against thinking about the result, but I suppose we do think about it – even if it's the result at that particular time. I don't think it's possible to think about the end product, but if you care or are involved in what's happening, you're engaged with the instant result. It's too difficult to think about the final result; you haven't got time to think about it when you're playing. You can base your decision and find influence for what you're going to do in the moment from earlier on in the piece. And you can have an awareness of the piece as a whole – where you've been. But I don't think you can be concerned about the final result. [04A]

I play this music to figure out things like 'What do I perceive when I play? What happens? What state does it put me into?' But I'm also interested in making singular, improbable music. … I'm interested in the rendering. But 50 per cent of the result also comes from what I've experienced. [47]

I mean, sometimes we've got our own thing, which we want to get out, and I think in a new situation the skill – if you want to do that – is to get it out in a way that doesn't force other people to play in a certain way, working with what other people are doing. You can do that, you can bring an agenda to the music and not steamroller them into playing it but find ways of either bringing people to your agenda or bending your agenda to them. [14]

Maybe in some way you project some ideal outcome of a particular environment, musically speaking, and you do whatever you can to make that happen. For example, you've had a great day and you are in a good mood, or you've been practising for ten hours or you haven't played at all. All those things are there and you try to work out what you can do to get into some ideal environment so that you can stop having preconceptions about what you'll play. I try not to have preconceptions. In some bands it's very clear what's expected of you and you can therefore, and very simply, make decisions to circumvent that or to take it to a point where it's good enough that it overcomes the preconceived idea by its own vibrational strength – or whatever it is that makes an idea live beyond its conception. Every group of people is a preconception. And in some groups, the necessity to improvise within a very clear perimeter is more obvious – early on and at different points throughout the course of a piece. Improvising is absolutely necessary, just as much as clearly conceived decision-making. [35B]

With the group Morphogenesis, we get on very well as long as we don't meet too often!

We've always had fairly different tastes. It's almost been that we don't have to tell each other to try and play differently. Part of the strength is that we accept whatever anyone is doing. There have been a few occasions when a person is doing something, and there's a general consensus that what that person is doing doesn't fit in and we say something about that.

The idea of the group was to find a musical territory where all of us could interact – because we were all doing different things before we joined the group. But having said that, we have a lot in common in terms of musical interests. We all have an interest in certain types of experimental music. I still like using that term. We all have an interest in that.

Everyone may have an independent idea of what they would really like to do if they were in control of the group. But we've always been interested in finding common ground – not a common language – and in developing situations where, for instance, you can't be entirely sure who made which sound.

We found, certainly back in the 1980s, that there were very few improvisation groups where that was true. You could say it was true of AMM, at least at one point, MEV and a few others. But with most improvisation groups it was always very clear which instrument was making which sound. Now I think a lot of that has changed. There are saxophonists that make completely 'unsaxophonelike' sounds – it has become much more the thing today. [11]

Having a defined purpose as a group doesn't mean necessarily having an idea of the form of the piece. It could mean having different tactics for creating a form but not defining what that form actually will be – for example, tactics like areas of sound, textural areas that could lead from one to another or a brutal cut to force the music somewhere else. [35A]

While you're playing, the form of a piece is a projection. You can only anticipate a possible result and try to work on it to make it happen, to shape the overall thing. But you can also fully concentrate on the details and on the moment – then the form is just the result of the process. But if I get into this process again and again with long-term groups, I can try to steer a development within these groups. I think it's more like an evolutionary thing: a group establishes a certain aesthetic and then comes up with certain results within their fields of possibilities. You can work on that and I'm quite concerned about that. I prefer to work in groups for a longer time mainly because of that. If you play with the same people again and again, over a long time, you have the possibility of establishing an aesthetic and fields of possibility within it. In some groups, there is a circular process – by revisiting an established area, this area becomes more stable in the sense that we are more and more able to cope with any kind of irritation; we learn to handle unexpected elements. It's still improvisation – but maybe there is a better word for it when we arrive at this point.

I think they're two levels of the same thing. When I'm playing, I'm trying to be 'in the moment' and to focus on it. In addition, there is also the level of reflecting on what we're doing with this particular group. And then you can recognize that certain elements reappear and that you come back to certain musical situations or sonic constellations and you can work on that on a reflective level. These are two parallel activities. [44]

Sometimes, while playing with someone, I feel as though I'm putting spikes or stones on a field. It's not about destroying but just about putting down a scale or a ruler. I still want to keep my distance from other things, I still feel like observing things. But not destroying things. I put down spikes like a machine but it's not very planned. It's like a machine but without the brain, a machine which can only put spikes on the field, without intelligence.

If you want to be funny, you have to be very serious. I think it's better to be a machine in order to have a better sense of humour.

'Result is result.' It's difficult to explain, but even with the spiked field, without any plan, you will have a certain result anyway. It's impossible to decide whether it was a good or a bad result, it's just what it is. For me, it's an improvised composition.

I make music where it's impossible to decide if it's good or not. It's just played as it was. That's all. [23]

My first problem is what I propose. When I'm practising my instrument, I have such-and-such a sound, but when it comes to playing, I don't hear it the same. The second problem is that when I'm playing with other people, it sounds different again. And third, it sounds different again when you listen to the sound as a whole. My relationship to strategy is defined with this in mind. Namely there's always something of the order of three things going on. What I analyse in what I'm doing, what I analyse in what others are doing and what all that sounds like. And I try to think about the rendering, except that that's not possible. I try to analyse the rendering while I'm playing. By saying to myself that there is an X that is being created. In your head, when you hear an X, you produce a Y, and the Y you're producing breaks down the X. But at the same time, you need the X, as it's the X that produces the Y. [39]

I'm very much interested in the result. But oddly, when listening back to the recording I am often surprised by the result because the result is not at all what I imagined when I was playing. So the result matters to me a lot, even if it's difficult to judge it. However, I'm also very much interested in being able to let go of control, not thinking. This is something that is only found in improvisation, managing not to think anymore, to release inhibition. It's a bit like being drunk without being sick, being drunk and being proud of it … . [13]

I've changed my mind about things. So, for example, what I would have considered a very successful piece of music a year or two ago, I don't necessarily consider successful at the moment. It's endlessly changing and I think that's important. [05B]

Human ingenuity is very strong. You'll find something to do. There's always something to do. For example, the concert published on the *AMM Live in Allentown USA* record actually felt like a terrible gig. Everything was running against us, we had played a concert the night before in Atlanta, Georgia, and it went late and we didn't get to bed until 4.00 am. Then we got up early to fly to Allentown to play an afternoon concert, not even an evening concert, so that meant an early start, everyone crammed into a small car and it was a beautiful spring day. I thought: 'I don't want to go into this concert hall, I want to stay in the park! And why are these people here? I mean they should also be in the park, why go into a concert hall on an afternoon like this?' So, we eventually got there and there were very few people in the audience – everyone was in the park! And then they showed us the instruments and they were awful! The piano was terrible and the percussion was so bad I put most of it back in the cupboard. I couldn't bear it; I just picked out a few things. And the gig was really really tough. I kept thinking: 'I don't really want to be here' and I think it was the same for John Tilbury and Keith Rowe too. But we thought: 'Well, we're here, there's an expectation, we have to do something.' So we just did it, got on with it, did the best we could and then left. About a year later, we heard the tape and thought: 'Well that's alright isn't it? That worked!' [07]

I think that it would be a good thing to interview people who only listen to improvised music. There are lots of people I see at festivals who only go and listen to improvised music. They're very serious about it. I'm quite curious about that. In London, for example, there are people who are out every night listening to improvised music. They might be able to give us more insight into what it is. [18]

I was involved with action theatre, which is like improvised theatre. In relation to what we do, it's a long long way away, it's a different world. It's theatre but it's improvised, and there was a discussion about action theatre. Basically we talked about the problems that arise when you engage in it. So basically we were talking about improvising, and a lot of issues were really similar to issues around improvised music: the relationship, the audience, how do you know when enough is enough. It was interesting to see, in something so different, so much common ground because it was an improvised discipline, an improvised form. [04A]

That's the good thing about improvisation: it really is open in terms of the spectrum of sounds and qualities. It doesn't need to be fixed to this note or that note. It's a different way of doing it: you're listening and others are listening and it's specific to that relationship. So you can't say: 'This is the formula you use for improvisation.' Improvisation constantly challenges this notion of fixity, of making a clear thing of: 'This is how improvisation should be.' And that's a good thing. [09B]

Hopefully something happens that makes you do something you've never done before. Those are the real magic moments. They don't happen every time. [18]

I take 'improvisation' to be an elusive term that produces instability. 'Elusive' in the sense that it has a very humdrum meaning – there always has been improvisation – but at the same time it's very connected to a specific scene that is very narrowly defined. So there is a broad understanding of the term. And I use it as a concert tool. I don't want to define the term, I don't want to answer the question: 'Are you improvising or not?' I'm interested in what you can do with improvisation, in these elements that go against the grain. If you do it properly, it will produce instability, it will destabilize previous ways of making music, previous understandings of music-making and previous solidified understandings of the context. It will slightly shift things and make things unstable or strange for everybody in the concert. As a performer, I am the one who has the possibility to do that – and that's problematic. There is a certain 'theatre' of what you are allowed to do but I'm trying to make this a strange situation in which everybody is in an unstable, uncomfortable position, outside the usual habits and behaviours one usually has. Improvisation is basically about trying to intensify the moment as much as possible through exploratory practice. It's the most site-specific form of activity because it's not trying to relate to anything else, it's not trying to achieve something apart from this densification of the moment – if we are idealistic. Of course, it's not that pure because we build up a persona in doing this. But we are trying to be in that moment as much as possible, in that situation, giving all we can to produce a different set of relations.

In improvisation, hopefully differences are understood and put in play within the situation. I'm interested in exploring these differences. We are different but we understand our differences and, in the moment, they become exposed. We all realize the limitations of our scope of action and that they are different. It's like allowing that difference to be there. It's not about forgetting those differences momentarily in order to create a nice collective moment. [24]

For me, one thing that's impressive in improvisation is that you're always separated from what you're playing. I mean, there's always a huge distance between your original intention and how the sound sounds when you listen to it coming out of your instrument … because you're also a spectator of the sound you're playing. And I believe that this unforeseen difference, this gap, is what makes improvisation move and gives it its subject matter. This is what you have to listen for each time. Since what I think I'm playing is not what I hear and what other musicians hear, when playing together, then I can always keep on running after this thing that I can't get hold of, because it's mobile. It escapes. [25]

What's exciting about improvisation is that I find myself within a flow of questions. When I'm not playing, I'm constantly asking myself all kinds of questions that I cannot ask myself when I'm playing. Because when I'm playing, I'm in another state.

What I also like is finding myself in situations, projects, where I have the impression that we're inventing music that does not necessarily belong to one person. Four people playing and that creates a sound world. [19]

When something gets turned on its head, when your agenda is open to being damaged or extended, for want of a better description, it can be really wonderful. [09A]

Improvised music still interests me more than composed music, although I find interesting things in both. Maybe I was previously but nowadays I'm not looking for any kind of 'pureness'.

I think improvisation is not only music. It's also a way of life. Everything is connected to improvisation. For me, the word 'improvisation' has almost the same meaning as the word 'life'. It's a very basic life energy. Everyone has to improvise. Music and life are really connected. When you meet new musicians, you have to improvise with them otherwise you push them into your own philosophy. But improvisation is not only a conversation. Inside my body and my self, a lot of improvisation is happening. When you walk through a city to go somewhere, lots of things are happening and you have to survive. I think that is improvisation. Improvisation is one of the most important tools for survival. When I'm playing, I never think about this. But before and after, I do.

We should never stop to think about how we survive. The important thing is not to be against something, like composition for example, the important thing is to keep thinking. If there is no thinking I am not interested in the music. Everything is complex. It's not about improvisation and composition. You can find more complex ways. I don't want to categorize improvisation or composition. I think Derek Bailey was considering very complex ways of survival. That's why he tried to play with anyone who wanted to. His thinking influenced me. I used to be a fundamentalist of non-idiomatic improvisation when I was young. Later I had to admit that non-idiomatic improvisation is an impossible idea. You can be non-idiomatic for maybe three or four days. But after five or six days, the non-idiomatic becomes idiomatic because we have a memory. But this idea remains very important as a starting point. It's like him saying to me that I have to think for myself, find my own way. In the 1960s and 1970s, free jazz musicians tried to be free or to make a revolution through improvisation but, of course, it doesn't work. It's far more complicated than that. But I really respect their idea because they tried to find a new way to live their lives, to survive – and they really needed that. But I have to find another way.

If you really want to change the world, you should be a politician, not a musician. But we can still have some effect on listeners. Maybe if there are young people are in the audience our music will make them think about something. We should always think about social systems. In festivals, musicians always play on a stage with speakers on each side and this is a social system to me. Why do we need this setting? You could play with just one speaker. Or you could play acoustic in the middle of the audience. Of course, some musicians do, especially in European new music festivals. But the system remains strong. For example, in techno festivals – everyone listens to the same rhythm. It's an automatic social system and there is no thinking about it. Musicians and artists can open up a door, ask questions: 'Why the two speakers?' Why is everybody dancing to the same tempo? Why noise or why silence?' It's important to ask these kinds of questions. When a musician plays a sound it's as if he was asking: 'What is this or that sound?' It's the beginning of improvisation and the audience starts to think about it. This kind of communication is important. [33]

In the early 1950s there was a story in the paper about a family whose little boy had never spoken, never said a word. After a while, they became concerned and they took him to all kinds of doctors to find out why. But they couldn't. They didn't know. And when the boy was six or seven, one morning at the breakfast table, he said: 'Would you pass the sugar?' So apparently he had been able to speak and had been speaking somewhere. What I want to say with this example is that there are so many definitions of what improvisation is but that it's very rare to hear what I believe improvisation is: improvisation is what man was doing before he learnt to write. So there is a chicken-and-egg syndrome, one came first. Doing the thing came first, then came documenting and writing. But even when you write music, there are dozens of ways to interpret the symbols. Jazz musicians never talked about improvisation, they never used the term, they just said: 'Let's play.' In the academy they didn't even mention the term. They used the term 'extemporization', that's the old word for improvisation.

What I play, no one can write it down, except me, if I feel like it. It incorporates many, many years of playing – I didn't always play the way I play now – and I invented my own language. If music gives you something to think about, it's worth it.

Don't forget that Bach had something like twenty children, and he didn't have time to write any music. So he learnt how to improvise a mass. A mass to Bach was just like a twelve bars blues to us. He knew the form. I don't think there was any mystery. Before composers became dictatorial about what they wrote, they were improvising musicians. They had to be.

I don't think 'improvisation' is a good word. I just think it's music. But you can't improvise unless you work at it. [34]

One of the reasons I play improvised music is that I don't trust third-party musical decisions. I feel like I'm from a music-less culture and I've been a heavy listener since I was eleven. My family were all musicians but it didn't make sense to me to play any particular genre because genre is like an alien import in my actual life, I think.

For me, the 'improvised music' style has just as much, if not more, cultural baggage than hip hop. [35A]

Initially, there was something that really intrigued me: going on stage and doing live stuff with studio equipment (synthesizers, tape recorders, mixers). I was improvising without knowing it.

But for me today, improvisation is first and foremost a way of making music. On the one hand you have composition and then you have improvisation. And then there are all these other terms. I think the idea of styles, labels, is a real danger. It's like you're playing 'improvised music', but you're not always improvising. Maybe the 'improvised music' style has worth in itself, but I'm not interested in being locked into a style, because improvisation belongs to rock as much as anything else. There may be something in the idea of the 'art of improvisation', in which certain specificities intersect, in which perhaps you see things that some people try to name, to define in some way.

I do not like the idea that improvisation, something that is too often the case (more for dancers than for musicians actually), is at the service of composition, that it helps you to compose, that it is a way of manufacturing material and appropriating it. For me improvisation is not necessarily something that is finished. It's something that's open, that's in suspension, in production. [36]

What I'm interested in in improvisation is musical thinking. If I had to define improvisation, I'd say that it consists in thinking about the music that I want to make and trying to make it without writing it. And reflecting, because that's part of the process for me, formulating, what I might call thinking, defining a whole lot of stuff, anticipating, analysing and putting it into a kind of reservoir, in fact putting the music under certain conditions. If there's any writing going on, perhaps it comes in the conception, the anticipation, before playing, of music that you hear and that you would like to make. And non-writing in the sense that I don't know what I'm going to play 90 per cent of the time. For example, I choose the first sound I'm going to make. And sometimes, I don't make it. When I start, I no longer hear that sound.

What I'm interested in isn't improvisation for improvisation's sake, but rather the relationship to the current situation that improvisation allows. What appeals to me, I think, is the idea that everything you have planned, everything you have thought about, even everything you're thinking about, is called into question by the situation itself. But Situation with a big S.

In fact, I don't like the word 'improvisation'. I reckon there's a big problem with this word. I object to everything implied by the word! The word, if you look at it as a statement, implies lots of things that I do not like. For example, the whole tendency in improvisation that believes it's 'communicating with trees'.

If you take a dictionary and try to define what improvisation is in some way, I don't think I have much of a relationship with that improvisation. What I want to do is to swing between thought and music, but without having a relationship with something that is written, a text so to speak. Or without having to be faithful to a thought. Which is to say – and this is important for me – that what can happen is that you have something in mind, but you don't have to be faithful to it at all costs. There are circumstances. It may very well be that something else happens.

For me, improvisation should be music that asserts the right not to define itself. Even if you can define strategies or idioms, you know that it's improvisation, you hear that it's improvisation, and generally I think that's a good sign. I think that, as material, it truly allows you to aim for that, to pursue an escape route, always push the framework of thought back a little, or rather the framework of listening. This is not something that written music allows at all. Written music also allows you to push back against the framework but not like that. Improvisation allows a truly unique way of listening. [39]

I am more attached to improvisation than to written music, to composition. What I find interesting is that you're in a particular state, a state of necessity, the necessity of the moment, whereas when you play a composition, you are in state of necessity of execution. Having this freedom of choice is thrilling. [37]

It's not us governing the music, in a way it's the music governing us, I think. [06B]

It's interesting to realize how much we influence ourselves sometimes, we think we do something consciously and it's not so conscious in fact. I go with Nietzsche's free will. What is free will? Not much, actually. There is something which we could call free will, which helps us not to commit suicide … but it's not much. Still, if you accept the concept of inspiration – some people don't accept that it exists, we can discuss that – maybe there is something like inspiration which is in between intellectual knowledge and empirical, emotional knowledge. Maybe there is something in between. Personally I think there is, somehow, something in between. I'm very interested in neurology. There are so many interesting questions. [27]

It's very difficult, impossible actually, to reach freedom; we are totally determined by language, social conditions, economic conditions and so on. But there are some moments, which can happen in improvisation or in a discussion or in another situation – I don't want to fetishize improvisation – where you get closer to it. We try to understand these conditions and it's a constant process. [24]

I would say it's a mixture: it is freedom but at the same time you always have the parameters to deal with, the relationships, the context, the environment. It's about how you negotiate your freedom within that context. Just because you've got to negotiate doesn't mean it's not freedom. It is freedom. The freedom is there, this little spark that's in you that makes anything seem possible. That's the freedom, not the chains. I've always thought I could be in jail and I would be free. That's a particular conception of freedom perhaps – it's not pure but it is freedom. [05A]

With some groups we've developed certain ways of playing – an agreement between us. If you recorded it and transcribed it and analysed it, you could probably describe certain rules that we seem to be following because all the concerts we do with a particular group sound similar in a way. Not the same, but there's a similar aesthetic. It's always the same piece and always different. And this is an agreement between us. But we also want to challenge ourselves, not to get stuck. We try to expand – but without making tasteless decisions, without losing our system of rules. This makes the music very interesting because I don't think it's possible not to have any rules at all. Imagine truly free improvisation – I wonder how that sounds! I don't think truly free improvisation is possible. There are always limitations or agreements, relationships. It's not possible to be completely free. Nobody is completely free so we can't improvise entirely freely. [17]

Freedom? Freedom is something that I'm not at all interested in. I don't know what it is. I don't see the point of conceptualizing freedom. What I'm interested in is thinking about what will determine what I'm doing, rather than thinking: 'Am I allowed to do that, can I, am I free?' No, what I'm interested in is dealing with causes, analysing them, examining them, having the ability to analyse them and anticipate them. The best definition of intelligence I know is from the chess player Garry Kasparov: 'The ability to analyse and anticipate.' I like this relationship, which is a relationship that I can have with music. And in music, I believe that this only exists in improvisation. [39]

I personally don't like to use the word 'improvisation' for the music I'm playing because I think it reduces the activity to one certain aspect of it. It brings this method too much into focus and changes the reception of the music. When people know it's improvised, they listen differently to how they would listen to it if they would know it's composed or if they don't know what it is at all. The other thing is that I think it has quite strong cultural baggage. The word 'improvisation' has been used in an ideological way for a long time. In the 1960s, when improvisers started to play, it was meant partly as a counterpart to the composed music world. I have the feeling that, nowadays, it's not necessary to place what we do against something. I think we can use the full spectrum, from composition or conceptual approaches to open processes. Of course, I don't deny that I improvise. I wouldn't claim that what I do is not improvisation. It's just about the way the term is used. Quite often, for people who are not involved in the off-mainstream scene, improvisation is just a 'second-choice method': if you can't do it properly or if it all fails, you have to improvise. And this is not what we do: we choose to improvise.

When I started, improvisation included the notion of freedom. But it changed with the experience of doing it. Because I noticed that there is a difference between the idea of improvisation and actually doing it. When you are actually doing it, you recognize that there's a strong responsibility that comes with it. Of course, you could do anything you want, but you're responsible for a process and for the musical outcome of the group. So you can't ignore what the others do. So you recognize that there are some limitations that come with the process itself. There is a starting situation you create in the first moment and, from then on, limitations are part of the process. It's quite ambiguous, but you are in this field of ambiguity straight away. There is still a lot of freedom but it's not so much about: 'I can do anything I want at any time.' There is a freedom in making decisions and stretching the boundaries, the limits that come with the process. The process doesn't force you necessarily to go in one direction and to follow it, because you are participating in forming the process. So there is some freedom but also a lot of responsibility. [44]

For me, improvising is not an end in itself. What interests me is making music, not just improvising. Improvisation is a way of making music. Improvising is part of the life of a musician, the challenges of music, but music isn't only that. Music is also composing on paper or tape, playing things that have been written. I have met many musicians by making music freely, without constraints, without a score or the premeditation of composition, with the sole constraint of the instrument, if you can call it a constraint, and the constraint of meeting in a given context. I have done a lot of it and at one point I realized that I could not spend my life improvising. Indeed, I have never only done improvisation.

For me, improvisation is a laboratory. Putting yourself in a state of improvisation is fundamental to the life of a musician. Moreover, in the history of music, all the great musicians were improvisers, whatever approach they had afterwards, whatever they did with these improvisations. Beethoven, for example, did a lot of improvising, Bach improvised within a framework and conversely, Igor Stravinsky and Giacinto Scelsi, who noted down their improvisations, recorded or transcribed them to turn their improvisations into a form in their own right, rather than inscribing an improvisation in a pre-established, pre-existing form. In short, there are lots of relationships to improvisation that interest me. The lab testing element allows you to discover other sounds, other ways of playing that you could not discover if you were on your own.

I have the impression that every day that passes is a lab test for the next days of our lives. We are constantly conducting experiments. Nothing is fixed or frozen. Everything has to be called into question. That's what you should tell yourself each time you start playing music.

Everything is very much interwoven. When you improvise, are you not playing from the score of that day's state of mind? When you play a composition, do you not find yourself doing things that are beyond your understanding? That's what we are trying to do, create something that transcends us, put ourselves into a state of playing that surpasses us. And improvisation is a means to achieving that.

What I find interesting about being at the crossroads of many ways of making music is being able to use the specificities of each way of making music in the other ways of making music. For example, when I'm doing 'pure improvisation', I try to imagine that I'm a violinist playing Bach, because then you have to be very precise in what you want to do, the sound you hear and that you think you now need to play. You have to play it as well as possible, and conversely, when I find myself playing composed themes that presuppose total control of the score, I tell myself that there's a natural way, a fresh way of playing them, and that this freshness comes from the fact that I'm improvising them for the first time. [42]

A while ago, I might have thought that music is a tool for improvising, but I don't think that anymore. I don't see improvisation as an end in itself. But it reminds me of something else I'm interested in: the idea that sound can be there in order to experience space. We normally think of space being there so we can hear sound better but it can be the other way round as well; when we listen to a sound, we always have an acoustic as well. I'm currently reading a book by Barry Blesser called *Spaces Speak, Are You Listening?* in which he discusses these questions. [28]

For some time now I haven't even been calling myself an improviser. I consider myself an instrumentalist who happens to play predominantly in improvised music settings. I am not sure how much interest I have in the absolute world of improvised music. I am much more interested in music – good music – whether it's improvised or whatever. [06B]

I don't feel that what I do is really improvisation. I feel that I have a certain palette of sounds and a certain range that I draw upon and that I know, more or less, the kind of outcome to expect. I don't really have the impulse to try and change that. The collaborations that I find myself in give me the opportunity to work in improvised settings without necessarily being a very competent improviser myself. I would never define myself as an improviser, in a million years, even if I work in improvised situations.

I do diffusion and multichannel works and things like that. There's always a live element that I bring to my work in terms of real-time processing. … So that I have something to do! Or else I just sit there staring at the computer screen.

There needs to be something to do! I need to be able to twiddle a few knobs and stuff. [22]

I am not an improviser. I do not improvise. I make decisions, but I do not improvise. I think we need to redefine the term 'improvisation'. For me rather it's communication. Improvisation is a word, a concept, but it does not exist. We communicate with our cultural baggage, a musical background that everyone has, and we try to find common ground for communication in order that what everyone is carrying with them can be asserted. And you try to get your own thinking to move forward, to get your own nature to progress, within the metaphor of music.

What then is improvisation? Starting from nothing? The usual conception of improvisation is that you start from nothing and that you improvise. Because indeed people say: 'Ah, you're playing without a score!' – that means that improvisation is outside of something. But when you tell them you've been working on something for several years, they don't understand.

We create ideas and that's what I'm interested in. We try to create thought. We try to create musical thought. [26]

I don't give a damn about improvisation. As a subject in itself, I'm not interested in it at all, and I find it very strange that people talk about improvisation in the singular, because it comes out of so many different practices. I do not even want to name the thing. It's becoming a foreign word. When I was a militant, I defended the practice – also because it was an artistic practice that received little support, that was little-represented – so much so that I had to wear the uniform of a certain poetic militancy. And now, I have the impression that it has become a foreign word. And the term 'improvised music' even more so. It's an expression that has been foreign to me for a long time and it even seems horrible to me. [15]

Improvisation was definitively not a goal. The goal for me was to play good music and to have a positive impact on the world with it. Nowadays I don't care if I do it with music or by whatever other means. But improvisation is not a technique either. A technique is something that you should be able to learn, at least to a certain degree. Free improvisation is something too vague and general to be learnt as a technique. It's just a way of making music among many others – and a fetish.

It didn't happen from one day to the next, but after a while I became disappointed with the improvised music scene, and I felt I was not achieving what I wanted to achieve. I was not touching people. I felt that what we did was not really moving anybody much. I didn't know what to do ... .

Everything became a bit pointless to me, a bit too abstract. But I had things to say. This music wasn't enough for me to say what I wanted to say. My ex-girlfriend back then was a dancer, and we started to communicate using weird body movements. We used to work together, me playing and her dancing. All of a sudden, during our performances, I found myself not only playing my instrument but also using those particular body movements we used in our daily lives. I gradually started to use my body while playing, then I added spoken words (excerpts of poems I liked or texts I used to write.) Then I came to feel that that was affecting the audience much more than me only playing percussion. The last concert I did with my instrument was at an art university in Jerusalem that is on top of a hill. I carried my huge orchestral bass drum all the way up. After that I said: 'No more for me.' I couldn't find a reason why to keep bringing the drum. The next 'concert' I played was in Tel Aviv, and I just didn't bring the instrument. I thought: 'OK, now I will just dance.' The concert was already organized as a concert, but I never brought the instrument. I did what I could.

Nowadays I'm improvising less and less and planning things more and more.

Improvisation is very open but at the same time very limited. Improvising is not about doing whatever you want. In the end, whatever you do, it'll be an improvisation. And it's not what I want to do right now. I want to be able to think in advance what will do to the audience if I do this or that. There are ways to keep things open without improvising.

You listen to improvised music or watch improvised theatre or dance and, paradoxically, it often seems all pretty similar. It's very difficult to get outside this abstract thing. Abstraction can be problematic. A way to avoid that is by working with concepts or ideas that the audience can somehow read. When you do that you reach the audience on an extra level, besides the material or the formal levels that are more characteristic of improvised music. It's never only about the concept or the idea, though.

Sometimes improvisers imagine that the materiality of the sounds they play is more important than what it really is for the audience.

Yesterday I went to a concert with a friend of mine. It was the first time she'd been to an improvised music concert. After the concert she told me: 'There were some nice sounds.' She is a very sensitive, intelligent person, and still she couldn't say or feel more than that. And the concert was not particularly bad. I'm sure improvisers want to go beyond this, but I believe we tend to imagine things that aren't there. We live inside this bubble. It's very unlikely that the audience will feel anything close to what you feel when you play. For most people would be just a person making sounds.

Lately, I rarely improvise. I do it only when I need to solve a specific problem where improvisation can be helpful, but nowadays, for me, improvisation is only a resource among many others. If I need to improvise, then it'll be something very defined that has a clear purpose in a piece. It wouldn't be something related to what is considered 'free improvisation'. [31]

Of course, improvisation is a means to an end because you're after a certain aesthetic result, but it always has also the element of experiencing yourself, again and again, in 'risky' situations. [44]

When we use generic terms like 'improvisation', it actually obscures what's going on a lot of the time. [21]

Improvisation for me is composition on the fly – so it's still composition, it's just live composition. [03]

I generally do quite a bit of preparation before an improvised concert – and in that preparation I will be practising constantly, thinking about composing, thinking about improvising and practising how to listen actively.

To me, improvising is real-time composition, and the strength of improvising is that there's little editing. That editing has to be done there, in front of the audience, in the moment. On the other hand, I feel uncomfortable if the audience has to sit there for fifteen minutes and have two minutes of brilliant music. I think it's possible – one practises – to edit spontaneously while playing, at least with one's own part and ideally collaboratively. So I'm composing, improvising, creating, I'm listening to what other people are doing at the same time, and while I'm doing that, I'm editing what I will or won't play. [40]

I don't find the argument about what composition is and what improvisation is very useful, because I think you're always composing, whether you're doing it on the spot or whether you're in a rock band and you're figuring out a song, starting with a bass line, then the drummer comes in, then the singer picks up a poem he wrote three days ago, or if you're in a five-piece improvising ensemble meeting for the first time … .

In terms of the traditional ideas of composition, with Germ Studies, a duo with Chris Abrahams, the composed elements are that we each figure out one technique or algorithms, and we dig into this combination as far as we can to find the common ground between this ancient Chinese instrument, the *guzheng*, and the DX7 synthesizer and we hope that over the course of five minutes we find that place. That's the aim. You could call that composition – but we have to improvise to get there.

With my group Hammeriver, which consists of seven people playing basic structures centred around the music of Alice Coltrane, we play a ten-minute piece called 'E' where every member plays E or bends just outside the note – absolute sustained high energy from beginning to end – but we all know the exact note that's played and the energy we're supposed to produce. Over the course of ten minutes, there's so much improvisation involved – where you place what you do, whether you hit or pluck the string, or the way it's performed. It has a very specific composition, but I would still say that it's an improvisation. I understand that it might sound like a contradiction to some people. I've asked these musicians to play these compositions because they are fantastic improvisers.

I find that I make more interesting music when there is some kind of restriction – so with my groups, Hammeriver or Germ Studies, I use restriction or structure while also embracing improvisation. [30]

In recent years, whenever I improvise, I digest my compositions – which are themselves partly improvisations. Sometimes they're also collective compositions, which can be very rudimentary: a decision may be made, for example, to work on a particular theme or idea. And when I work with someone for longer, our improvisations become new compositions. Together, we develop something that will influence upcoming pieces. It's a long process in which improvisation influences the composition that itself influences the improvisation and so on.

There are a lot of compositional rules in our improvisations. Even when we're playing with someone for the first time, we respect these rules. And when you work with someone for a longer time, what's interesting is finding new ones that don't exist yet. In fact, they're not really rules. Rather they're small planets. When you're with this or that musician, you're on this or that planet. And, when you're working together, you may discover a new planet, that you didn't know yet. Even if all these planets are part of the same system. [48]

When I was studying music, it seemed strange to me that everything always had to be pre-arranged in music while, when we speak, it's not the case that we have everything written first, like in a theatre play. That's one of the reasons I became interested in improvised music.

I don't see improvisation as an utopia, as a model of a perfect society. I also know from working in classical contemporary music that the model doesn't really exist anyway. It's usually an exchange between the musicians and the composer. It's not about the idea that the music belongs to one person. It's actually a construct that the composer has to complete a finished work in its eternal form before writing it down and giving it to musicians to play it. I don't think this was ever true, even with the icons of classical music. I don't know when that myth developed, really. But it has and I think it was healthy that improvised music challenged it.

I don't necessarily separate improvisation and contemporary composed music. I just try to think about what makes musical sense. In improvisation, if you work with someone over a long period of time and really develop your playing together, it's a sort of composition anyway. And in terms of composition, I'm increasingly interested in finding strategies of making composition more like a set of rules, like in classical Indian music, within which the musician improvises. I am interested in finding some ways of making those rules more conscious, because when we improvise there are rules anyway. I don't think really free improvisation ever exists. I call some of my composed pieces constructed improvisation. But what I don't want to do is to compose a bit and then say to the performer: 'Improvise' and then compose a bit more. I find that really unsatisfying because the second time you play the piece, you've got the memory of what you've improvised before. I'm much more interested in looking at traditions where improvisation is inherited within the tradition like the Indian music tradition. One of the things I find interesting and also frustrating about improvised music is that the criteria are not clear. So much is left to intuition which is nice, in a sense, but sometimes I want to know what the underlying rules are in order to change them. But I'm not sure I'm going to analyse what the rules are in improvisation. I think they change too much. But I certainly want to write more pieces, which I see as a kind of game. When you play a game of tennis, you don't think: 'Now I'm playing a game – a composition – which was invented by somebody and I'd better make sure I respect the rules because that's the way so and so meant it to be.' I don't even know who invented tennis. I suspect it was invented over a long period of time and not by any one person. Language is not invented by a particular person either. [28]

I don't always make improvised music, even with people who improvise. I don't want to forbid myself to step outside of the context, the intention or rather the image of the intention, in which we are playing. What I'm interested in is what I get back from the sound, and if I feel that's of interest, then it's not off-topic.

I think more about improvisation when what I'm playing is not improvised. Improvising itself is what seems most natural to me. If it takes on importance, it's like when I speak English – and I speak very bad English – it becomes forced, which necessarily implies an aesthetic. When I say 'natural', I mean a mode of listening, not something that is at all conceptual. You just listen to how the sounds are placed ... and they position themselves there. You listen to sounds you are making, those your colleagues are making, those the fly is making. ... 'Pure' improvisation is when I don't have any idea of what I want to do. And when the people who are with me don't either. But there are different styles of improvisation, protocols, styles of improvised music. There are quite a few people, I think, who are going towards somewhere where these protocols don't exist. A lot of musicians make improvised music knowing what they want and what they do not want in advance. That's not what I'm interested in when I'm improvising. I'm involved in projects in which you deliberately decide (and this may itself be a concept) not to talk about what you're playing together, but simply play in the same dynamic. Aesthetics do not result from a decision. However, forcing yourself not to deal with conventions and aesthetics also goes against the idea of not worrying about them.

It is possible not to have any idea at all of what you're going to play – and often the results are not very successful. You may find yourself in this kind of state, but often the music you make is not much of a pleasure to listen to. In fact, it's not really possible not to have any idea at all, but it's possible to believe you don't. It's like loving someone: Is it really possible to love someone? Yet we believe it. It is possible to try not to have a conceptual intention. The question is rather: Does improvisation exist? But that's not the question you asked me.

Are we talking psychology? I am the way I am. Whether with my instrument or without it, I'm still the same person. And if I let myself go and express myself in anything other than Alexandrine verse, I express myself in my own way. Does that make it improvisation? No, it doesn't. It's the accumulation of the components that make you up. Like all your actions. Managed in the same way you manage your day, your sleep ... . Are all our actions, daily or not, improvised? You could say that yes, since they're an accumulation of what we have learnt from existence. If you agree with this idea, the way you hold a clarinet note in the middle of a phrase of an ultra-written contemporary piece is also improvisation in some way – if you use a microscope to look at the way you're blowing into your clarinet. It's very fast. You think your brain doesn't move that fast, but actually it does. In fact, it's your consciousness that doesn't move that fast.

Personally, I'm not a 'score player' so I wouldn't go as far as to say that when I'm playing with a score it's the same as when I'm improvising. [12]

The relationship between composing and improvisation does interest me. And where one starts and the other stops, that's something that has always fascinated me. [06A]

I think that the concerns of improvisers are in general not so far removed from those of composers or even jazz musicians. For me, they function rather similarly.

I think that from a certain time, composers have asked themselves the same questions: 'How do you free up the performer? How do you give them more freedom? How do you not give them choice?' Or the opposite.

Actually I'm not interested in how the performer plays a composition. I'm not interested in musicians who perform music composed by someone else. On the contrary I am interested in composers who asks questions like: 'Why do I write? Why do I do that? Why do I offer what I write to be played?' Or conductors who will confront themselves, put themselves in a position where they have to offer their own reading of the work. [26]

I compose as well. But I never think of myself as a composer. So it's one way to improvise. I can't say what the main difference between composition and improvisation is.

It's not necessary for me to be a composer because, when I'm improvising, there are some limitations and some rules as well. For me, composing is just about setting rules and limitations in music. I think the difference between composition and improvisation is just that you set those rules before the music is played or during it.

I think I am an improviser, even if I've composed several pieces for instruments. I write scores but I feel like I'm improvising with writing. When I'm composing I don't know the result, I don't know how it will be played even if every note and every second is written out. My impression of the result of the music is not so different from total improvised music. If I had to choose between the words 'composer' and 'improviser', improviser would seem more familiar for me, but I think it's not important to give an answer. [23]

I don't even think about the idea of improvisation versus composition anymore. It doesn't even interest me. I used to think about it all the time. Actually it depends if you're talking about 'improvised music' as a style or about 'improvisation'. When I started to play improvised music, it was really interesting to learn a lot of things, sonically, texturally, and to play with a lot of people from different backgrounds like, for example, playing drums with someone from a classical flute background – a very bad idea, yes! All kinds of weird groupings. It was like: 'Anything is possible', the music could go anywhere, and it did, and I made new discoveries. And then it took me quite a while to realize that I could improvise more, sometimes, playing in a really conventional jazz band or with the flamenco dance company I worked with for a long time, which for me was really serious improvisation. I had a lot of stylistic problems back then. I asked myself: 'What music do I do? Am I a jazz drummer? Am I an electroacoustic composer? Am I an improviser?' I felt I needed to define what I did. Nowadays I think I'm an improviser. Because when I try to do compositions live – in the studio it's different – when I try to set what I'm going to do, I can't do it. I often do it solo because I have a lot of problems playing solo. It's really difficult. And many many times, I've said: 'This time, for once, I'm going to say what I'm going to do and I'm going to do it.' And it's the worst music I've ever made in my life.

But I don't know if it's possible for me in my music to really improvise anymore, to be at that point where I think: 'What am I going to do next? I don't know.' [35A]

If the goal isn't to index the place and the moment in one way or another, I don't see why we use improvisation. Of course, you can compose. That's just as valid. ... In fact, you can always say that the context is the ultimate instance of any artistic experience but that's summarizing a bit too much. ... I'm not, for all that, a fierce defender of context but nevertheless I think that simply reducing the distinction between improvisation and composition to context is a catch-all idea. Some finished objects resonate with a context in a fantastic way and some improvised moments don't get beyond the edge of the stage. ... For me, it's the realized form that counts, the interface you need to 'experience' something. Without form, you don't experience anything in space and time. [25]

Composed music and improvised music are both very beautiful ways of making music. They are very different but not so different – it's almost a paradox. Of course, in a composition you usually get a piece of paper in front of you – it could be a monitor also – but information, in any case, and that information tells you to do a certain thing at a certain time. Before you start, you know you're going to do a specific thing at a certain time. In improvised music, you don't have the piece of paper, but still there is the feeling that I'm going to do more or less this or that. I know that, you know that, we all know that. That was the reason why I left so-called improvised music because it became too static for me, too idiomatic. You have to do this in order to be free and certain things are not allowed. And it became a cliché of a cliché of a cliché after a while. The first generation actually did the most interesting things, and then the second as usual, like everywhere else, started to get idiomatic and to replay the first generation. And when it's stagnant, so that there's no evolution possible, this for me is the time when I hear alarm bells ringing: 'Get out!' [27]

Nowadays in professional classical music we have musicians who are very good at playing notated music, and then we have musicians who tend to improvise. And it's quite rare to have musicians who are interested in doing both. This is a relatively new phenomenon, and I always remind myself that for most of the history of classical music (and of course all the rest) improvising was invaluable for musicians. The idea of not separating too much what we do in performing, composing and improvising music is quite an important aspect to me. [40]

We all know that historical distinctions change over time and that they are often based on cultural assumptions. So how do we get beyond the cultural assumptions of our time about what constitutes music or text or signs? What happens when you bring those aspects together so that the fabric of it puts you at the edge of distinction?

One thing I love about improvisation, which is really different from working with composers – but it depends on the composer, of course – is the openness about questioning the nature of the activity and trying to find new distinctions. [21]

If we're interested in improvisation, then that suggests that we're not quite sure what music is. We've got some idea but we'd like to find out. So every time we play, what music is is open to a certain freedom of discovery, open to question.

The possibility of being surprised by oneself or by the situation – this is what we hope for. [16]

I do sometimes wonder what the purpose of music is. I don't really understand why music is so important to me.

When I studied music, most of my teachers seemed to think that music is basically about self-expression, a tool for self-expression. But actually you are expressing the self that you become through playing. [28]

What interests me is what's behind what is written. My intention? What's behind the sound, beyond the sound. What that is? I don't know, I cannot name it. That's why I play. For me, that's what music is. Music is not sound. Sound is just its aspect. There are other things behind it, otherwise there's nothing of interest there.

I have the impression that it depends on how you define music. I cannot define it. But I like to call what I'm looking for 'music'. There's a lot of stuff in there, but I have a hard time defining it.

Sounds are elements that I use as means to make music. I do not like the term 'improvisation'. What I do on my own is composition and, inside that, I improvise. When I play with other people, I don't know if I'm actually playing with them. In fact, I don't quite understand the term 'improvisation' or 'improvised music'. Because, for me, it's not improvised. Improvisation is, for example, when, in the street, you meet someone by chance, and you start talking with them. It's an accident, it's improvised. At that moment, you're improvising. But when you play with someone, you bring your instrument, you know pretty much what the other person is going to do and there are things you can predict.

Instability is what I'm really interested in. That's the dynamic that I'm interested in. We tend to think of many things in a static, analysed, fixed way, when in fact things move. Objects want to move and I try to silence them, to obtain silence. If I don't think about objects, they disappear. That's how I experience it: I have to think about an object, otherwise it won't want to respond to me. I communicate with them. What I do, if I analyse it, is what is called gestural music. I have a special relationship with objects. I kind of do Sufi music. The music itself is not animistic, but the relationship I have with objects is animistic. I'm interested in listening to objects. Objects also means our bodies. When I hold a cymbal, I control neither my hand nor the cymbal, but there are connections between the cymbal, my hands and my body and what's strange is my mental, psychological, stability, which is very important. What's most important is my own stability. It's like calligraphy, it's connected to the brain, and there's also a kind of action-reaction with objects, with percussion. It's that too: how to catch the rebounds. [41]

When I'm not making music, I really want to, right away. Because I don't have any doubts when I'm doing the music that I do. I bathe in a kind of self-evident obviousness, while in life I very often doubt. Making music in this way can reassure me inwardly, intimately. And help me find myself. I am rid of all the contexts that disturb me and I exist in a self-evident obviousness. I may have difficulties with words for example, but in my music I am somewhere beneath words. I find myself within a sensory perception that does not need words. Words aren't easy to use because there is too much missing. While in my music, I feel complete. I'm in a complete existential mode, and not in something unfinished like language. [45]

What interests me in life is that which I am not yet conscious of, that which is beyond my consciousness, beyond my analytical capacities. I've transposed that to music, which is to say I'm excited by things I don't understand – even though understanding is not the goal at all, but rather being aware is.

What does 'understanding' mean? That's what's a problem for me in language and that's where I found a solution in sound: you can express something that's beyond understanding. You don't need to understand. You need to feel a presence. The only thing there is to express is a physical presence.

I see music as a tool that will help me go towards those things that fascinate me. And only improvisation offers me the possibility of finding that which I am not able to have consciousness of when I'm on my own. Improvisation is a tool that allows you to destroy the framework, the framework of received, accepted, acquired, thought … of received thought as I am aware of it, of course. What I'm interested in is being surprised, someone overwhelming me, making me see the world differently. I really think you can see this apartment, an urban, rural, whatever landscape in different ways – that you can change the vision you have without going anywhere. I need to mix my reality with that of other people to enrich my reality. I want to be disturbed, to be modified.

Behind all this, there's inevitably a weariness in seeing human beings live as they are told to live, using objects as they have been designed to be used and not inventing things, without even going so far as to make art, but simply in everyday life. [46]

After a moment, I thought: 'Maybe what I'm doing isn't music, or maybe it's not important to be sure whether it's music or not.' There's something that's much wider than music and that's called sound, quite simply. And in sound, there's something called music. But before and after that, it's not called music. It's something else. What is called 'music' is defined in dictionaries and schools. It's learnt. It's transmitted and it's above all defined by the person who listens to it.

The listeners, who receive what I do, are working as much as I am, and they have to manufacture something with their perception of everything that I'm doing. It's them who are making the music. I make sounds and they make music. [36]

Today, I use other mediums. I mean that there's not enough latitude in music to allow me to manufacture meaning. That's a big limitation right now. [39]

The goal is not music. It's the expression of something that has no name. I'm not saying that I'm not interested in music. It's not as simple as that. I don't know. I didn't choose to make music. I have always done music and that's fine by me. I even stopped, then I started again. That's how it goes in my life. [43]

It's very difficult to talk about expression because whatever you're doing you're expressing something. So it all depends on your perspective, on what you see yourself doing. [04A]

When you're involved in the thing, you don't have time to think about what you're expressing. That's for the Hollywood movie. And you don't know what you're expressing anyway. Music is something that you can only hear. You can't see music. We see symbols that we say represent music. But music can only be heard. You can't touch it. So when we talk about expressing ourselves in music, it's a rather haughty kind of a thing. Even if you play a composition the opposite way to what the composer said he wanted, you've still made music. In music, people are always giving you things to represent what the music is. Music only expresses music. [34]

In this scene, there is no much separation between what you do on stage and what you do off stage: a lot of musicians feel that their music is an expression of what they are, or that their music helps defining their identity. I personally feel my work to be something quite separate from my own life or my own self. It's like another life of my life – a place where I cannot recognize myself. I don't confuse myself with my work (which doesn't mean that I don't stand for it or that I make a work/life separation). I just make use of my work. I call for pragmatism in art. And free improvisation is one of the furthest points from pragmatism you can get to. Sometimes it can be useful in order to think certain things, but most of the times it's frankly useless.

I want to express love and happiness. Love and happiness have to do with having more power, having a greater ability to do and think things.

It's about creating a collective experience where we can all develop. It should be very concrete: we think about this, we speak about that and when we leave the performance we have something to process. When the performance is over, something should be different. If everything stays the same, it's like doing nothing. It should create movement in the sense of making a real change in the world. I often see art and it's just nothing. It's neutral, which is worse than bad. If something is terrible at least you go out and you say: 'Why was this so bad?' When it's neutral you're wasting your life. Most art is neutral. [31]

6

Talking about improvisation and music in general

I think our talking is a laboratory. When we listen to CDs, or even when we listen to other people's music, or even when we are out with our girlfriends, this 'laboratory' is always there, whether we are talking about music or not. [06B]

It may be a learned music, but there aren't many scholars who make this music. You do the work while playing. You can talk about music with the musicians you play with, out of politeness, but the discussion takes place while you're playing. [01]

We don't talk about the music after a concert. There wouldn't be a post-concert autopsy, ever. You feel good or bad, or indifferent, it's just something that happened. [06B]

It's actually quite rare to really talk about the music with the group members. It's something that develops through the playing. [14]

There are things which we sometimes talk about after the concert, when we all agree that such-and-such was a good moment or that we all liked some other moment. That happens. [17]

Some musicians do tend to talk about the music but I tend to be like: 'Oh shut up. We'll just do it and see.' It might be that somebody has done something you don't like. Do you tell them? [18]

In my weekly workshop, I don't do anything. Well, I guess I do but I don't know what it is exactly. You would have to ask the people that come because I'm not sure. But I'm there, and we keep the talking to a minimum, we don't ever really have big discussions. Every now and again we might get into that area, or if I'm obsessed with an idea I might bring it in to get some feedback, but it's all about practice. Its main value is as a space where people can come and play, and meet people of a similar mind.

It's all about us being there, being open enough with each other, open enough to realize that there are lots of different ways of understanding what music might be and being open to the possibilities. I always encourage people by saying, and I say it to myself too: 'Every time you play, try – even if it's only in some small way – to do something you've never done before.' [07]

There's a degree of, what's the word, there's an unknown quantity, some factor that doesn't fit into the type of language we're using here. Uncerebral. When we play, it's one hour or so of phenomena and it's really hard to make a generalization about the whole event and what's going on in my head. [09A]

I really want to believe that we can 'augment' music by injecting elements that are external to it: philosophy, politics, mathematics or whatever. And I don't believe that that produces 'philosophy-as-music', which would be very dubious, but rather something like non-music, music that isn't only thought musically, but that you might find beautiful or interesting, philosophically for example.

In fact, I think there's something that resonates with the questions of language and meaning; music also has its own way of making sense. I believe that there are things that can traverse music. I don't see why it should be more hermetic than anything else, even though this is something I often note. ... But hey, a bit of lexical precision is needed here ... because the analogy with language is a slippery slope, although exciting in my opinion. [25]

I think that the kind of analogy often made between conversation and language in improvised music is wholly flawed. I think it's not the right way to be thinking about it. That said, just as I'm trying to articulate what I do, I'm going back on it, changing my mind. Because as I try to formulate an idea and then articulate it, by the time I get to it, I'm not even sure that I agree with it. It's very much the same with what I play. [05B]

The analogy with speech and conversation is a very attractive one. But, of course, it's not conversation, it's not speech. If it was simple one-to-one correspondence there'd be no difference between speech and music – and there is an important difference, namely the abstraction of the material.

So all of these analogies break down at a certain point. They're useful but if you push them too far, they distort; they don't help anymore, they do the opposite of helping, they're not telling the truth anymore. So when the conversation or speech analogy breaks down, we move to some fractal nature or some other analogy that fits, usually to do with what we've been reading somewhere else, some great poem or some great piece of science, and we try and make a connection between that and the music. Because there are natural connections always, I think, between different human activities. [16]

For me, there's no connection between music and language. I believe that music does not say anything. It can say things, but things that are not of the order of language or communication.

A few years ago, I worked with a composer who wanted to write a piece for me. She had asked me to show her some of my sounds. So I showed her some sounds and I said to her: 'Look, I do that and I do that.' Then I wanted to push that further and I tried to draw up a correlation table between, for example, ten ways of positioning the lips, ten ways of positioning the tongue, ten types of fingerings, so that such-and-such a position of the lips could be combined with such-and-such a staccato technique and such-and-such a fingering. And I quickly realized that it didn't work. ... So it's not like a language where you can, for example, combine letters in the way you like in order to get sounds. You'd need a linguist for that ... but I'm not able to draw the analogy. [47]

I don't know if it's a language, but in any case talking about non-idiomatic improvisation is I think a false problem, because there is always an idiom. In fact, I have trouble associating the word 'language' with music. I did earlier but that was just in association with the word 'idiomatic'. In the end, I don't think that there is any meaning in music.

For me, there's no absence of idiom because there's all the learned stuff. ... I mean, there's a pool of learned things, you could even say a large part of learned things in what I hear or believe I hear. Learned things that are reorganized differently, plus an element of chance, of failed attempts – for me that's it. It sounds very simplistic, but in fact not at all because I don't think we're in a conception of things where we're supposed to be geniuses who recreate themselves anew every day – that's a complete myth. I do not fundamentally recreate myself every day. I'm only a person, an entity, something which has learnt things, experienced things and suffers from paranoia. I'm not saying that there's a continuity. There's nothing continuous about it. It's constantly called into question, but I never question myself about what I have accumulated. [37]

7

Non-idiomatic improvisation, experimental music, genre labels

I don't believe at all that we play non-idiomatic music. Our music is improvised in the sense that the layout of events, the temporal organization, the form, the structure, is not defined. We're trying to figure out what it *might* look like, but not what it's *going* to look like. It's a field of investigation that we have narrowed little by little while working.

I do not believe in fresh and spontaneous, free and liberated ad hoc meetings. I believe that all improvisers who devote themselves exclusively or principally to this music are instantly recognizable. In that sense, they have their own idiom, and they are working on something that they're interested in. It seems to me that for them, improvisation is more a way of making music than an aesthetic, a style.

There is a practice of improvisation, a culture of improvisation. Everyone plays with it in their own way, I think. [47]

In a way, I guess some of the philosophy behind some groups like John Stevens' Spontaneous Music Ensemble was about an extreme collective music where no individual voice surfaced, nobody soloed. Everybody is in a non-hierarchical instrumental structure where any instrument can take any role. But that music only occasionally worked in the more static areas which are being explored more by improvisers nowadays, and it seems to me that to push into one of those static areas and add your voice to it is a bit like the old Spontaneous Music Ensemble, just without the rhythmic input. You're prepared to add to the sound, to try to turn it into something new.

You shouldn't be scared of doing the obvious, it can produce great music – because improvisation shouldn't be too much about the search for the different in the obvious sense, it's the difference in the total: the total music needs to be different, not always the individual elements. [14]

Many people use the term 'improvised music' to designate a relatively precise aesthetic that, in any case, detaches itself from jazz. But language is constructed through usage. So if jazz musicians use the term 'improvised music' to define their music, they have a right to do so. Jazz and improvised music are not the same music at all. I think, unlike some people, that improvised music has an idiom. And the language of improvised music is not at all the same as that of jazz. Improvisation in so-called improvised music has a preoccupation with form, in terms of research, of aesthetics, that is completely different from that of jazz. [37]

When I'm in an 'improvised music' type improvisation situation, it wouldn't, for example, occur to me to play a melody. This may be due to formatting or a lack of maturity. But I don't hear melody – so I don't play it.

Rather we draw on the sounds of nature or industry. Or we find sounds that could be notes, but do not take up their place in a system that Western music has used for centuries. [01]

I think it's like an argot. It's a musical language, a kind of a deviation in which there are no rules or anything. You have to find your own way of dealing with the language. Because this music is quite abstract; you decide what you want to get out of it. I find that this can happen in improvisation. [09B]

All the music I hear is like a version of something I've heard before. It's hard to be enthusiastic about music when it's so familiar to you. It's OK but it doesn't excite me in the way that music should be exciting me. It's not that I'm old or tired just that I don't think the music is as truly innovative or exciting as it was. When the technology was poor, when resources were less available to people, for example. Today seems like a time where we have fantastic resources but the music isn't benefitting from them whatsoever.

I think experimental music is a bit of a ghetto for a lot of people who think they're innovative or provocative. Experimental music is very tired, the people are tired, the audiences have dwindled to nothing. It's the most irrelevant music I know – no one is interested in it except a handful of people. But to me that doesn't lessen the possibilities that experimental music can provide. But some of the most experimental music of the last twenty years isn't in experimental music – it's in R & B and hip hop and metal and popular music. No one refers to the processes that these music genres have actually embedded in popular music production. So a lot of what we're discussing is related to modernist ideas, things we could have been discussing in 1958. It's 2007 – can we go somewhere else with these post-Pierre-Schaeffer, post-John-Cage discussions of music? [22]

I claim the right to use the word 'experimental': the idea of observing and creating something and at the same time being the witness of it is what I'm interested in. But I don't see this in improvisation.

I'm not at all interested in over-elaborate improvisation. I have the impression that I'm faced with the same problems as in other musical idioms. That's not what I'm interested in. I chose music by chance, through unconsciousness. I had no reason to make music, but I stayed in the field of music, then sound, which is much wider than the academic musical terrain, and now what I'm interested in is reinjecting other forms of interest into a field that I now master, other interests that I may have in relation to painting, architecture, sociology, philosophy.

What interests me in painting is the idea of the surface, the frame, a certain idea of space, that which is outside the frame, and then there's the whole relationship to the transmitter and the receiver. There was a whole field that I had not experienced in music up until a certain time and experimentation led me to exit music. What I'm interested in is when music projects me beyond music. It's not the music that does that, it's because you enter the field of matter and from there, it opens onto quite another thing. [26]

There was a festival around here not so long ago organized by three not-so-well-known musicians. They're a little apart from the improvised music scene here. In Berlin nowadays there are somehow two improvised music scenes: the 'official' and the 'unofficial'. The official one is the one you know, the one we normally talk about. The unofficial one is where hundreds of other improv musicians play outside of this more recognized scene. So one of the guys from the unofficial scene organized a festival which was an improvisation competition. He said: 'I will organize a competition, you will have to apply, you will play in duos, the audience will vote, and the best duo will win 1,000 euros.' The people from the official scene reacted very badly. They tried to boycott it. Since then there has been this discussion about whether it's possible to say if an improvisation (or an improviser) is good or not, and who has the authority to say so. For me, it's about whether it is possible to say that something is better than something else, and if so, how can that be said? What arguments do you have? How do you think about it? Why is something better for you? Improvisers don't take criticism very easily, and I find often they're not very self-critical.

Many people chose to play improvised music simply because they have authority problems. They don't want to have anybody tell them that what they're doing is wrong. It's a safe space. Nobody will be able to tell you that. You'll always be able to say: 'No, for me it's right.' It's not possible to tell someone that this or that is wrong or bad. The consequence is that then you have this huge amount of bullshit music presented even in big festivals. A lot of people are doing bullshit – not just people from the unofficial scene. Lots of very well-known musicians play shit, and they keep being invited because they were there before, or because they are charismatic, or because they are good at doing public relations and what not. Nobody will ever say they play shit. [31]

8

Silence and dynamics

Once you come down to a lower register, or whatever, the quieter you get, the bigger your world is. The dynamic is much bigger. And there is more space for details, your vocabulary is much bigger. You don't have to feel like you're pushing or jumping through hoops or whatever, or playing energetically. I think it has something to do with an idea of self-expression.

When the pulse slows down, the dynamics of the pulse are bigger. It becomes much more three-dimensional. [04A]

I think playing long silences was about altering musicians' expectations – and the audience's too. [04B]

What I felt was that the silence was really necessary in order to increase attentiveness. Some musicians think that you can only really achieve that attentiveness in silence once you've gone through something but I was saying: 'No, the attentiveness can come out of the silence.' You're bringing attention to that sound world, it's a tool … . That's one of the issues but there are lots of reasons why silence became important. Another thing about so-called reductionism is that it can make the process a lot more obvious. So you can really bring the audience with you … it's more transparent. [04A]

When we started, people thought we were deliberately playing quietly, when we were actually playing as loud as we could with our instruments. I'm not interested in just playing one dynamic anyway, I don't think it's interesting. I'm interested in framing sounds with silence.

One thing I'm working on is getting away from gesture, the busy gesture, trying to find another way of working. [06A]

Recently, I've tended to play with a lot of silence. I think I need silence – not to make meaning, because if I play two sounds very close to each other, the meaning is a difference between pitch and dynamics. And I like that to happen, but not too much. I think that I play the next sound when I've forgotten the previous sound. I don't actually forget it, but it isn't so present anymore. Sometimes I'll also be waiting for the sound of the air conditioning to stop. Your sound is not silence. So if I wait for silence while I'm playing with you, I'm also waiting for you. [08B]

I work on pushing myself into an area that wouldn't be instinctive for me. I try to go to the limits of the sound or the limit of the silent. When I first started improvising, it really didn't have much silence at all, and it was always changing. It was very difficult, for me to be silent because it would mean that I wasn't playing or doing anything. So now I try to use silence as well and try to push that even more.

Silence and quietness are quite different things. What I can say is that I like playing softly or in detail because it's a different type of listening than listening to something very loud. I think that what interests me at the moment is to play something very quiet, subtle and detailed, because it draws a different kind of attention. Sometimes if you have something loud and in your face, an audience can easily switch off, whereas if you play something with a real sort of texture, it really makes people want to hear it and wonder whether it's silence or whether there is actually something there. Playing quiet sounds is quite interesting to explore people. Maybe they don't really say anything about the music. Maybe they don't actually like the music, but they start to listen in a completely different way to how they would every day – because we're so surrounded by noise. It's impossible to go anywhere without some kind of noise. Whether it's an aeroplane or traffic. I think we lose our sensitivity with listening. I wouldn't want to consciously force someone to listen in a particular way, but I guess it's a tool to draw an audience closer, to draw them in.

The silence depends on what I've played. There are different types of silence. I don't see the silence as the main thing, I use or utilize the silence to do something. I can use it to give form to what's gone on before, what's come in. Or as a space, like a little mini break before you go on to the next thing. It's definitely musical. [10]

I think with our music it's very important to have that sense of dynamics – not to be bludgeoned over the head with one sound necessarily. Sounds should interact and come and go, there should be common ground for sounds to meet and interact and that, of course, depends quite closely on the mix being right. So there are often disagreements about mixing.

Whoever in the group does anything with the mixing desk is ultimately controlling the degree of sound that somebody is making. Ideally, we should feel that when we're mixing we're doing so within some sort of commonly agreed realm.

It's not like we take it in turns. I think anyone can do anything they want. And someone else can change it back again!

I think each of us in the group has a slightly different feeling about how the improvisation is progressing in time. I think it's actually slower in a certain sense than other improvising. Things unfold slowly over a period of time, like layers.

I think we're interested in building up colours and textures and slowly changing those.

We're not looking for rapid events.

Sometimes, though, I think it is quite frantic, within an idea of stasis. It's like: 'Is this static or actually quite frenetic?' You can't really decide!

We came to play like that. I don't think we ever sat down and said: 'Let's play slowly.' It was something that emerged. [11]

If I played with a relationship to silence, I feel that it would be artificial. Playing a sound, making a silence, making a sound again … playing like that would be artificial. It would be voluntary. It would not be natural, so I would stop playing.

The ideal is rather that the two coexist: occupation of the duration by sound or silence. Whether time passes filled with sound or silence is the same thing. It's a progression of time, but I still have a hard time conceptualizing it like that.

It's very hard to do: to hear that silence has the same weight as sound, at least in improvisation, because in composition this is something you can do.

This is my existential, initial question: silence, to be silent, to be able to be silent in a silence that opens onto the real possibility of something that renews itself, even in terms of thoughts. That silence intervenes as a space from which something can emerge. If I think about human relationships, there's a link between my speech relationship with people and making the choice to play improvised music, to get out of the discursive aspect of music. Choosing not to speak as much also represents a certain deliberate desire that I have outside the field of music, the desire to keep quiet, something I'm unable to do.

For me something gets lost in bustle. It's not related to the amount of activity, the density, the sum of information, the accumulation. It's linked to loss, drowning, the feeling that you're *dominated* by activism. [26]

I hate loud music. So if a static piece is loud, it's the loudness I don't like. It hurts me. I don't like to look into the sun without sunglasses. [27]

I've noticed that if I'm feeling lethargic, quiet noises can wake me up, but I don't know why. [28]

Today, I'm more open to harmonies and notes than a few years ago. I think it was one of our characteristics, in Berlin in the late 1990s, to say no to things. For example, there was no such thing as pitch anymore, everything was based on noises, and the silences were very important, at least for me: I only played when I really wanted to play and not just because I was on stage and I was supposed to be doing something. There was silence and noise, with the idea of being inexpressive, or rather of playing 'like machines'. I think that was in relation to the improvised music that was there before, where it was almost always the same schema: 'We start, we play louder and louder, faster and faster, with more and more energy' – a bit like a big orgasm that never ends. And I felt that there wasn't anything of interest in it. We had already heard it too often, and there were people who played that style very well. For us, everything had to be clear. That was the idea: if we combine one sound with another by playing 'like machines', we can really focus on how it's assembled, while if sounds are too unstable, they mix, and you can't really focus on the details anymore. There was also the idea of ensuring that there was no soloist, that each member of the group contributed to the sound of the group. Clarity also meant trying to find interesting structures, but without composing them, in the moment. [29]

With ancient Korean music, for example, the idea with silence, or with music, was that you had to have a sound that respected the silence enough to break it or to meet it – that's something that made a great impression on me. I don't ever want to be making sounds just to fill up space – because silence is so powerful anyway. [30]

For me, non-action generates tension. Silence is for me a source of tension in that even if it's long, you know that an event will take place. You're expecting something to happen. So it's a source of tension. When silence is played, it's a source of expectation, an expectation that therefore generates tension, anxiety even. [38]

Sounds as material

Well, what makes a melody? It's not only the pitch, it's the rhythm and the length of the pitch, because if you play a note and a month later you play a different pitch, it's a melody but you don't think of it as a melody. So melody is putting different pitches so close together that you realize the difference very clearly, you don't have to make a drawing. So if I play a long low tone and two minutes later a slightly different long low tone it's a melody but it's not perceptible as a melody. So I don't think in terms of melody. I think in terms of colours actually. I use pitches, I like pitches very much, pure clean sounds, so when I make one I think in terms of its presence now, how it fits, how it sounds. Then when I've finished, it's gone and I forget. [27]

Derek Bailey came up with a way of playing where he could play with anyone in the world. He could improvise with any other musician in the world and make it good. He said to me that he'd often tried to recapture the innocence and excitement that the Joseph Holbrooke Trio with Gavin Briars and Tony Oxley had. Derek wasn't worried about repeating a certain pattern of notes in every piece. If he thought: 'Oh, this would work now', he'd do it – because it was that precise moment. I think Derek could get away with it because, over the years, even if he repeated the same patterns, he had a way of doing it, which was different in every piece. [04B]

I like drones, I like mechanical drones, I like accidental percussion, natural elements, I like the effect that wind has on other things. You don't hear the wind itself but you hear the cable bouncing on the flagpole or the fence reverberating in the wind – you're essentially listening to the wind but you don't know it.
I often manipulate the sounds. It's a way to artificially highlight certain characteristics of the sound, like heightening the colours of your photographs. Of course, there's no such thing as the sound itself. There's only your perception of it, there's only the way you hear it. I use quite simple effects that leave the

quality of the sound intact – because otherwise what's the point? I could be using any sound. You can make just about everything sound pretty interesting with a stack of effects and a really good equalizer, but the reason why I work with this particular sound is because it attracted me, so in my manipulation I want to highlight elements that are already there, not impose something that is completely alien to it.

In an improvised context, though, the sound itself isn't as important; it's a question of serving the relationships between sounds. [03]

You throw away as many ideas as you use, I guess. After a while you come to figure out if something has any kind of long-term use or not. The thing that depresses me most is that I've been playing for a very long time and there are still moments in a performance when I do something I've never done before and I think: 'How the hell haven't I done that before?! I've got this limited amount of material and I've been blind or deaf for thirty or forty years never to have seen that before – how can it be the case?!' The limitations are only in the head … . [07]

I have two sounds – 'high' and 'white noise'. I have a very reduced vocabulary – but who needs more? All the possible qualities of sound, I can bring them to bear on my playing but, in simple terms, what I play is either feedback or white noise. I play with the parameters of these two sounds. I'm really interested in having a small sound repertoire, which other people might think is quite reduced, and trying to get the most – or what I think is the most – out of it.

I keep working with feedback and I keep finding new stuff. The qualities of sounds that I want to play with are quite residual, what in mainstream music would be unwanted. Feedback, or white noise, they're sounds that don't have much value – what they call 'dirty' sounds in other music – and I want to really work with this. I try to avoid sounds that I've heard for a long time in improvised music. I do want to try and do things that have some freshness, something that hasn't yet been fully explored. I still find it interesting. [09B]

The cultural baggage matters. It depends who you are: some people would much prefer to listen to some feedback noise than to the Spice Girls. [09A]

When I use a preparation I have a slight idea of what the sound is going to be but it's never exactly the same. It's improvised within that, because it could be that I haven't put the preparation on exactly the same as I did yesterday or two months ago, so it changes and I work with that new sound. Maybe it all sounds the same to everybody else but I try to make a different sound, even if it's the same preparation. [10]

I have some kind of stupid theory … to define my conception of sound: there is *one* sound, a single sound, which we delve into to remove what we don't like. You can look at things differently and say that there isn't any sound, that all there is is architecture and that we are building a structure. I rather have the impression that it's sculpture. And that's the block that I'm interested in. It's a theory, not the truth. But that's the way I see things. I'm more interested in seeing things like that. I spend my time emptying my mind. [12]

Trying to play long sounds is a major constraint. There's some quite physical stuff, maintaining the pressure of the fingers, continuous movement. And that's something I like to play around with. Sometimes I wish I could avoid 'taking a breath' in order to do something really continuous – whatever that might lead to – but it's difficult.

Lengths are what are most obvious when listening, having durations, always the same proportions, the same mode of operation – I don't see any way of avoiding that. [13]

Derek Bailey once said that he was searching for material that was infinitely flexible and, in a way, that's what he did. The changes are all small changes, but a lot of small developments and small changes add up to continual change. I think in the earlier days people didn't want to draw too much attention to new sounds although they were there, because they got in the way of the music, because the music was about how you were connecting sounds and how you were relating to other people through those connections. In early works, I was excited to discover unusual sounds on the saxophone, but I didn't use them because they were too strong, the listener noticed them too much in a piece of music and I didn't want that, for people to notice just these sounds. I wanted them to notice what I was doing with all this material. [14]

If there is no backbone, no structure of known material, what you're dealing with becomes a fog, a jelly, there's nothing there. So there has to be this known stuff. But the known stuff has to be dressed and presented as if it's presented for the first time. So it's a question of presentation and organization. I think of some of those materials as armature, when the sculptor makes something, fixes something – he knows there needs to be a limb in a specific place. So you need something to support that, otherwise the material will just collapse. So some of these learnt materials function like armatures in the sculpting of the music. [16]

When I do improvising workshops, I like to work on the opposite of a sound. What is the opposite of a sound? Usually if I go: 'Aaaaah', people go: 'Peep peep'. Or if I go: 'Chwiiiee', the opposite is: 'Mmmm'. Little ideas like that. I usually try and come at it with an angle – counterpoint. I like that word. So it will develop then with everybody working with that counterpoint. If you hear everybody just doing the same rhythmic ideas or the same colour, pitches, whatever … that's why music is interesting, because of this counterpoint. Abstract impressionist music. That seems to fit quite well. [18]

Playing with musicians who work with noise, I've tried to make the voice not sound like a voice. The question was this: 'How to make the voice function in a non-typical way?' At the moment, I can't stand the virtuosic vocalists doing their thing, these series of 'bags-of-tricks'. I hate the 'diva vocalist' thing. So there have been different things that have come out of it, like exploring new sounds, looking at language in a more microscopic way. But I do question this constantly, asking myself: 'Am I actually just being decorative?'

I developed this system of 'impro-texts' as I called them: I would bring along to the gig a big wad of texts, of which I would use perhaps 5 per cent or 10 per cent, or maybe none at all, depending on what would happen. To me, it was a store of ideas that I might or might not bring into the improvisation. I liked this idea because it made the whole thing richer. One couldn't just say: 'Oh, there goes the vocalist making music.' Sometimes, I also used to think: 'I'm going to use the musicians to make a new text', in order to complicate this idea of what the activity is. [21]

Often when you listen to what I do in concert or on a recording you might think that what you're hearing is one sound whereas it's an amalgamation of four or five different sounds, all subtly intertwined. In the mixing process, I emphasize particular aspects of that sound but it's an act of listening; I don't know whether I'm actively thinking I must do this or I need to do this – I find it difficult to work in a predetermined fashion. But it's not pure improvisation either – I've got many prepared sounds, and I know what the outcome is likely to be 80 per cent of the time. The context and situation determine the outcome – and the outcome is always different even though my palettes of sounds are often similar. [22]

How do I choose sounds? How do I decide that this sound is better than other sounds in this situation? How do I choose a particular timing? How can we decide if it's bad or not? And also the value of sounds – the quality of sounds: Why is the sound of a Stradivarius good and the sound of a cheap computer bad? This is a totally cultural or social thing. I think there are no essential differences between these values. Mainly, my recent work has been related to attempting to avoid these decisions.

On my CD *Malignitat*, the title track is kind of sampled music. I just went to a CD rental shop and I rented a sound effect library CD, at random. I used the first track of the CD and tried to make a composition with those sounds without choosing them.

These past years, when I've played improvised music, I've only played a few, very limited materials. I mean just one pitch or hand clapping. If I play guitar, there are many possibilities, many kinds of possible sounds. But recently, I've been playing with very limited, very few sounds, sounds you can count on the fingers of one hand. With these few sounds, the structure of the piece as a composition will be clear, very simple, schematic.

I don't like improvised music that develops, changes, finds something, changing and changing. I don't want to play like that, don't ask me why. So one of the reasons why I play with very limited materials is as follows: if I play with very few notes, you can find the same material from the beginning to the end, it's like the same block to make a building. So if I use the same thing, in the end, you will find a building of sorts. Of course, it's not like a building, it's very unbalanced, not mathematical. It's not like a machine – but the important thing for me is to use the same bricks to make music.

As a result, it will be a very strange building but it will be built. I think this is interesting. To make a building, the bricks need to be clear, stable. So I choose really clear sounds. Of course I have my own history too, and I can't escape from that. [23]

Playing a pre-recorded forty-five-minute sequence in an improvised ad hoc meeting is not a problem for me. You play it, you're not just in the transmission – that is, making something heard that's there – you really make something heard in a particular way. You get involved, you really want it to be heard. From the moment this intention exists, you transmit something different to the listener …. [36]

The choice of material is what has been accumulated as experience during the various improvisation, work and concert sessions, and the accidents that have meant that, without even paying attention, certain things have appealed to me, touched me and others less so.

The same note doesn't have the same meaning in different contexts of improvised music. It's not the medium, but the environment that gives meaning. [37]

When I play piano notes on the keyboard, I don't hear them as melody or harmony. Rather I hear them as sound, as material.

For me material is made up of the different types of sound that I am able to produce with the piano. Which is to say everything that's available in terms of the sound palette, different types of sound, timbre. I know that there's a field of possibilities in front of me with different categories. I know, for example, that I have access to ten or fifteen ways of making continuous sounds, so I know that they're available. But I don't have them all in mind all the time.

Actually, I'm very much aware of what a sound will sound like before I play it. Except for the fact that all pianos are different. But I don't have any desire to control things because it isn't interesting to do so and, moreover, it's strictly impossible. [38]

I constantly work on 'mixing up' my different modes of playing so as to avoid repeating certain 'mechanisms' at different times of the concert. Actually I play the same material, which itself changes, so that the listener probably doesn't have an impression of repetition. I prod this same material and many small changes are generated through this dynamic, and suddenly I am no longer worried about not playing the same thing I have already played previously. Trying to 'mix everything up' in this dynamic is an important area of work for me today. In fact, it's more of a dynamic than a material. For example, if I work on a playing mode based on jerky sounds using an object introduced into the bell of the saxophone – like a bottle – I have endless possibilities. So, I know that I can vary my playing without the listener knowing or noticing whether there has been a change or not.

This is more a way of working, a paradigm of a technical nature – such as muting the saxophone or working on 'breath' sounds – that changes a lot of things for me. They act like registers of an organ that I choose to play. Within each 'register', there are many possibilities, those of the whole instrument. [45]

Quite an important thing for me is that if I do a piece, I don't want the next piece to be a repeat. That's always my big paranoia about improvised music – the first set could be the same as the second. I actually save up material by deliberately saying to myself: 'This piece might be going on for half an hour but I'm not going to go near that area of material because I need to save something for the next set.' Maybe that's a compositional thing. I think it is. [04B]

I think the reason we usually choose to break up the sessions is so that the two sections will be different.
I always use different instruments, and I usually split my instruments between two sessions.
Speaking for myself, if the first piece has been very dense, I would be inclined to do little isolated sounds in the second one. And it's going to start differently because of that and then maybe you get carried through differently because of that. You want to contrast, for your own sake, quite apart from the result it will provide. [11]

When I play two sets I don't consciously save some sounds for the second set. For me, it doesn't depend on the sounds themselves but on what you do with them. [28]

Ideally, during the first set, you don't think at all about the second. It's not an issue for me if the two sets are identical. It's when I have a memory of the first set that I often find myself stuck. I prefer to use up all my ammo in the first set so that the second is all the more improvised. [46]

10

Instrument and technique

With this music, I have learnt that it's useful to have some technique, but not necessarily romantic music technique.

In fact, I went from double bass to cello because I found that as I'd done a lot of jazz with the double bass, there was always this jazz idiom going on in the background on the double bass, even when I was immersing myself in noise-based improvised music. No doubt more because of my personal history than that of the instrument, but it's true that a beautiful double bass sound always makes you think of jazz after a while. I don't know if, to make this music, it's necessary to detach oneself from jazz. It's just that I did not want to hear it anymore. When I'm tired of doing something, I don't do it anymore. I don't know if I move forward, but in any case, it's a change.

When I stop practising the double bass, I lose my cello technique. That's why I defend multi-instrumentalism. I think that aesthetically, it offers you something, and physically too: it remains a sport that we practise as much as a discipline. Even entertainment is a sport.

I also play guitar. The guitar and the double bass are very much associated with popular music. I only really go into the realm of music that's a little less popular with the cello. What I call popular music is in my case when there's a rhythm. Or when we know why there's no rhythm. When you use a system of rhythmic values and chords that everyone recognizes quickly enough. [01]

Playing percussion opened all the possibilities of sound bodies, objects, tools to me, and I poured all that onto the guitar. I don't like to prepare things. I don't like to plan and know exactly what sounds I'm going to produce. I know that if these objects are there, it's because I have already tried them and that I can get a certain kind of sound out of them. But in most of the sounds that I make, there's a huge margin, a multitude of variables, of possibilities, which means that I don't exactly know what sound will come out. Take this dismantled Walkman, for example. If I play with the short circuits, I don't know which sound we're going to hear – because it's unpredictable. With simpler objects, such as a piece of wood on a contact microphone, for example, I know approximately what to expect but there are still all sorts of parameters involved, the pressure on the wood, for example – you can even feel my muscles or my nerves through the wood and the microphone. A whole sound world is lying in wait and once it's there, it's a matter of listening: I head towards something because I hear something that I have not heard yet and that interests me. So there's a lot of unpredictability.

Let's say I allow myself a frame of reference that I control. Let's say that the control is in the frame of reference that I'm holding in place. But within all that, there are elements that I do not control. There are too many parameters for me to know exactly what sound is going to come out. The guitar pickups will take in everything that is going on above them, and the contact microphone will amplify the body of the guitar. But sometimes, putting weight on it also amplifies the whole table. So there's a sort of control and at the same time a letting go because all it needs is just an unexpected knee kick and I lose control. But this will go into my set-up and become something that I actually accept too. I also have accidents, especially with electronics or, for example, with e-bows. Sometimes high-pitched sounds get released when I don't want them, but it's very difficult to prevent them because it's a question of millimetres one way or the other. So there's a part that I do not control.

The control comes from the fact that I know something about all the objects I work with – even though I often bring in new ones. But in the end, it's the ear that determines control.

I don't know if the experience, actually the technique, yes the experience that I acquired with the guitar a long time ago helps me control my sounds. I believe that the guitar pickup and my objects form a totally different instrument because my listening has changed radically. At the time when I played the guitar in a conventional way, I thought in musical terms, in terms of style, music, very coded stuff, whereas now I focus on the sound, on the sound matter. And it feels as if I've forgotten everything that I did before, even if it isn't totally new in the sense that I have use of all the timbres of the guitar … .

What I do remains instrumental, in the sense that I feel that the gestures that I make have come from my time playing percussion. For sure, if I take a lid and a brush, these aren't instruments used in percussion classes. … In this case, it may be more the technique of brushing teeth that helps me. … So some of the gestures come out of the objects themselves. But it remains instrumental, although I cannot say exactly how.

The guitar is getting diluted. It's been a while since it got diluted, with contact microphones on it, me playing it horizontally and putting a bunch of objects on it – the objects end up burying the guitar – so much so that today, all that's left is the guitar pickup: there's no guitar there anymore, but in fact, for me, that's the essence of the guitar. What I mean is that I don't play the guitar 'guitaristically' and that everything is in the guitar pickup.

I believe that when I use all these things on this table – in fact maybe it's a prison – I cannot imagine any other music than the music that comes from these objects. [02]

I think you improvise differently if you're on a different instrument. If you're playing a trumpet, you improvise differently to how you would improvise with a sax.

Having that experience of playing electronics was very important for me because it gives you a different relationship with the energy. You can press a button and sit back – and this informed my trumpet playing. Even though I have to make the sounds, I get a sense of my relationship to the energy involved with the trumpet, which is really important. [04A]

I really like electronic sounds. There was a while when I was using electronics to expand the violin. ... But at the end of that period I found I had the violin under my arm and I was scratching the strings and pushing faders around to alter the parameters of the treatments and I thought: 'Wait a minute, why do I need this bloody violin?' But also, in order to be flexible enough, I was taking tons of gear around – switching with volume pedals between two different settings – and I thought this is ridiculous so I dropped the violin and used samplers and treatments. Then when this computer came out, it was suddenly powerful enough to use software live. And it's portable! But I've always loved electronic music, and it's informed the way I played the violin throughout my career – I've always imitated and been influenced by electronic sounds. [04B]

With the trumpet, it's very rare that I do something completely different, but within certain sounds, sometimes I arrive at a new place. I definitely don't avoid that. [04A]

I think that it is a real agenda to be able to really improvise. I don't practise anymore, ever. Because I think that if you have no patterns and no licks and no repertoire it really changes your playing. Every time I take my saxophone out, I try to do something I've never done before in terms of procedure. I'm not remotely interested in playing any other instrument, but I am interested in generating as many possibilities with the saxophone as I can. My saxophone is falling apart as you can see but I don't want to fix it. It's evolving, it's changing, it's always different. So in a way it takes away some of the premeditation and some of the patterns and the confines of what you're doing. So it's not truly free but … .

I still personally have doubts about the battery-operated fans and the pen I sometimes use in addition to the saxophone. Things like that still bother me. The reed is fine and the cap is fine because they're part of the saxophone, they come in the box. Even the box itself is fair game because … that's the kit. You've got it anyway so you might as well do something with it. But other stuff I'm not so sure about. [05B]

I have reached a stage in my playing where I'm pretty bored with what I play, and with my sounds. Part of what I have been trying to do with the harp has been to escape the instrument, get off-trained and try to find a new way of playing it. And in the end you reach a stage where it's such a different sound to the intrinsic instrument that it begs the question: Why not play another instrument? Or invent an instrument? But I am as much bored with the way I'm playing as with what I'm playing … .

I used to have some psychological thing – that I could hide behind the harp. [06A]

You either have command over the instrument or you have a relationship with the instrument – very different attitudes. Having a deeper relationship with the instrument is maybe thought of as the same as having technique, but it is a different emphasis. This is a very old metaphor, but I remember a physiologist talking to me about the human body, and he said that if you had to think through all the movements you needed to walk down a flight of stairs, you'd fall down. There is no point in thinking about it, you just do it. And that's what I mean about having a relationship with the materials and the instrument: when you do your practising, you're actually facilitating and formatting yourself, all those neural connections are all being made. It's like in golf, you have muscle memory, you practise something until you don't have to think about it anymore. In fact, once you get to that point of not needing to think, it just sort of flows … .

If I'm in England or I can travel in my car, I can take more stuff, but I very rarely play my own instruments outside of Britain. So what I tend to do then is look at it as if it were a workbench. So I tend to use a very large concert bass drum and a gong, then I use things on that. At the concert venue, I look at what's around me, you can often find good things there, or even the stage itself, you can play the stage – there are some good, resonant stages. Again, it's about not being limited by a mind. I mean a drum is a box, and a concert hall is also a box; you can play the concert hall – why not? You're only limited by what you think is possible, by your own imagination. Sometimes you find a stage that is really fantastic, a lovely wood stage, with a hollow bit underneath and you can make it vibrate and it's beautiful.

I could do a whole concert with just a snare drum. I mean, I could do without that even but then it's a bit limited. I have a personal relationship with these materials: they are familiar, I've spilled blood on them, my sweat is in them. For example, one saxophone is different from another, you have a relationship with that specific tube, and I have that with the drums, of course. [07]

For me, the computer is an instrument too. It's not closed, it's moving. I also modify my program all the time. But your sounds are limited, of course, by the equipment you use. So, finally, I use the material I find. It's possible for me to change instruments. Today I played guitar and maybe tomorrow I'll play computer. I also play piano, banjo, mandolin, guitar, steel guitar. With the banjo, I play country music. The techniques of country music are very interesting. For steel guitar, it's the tuning that is of interest to me. I like string instruments. Not only for improvised music. On the piano I play Bach sometimes – but only for my pleasure. [08B]

When you improvise, you discover a new way of dealing with the instrument. You're testing it. Perhaps other types of music aren't able to do that. This is the only music that allows you to keep exploring.

I'm pretty open to playing with whatever. I used to play guitar, I used to play bass, whatever. Or even an instrument I don't normally play. I played an axe once, trying to bring intensity to the performance in any possible way I could find! I can scratch the computer, I can bring something else to it, or I can put a microphone on the lid or … . Usually, in performance I stick with what I have, but I'm open to other qualities too. [09B]

I like to limit my palette, to stick with just a snare drum and cymbal, because I've found so many things I can do with that. I'm really glad of that. I still play a big drum kit quite often – a kick drum with a double pedal then a kick drum on its side, like a floor tom, two ride cymbals, hi-hats, usually three snare drums, two floor toms, one rack tom, two smaller toms and quite a lot of cymbals. Then I have a lot of different beaters. I used to have a guitar as well with an amp and effects unit – but I haven't used that for years. I use my voice too. But even when I've only got the snare, cymbal, beaters and my voice, that's still a hell of a lot. But there's something I really like about that, to have this restriction and discover more and more things. Especially if they're good quality things. It's not like I'm saying: 'Oh, I can rub my elbow on the drum.' They're actually good results, results that I'm happy with. They're a means to an end – making music that I like. The end result is sounds that I'm really happy with. I haven't really jettisoned standard percussion vocabulary. There are lots of things that I don't do, but one good thing about this music, or improvised music ideology, is that it encourages you to think laterally and to persevere just with one drumstick or to think of ways of solving a problem without adding to your tools. This approach to problem-solving can be handy. But you've got to be careful – you could have a lot of other things going on in your mind. [09A]

With every instrument, or set of instruments, there's always a limitation to what you can do. And I think some criticism of improvisers is actually rather unfair. This is just one example: if you take someone like Evan Parker, who plays only saxophones, by and large anyway, and he's been performing since the early 1960s, I think it's rather unfair on him if people say that they went along to a concert and he did nothing new on that occasion. It would be impossible for someone to do something totally new or different in every performance. Simply because the saxophone has a certain range of sounds. There will always be limitations. It's not absolutely infinite.

Yes, that's the interesting point. Improvised music is like leaves on the tree. They're all similar but they're all different. [11]

I don't see why I should conceal my instrument. *Détournement* isn't the same as concealing it. I don't see why I would insist on playing the electric bass if it were to conceal it. There are a whole lot of other instruments that I could play. It's easier to be less deliberate and more abstract when you play instruments that don't require technical skill and knowledge of musical theory. When I play tapes or the synthesizer, it's a lot easier not having all the musical baggage I have when I play the bass. I had a period when I added lots of electronic effects to the bass in order to get particular sounds. But today, I prefer to play bass without electronics and electronics without the bass. [12]

I like small variations because sometimes I'm a little embarrassed by the sound of the instrument itself. So, learning to vary it, in a very small way, is a kind of way to escape this sound. When I work at home, I play sequences of varying length, and if I come across something good, I try to go into it more deeply, to be very focused on these small changes. The fact that I have not quite managed to conceal the guitar yet prevents me from playing a guitar note such that it can be recognized that I'm playing the guitar.

I first started improvising on the electric guitar, on which I quickly started using the guitar pickup as a contact microphone, against which objects tap. And since it's something that's very localized, sometimes just a fraction of a millimetre or a different pressure will make the sound change dramatically, and this makes it very difficult for me to have a pre-established vocabulary. But I am more satisfied in general by the sound quality of the acoustic guitar, which offers fewer possibilities for preparation. This is a way of allowing for chance. Maybe if I had a disposable guitar, I could do different things with it.

Practising the instrument can lead to a state of reactivity and consciousness of music, a state that helps you function well in improvisation.

Why do I play guitar? Because I started with this instrument when I was six and I'm pretty happy with it because it can integrate chance physically. It's a very open instrument. I suspect I'm seriously attached to this instrument. At one point, I had the idea of taking up the cornet, for example, but I didn't have the instrument to hand and the times I tried, I didn't play it with the same ease. [13]

The saxophone is connected to the breath. If you want to start a sound, it's never the most perfect beautiful clean beginning so there's a little piece of drama at the start of your sound. I won't use the word 'emotional', but even if you're being as cool as you possibly can be, it's going to sound like … a human body. You're going to hear breath, you're going to hear the physical effort and some of that tension is going to go into the sounds.

I very much like the fact that, if you play the saxophone, you've got a restricted tool and you've got to force things out of it, wherever you're imagination goes, you've got to try and force something from it. For me, whether you're working with harsh multiphonics, spit, or breathing or bad frequencies, it still sounds like a saxophone; it's got that cohesion because of that fact.

People ask: 'Why don't you add electronics to it?' But I think you can get enough timbral interest out of the thing as it is, and it means something if it comes from one sound source. I suppose it's a bit like the thinking of the old music concrete where you suddenly have the world of everything you could record to turn into a piece of music and a lot of them just thought: 'OK, we'll use one sound source and manipulate it and produce the music from that.' [14]

If I carry on playing this instrument, it's because I know that I haven't got to the end, if there is an end. On the other hand, it's true that increasingly I feel the need to extract myself from the instrument. Not necessarily physically, but internally. The instrument question is a central question. It's both important and absolutely not important. We know that it's a tool you can use to construct yourself. When I play it, I don't play it as an object. It's an instrument with which I have an animistic relationship. But it's still a metaphor for oneself, in spite of everything. The West is relocating and in the future none of the work that is done here will be manual work: manual work will be done in the third-world countries. In music, in art, the same thing is happening. That's to say that, nowadays, the medium of the body isn't necessarily needed in order for something to be produced. [15]

What I'm interested in is having access to as many tools as possible in order to be able to roam around. If you only have one tool, it's possible – in a lot of music people work with very little equipment and the music is beautiful – but I like increasing the number of tools, to be able to head off in all sorts of directions ... .

I like microphones. I think a microphone is a beautiful instrument. And so you just have to accommodate your gestures to the microphones, that's all. I'm never unaware of it. I know where it is. For me it's really as much of a tool as an octave key. It's like a reed ... .

I like amplified sound too, and for me amplification doesn't mean denaturing the sound. I'm not denaturing anything when I work using a microphone. I'm playing the microphone. It's there. It's part of the work.

It's a space. You create a space.

The clarinet is an instrument that allows a lot of virtuosity. You can play very fast, and you can change your mode of playing very quickly. When I work with loudspeakers, it's the opposite. I feel like I'm driving an old truck and I have to pay attention to the gear changes because it could go at any time. ... There's no virtuosity. Even if I want to go fast, I can't. [19]

Technique and musicality are entirely the same thing. In non-artistic everyday work, your relationship to the tool is really purely functional, that of a craftsman. And the tool is not even the tube because the tube is fixed, the mouthpiece is the same. I don't change it. The variables are the body, which changes, and the reeds.

If I put so-called technique to the fore, it's also so that I can move forward with discarding stuff that's purely artistic. For me this is craftsmanship and I like it like that. [20]

The voice is a unique instrument in that it can synthesize musical, semantic and analytical structures within one continuum. That's what I've been particularly interested in playing with in my improvised work with musicians. [21]

The computer is something specific that I refer to when I'm outside Australia. It's a convenient tool in many ways because it allows you to do many things efficiently. This is normally something that doesn't interest me – I like technologies that are cumbersome and difficult to work with – not necessarily difficult to master but to have some kind of relationship with. In Australia I have a broad range of technology, vintage synthesizers, electronics, tape recorders, all kinds of redundant and very inefficient ways of generating sound, which I actually use in concerts there, but which is not possible to bring to Europe. The computer allows me to have a predetermined set of sounds that I can call upon in the concert. They are, for example, prepared field recordings and sometimes I run them from start to finish, sometimes I stop them. I see myself more in a supporting role when I collaborate with people, rather than as a leader. I don't feel very confident or comfortable driving a particular performance with my own gestures, sounds or concepts. So I often listen to what the people I'm playing with are doing and then find an appropriate form of response. Not necessarily complementary but something that can be contrasting or awkward, or something that doesn't quite suit that particular moment. For me, in performance, a lot of it is based on the act of listening, and not actually making a lot of sound – but when I do make a sound for it to have a very specific function. Once again, the computer allows me to have a whole range of options to do that, which is very different to working with other sorts of tools or equipment. This is another thing with the computer. ... I use colour codes so that I'm not constantly staring at the screen. Because when you're staring, you're not listening. [22]

For me, it's not a big difference to play computer or guitar. For example, when I'm on tour in Europe, I don't bring a guitar with me because it's just too heavy. They are different materials but how I use them is the same, it's the same music. [23]

The saxophone appealed to me because it allows you to manufacture sound, unlike the piano, the instrument I used to play before. The saxophone sound is much more malleable. For me it's easier to shape than the piano sound. The parameters are very organic, very corporeal in fact.

At some point I stopped playing, I stopped practising the instrument. I sat down and I asked myself what it was I didn't want to do anymore, what it was that no longer interested me in the instrument. In fact, I had the intuition that if I could approach the instrument in an electroacoustic way, by changing my way of blowing, it could work. So I decided to put it to my lips differently, to pinch the reed, to put my teeth on it, to work on the idea of a permanent high pitch. To see how, by basing yourself on this frequency, you can achieve an acoustic distortion and see what can happen inside it.

The result that I'm interested in is similar to electroacoustic music, but the means of getting there has to involve the body. I have a certain fascination for electronics, but in terms of instrumental gesture electronics isn't something that suits me at all. I tried the virtual synths … .

When I get to the point of feeling that I'm no longer active, that's something I like. But in fact I am being active. I'm playing with distance.

It's a circular phenomenon between the body and the instrument. There's something that extends into the instrument but returns to the body, continuously returns to the body.

I chose the soprano saxophone because it's easier, more malleable than the tenor. I cannot do what I do on the soprano on the tenor. It doesn't work. Similarly, for the high frequency that I play: it's a consequence, it's not really a personal choice. I think I prefer the low pitches! [26]

I wanted to play the trumpet and they put me on tuba. I was only ten years old. It wasn't my fault really. … I liked it at the time before I realized what that implied – much of the tuba repertoire is terrible, at least outside the orchestra. There is a slowly growing number of very good pieces. The tuba is almost a caricature before you begin, and it's so easy to confirm that cliché and just do something funny. It's a problematic instrument. But nowadays – apart from carrying it around – I'm very glad that I play the tuba. [28]

Sometimes I'm sick of my instrument, which was built for me. I want to give it up. And when I come back to it, I'm very happy. My relationship with this instrument is very close and it influences my life a lot – because of its weight!

My instrument is very rich in terms of sound. It's quite easy: when I have enough imagination, I get good results out of it. [29]

I didn't listen to classical harp, and I wasn't interested in the harp as such or its historical placement in music – Harpo Marx was the reason my father agreed to help me pay for the lessons. He was a big fan and my teacher actually banned me from watching Marx Brothers films due to Harpo's bad influence … .

I was doing a lot with the harp to shock people, not for the sound necessarily – sticking corks on it, plastic bags and cutlery … preparing it in a way that was very theatrical and physical. I got bored with this and felt like I needed a break – then the *guzheng* came into my life. … Of course, it's an instrument with an incredibly long history – but I had no training on it, no background, and sat at it feeling this great freedom and opportunity to make music without the traditional traps that I felt on the pedal harp. I loved this and ran with it. Since then it's been my key instrument. Practically, it's easier to travel and tour with but also I think I've found my character with the *guzheng*. With the pedal harp, I still feel very much connected to its history, its cultural baggage. [30]

When I started to improvise I'd already moved from drums to percussion.

When I started to dance or perform body movements, I understood that whatever you do involving your body will be much less abstract than playing sounds.

You could reach a certain level of abstraction with your body, but it tends to be less abstract because people see a body and can read more into it than when they listen to sounds. [31]

I started with samples, mainly speech, cutting up things, trying to do different manipulations. I was interested in making music with speech and leaving out the semantic aspect of it, focusing on the way people talk. At some point, I wanted to be more flexible and decided to work on additive synthesis, creating speech with sine tones, and I discovered that the sine waves sound so nice that I gave up on additive synthesis. The software I use was there before. The first patch was a sample looper, this is why I called it 'lloopp'. When I started to use sine waves, I developed other patches. I still work on my software, and I think it will go on forever. Now, from time to time, other people develop patches for it as well. But it never became really popular among Max programmers. I'm working on making it really useful for them.

I think sine waves are beautiful. In a way they are 'without character'. Of course, that's not really true, but still. Acoustically, in a given space, some very interesting things happen with them. Different frequencies react differently, quite obviously. I also like the fact that I don't have to do much and people have a lot to experience. Different people listen to it differently, depending on where they sit in the room or if they move. With sine waves, I also don't have to think about the sound itself, about the timbre of the sound.

I try to avoid equal tuning. There is no scale, it's open. Pitch is one of the two parameters I can choose. My choice is a matter of mood, I have no concept about it. In terms of harmony, I listen to the sine waves I'm playing, delete one or add one, trying to guess how it will be when I do so. I don't try to create a particular harmony and I don't use any presets.

If there are three or four pitches that don't move for a while I change the volume of one of the pitches a little bit, for example, to change the quality of the sound. This has to do with levels of perception. I also like to play a sound very softly so that one doesn't know if I'm actually playing something or not. These things have been in my mind for years but I never conceptualized them. [32]

When talking about the objects I play with in the broad sense I use the word 'set-up'. I don't speak of instruments, because – beyond the term 'set-up', which extends outside the realm of the music – they're not an instrument in the sense that an instrument is something that's taught, that's learnt, a knowledge of which is passed on, while my set-up is really related to me. I manufactured it. I did not manufacture the devices themselves, but rather the links between the patches. I came up with the idea of the links empirically, by dint of experimenting. So, for me, there's a difference between it and the idea of an instrument.

I could press the play button, go to the bar and drink a few beers, come back three hours later and it would still be working, which is something that a pianist can't do – or a violinist, or whatever. When I play with instrumentalists, I try not to be necessarily in the logic of the machine. I try to 'instrumentalize' it. To try to 'instrumentalize' it is to try to limit myself in the same way as the person I'm playing with – 'limit' not being a negative term – to try to involve the body more in playing, in the making of sound.

For example, I work with feedback systems a lot. But all you have to do is move the microphone in front of the speaker to create different types of feedback. And because moving it the slightest millimetre changes the sound, it has to be very precise … .

Most of the tools I work with are not designed to make sound. They are sound reproduction tools, and some are even high-fidelity reproduction tools. Thus I use the idea of 'instrumentalizing' them, hijacking them, using them to do something other than what they were invented for, to flip them around.

There is always a moment when I'm not fully in control, because of the feedback phenomena. There are times when there are phenomena that get out of hand. This is where improvisation comes in, because you can react to the sound phenomenon that's going on in front of you, take things somewhere else or react differently than you would do to something you could have predicted beforehand. [36]

I'm not looking for a difficult relationship with the instrument. On the contrary, the easier it is, the happier I am. I wanted to gradually eliminate everything that was symptomatic, all resonance phenomena, all play on the strings. And what allowed me to stop this was putting the bass on the floor and only using the concrete material of the bass. The wood, the tailpiece, but not the strings anymore. Even in the end – I say the end, but it may not be over – I almost always put a towel on the strings so as only to produce dry sounds.

I think that if you listen to the sounds that I produce, they do not sound like a double bass, but at the same time, only a double bass can make sounds like that. It would be possible to imitate them, but you could only *imitate* them.

Even though I don't use the instrument in the way it was designed to be used and I look for sounds that could be described as abstract, what I'm really interested in are double bass sounds. It's almost absurd in fact.

I want to be able to make all the sounds that I want to make in the second that follows. I can't use a clothes peg, for example, because you have to think to make a gesture to make the sound. If I'm using a bow and I want to stop a sound, all I have to do is remove the bow from the strings.

In fact, it's all about compromises. Laying the bass on the ground is a compromise; it's the best compromise. If I could have done all this by keeping it upright, maybe I wouldn't have changed anything. But there were too many things I could do in this position that I was interested in for me to be able to continue playing it upright.

I think what I was interested in was treating the instrument as an object. But I still kept a very musical relationship with the instrument, very instrumental in the musical sense of the term. Even if all I am aiming at is a kind of withdrawal, to treat the instrument like an object, like a sound generator in space, my relationship to music is very much influenced by the instrument in the traditional sense of the term.

What encourages me to lay the bass on the floor is that at some moment there's a problem, sounds that I don't want: everyone makes the same ones. ... And the sounds you use imply an enormous number of things in terms of form, the music you make. And then there's something much more complicated than that, something that would need to be dealt with separately ... .

Then, there's something else again that has also influenced me a bit: Arte Povera. You have something and you have to make do with it – and then there's the impoverishment of the material. As the double bass is a very complex instrument, I like to put it down on the floor and impoverish it, to reduce it to a minimum, a bare minimum. [39]

My first instruments were electronics and the violin – although for a time to get into university guitar and piano took over. I was already into creating my own sounds, unusual sounds not learnt from notation. The first time I heard a hurdy-gurdy, it was like hearing an acoustic synthesizer; I was drawn to it like a magnet, such an unplaceable sound. So I saved up and eventually bought one. There is nothing stable about this instrument – from any obvious teaching tradition through to how to find strings for it and choose their design. In struggling to learn it one discovers that it was a really experimental instrument with many different techniques, even in the Middle Ages. In fact, the way we play it now is very conservative and simplistically tonal – if very virtuosic – which rather misses the point. For example, most players change the pitch only with keys – and that's only one type of the instrument – there were some instruments with no keys and that's a very different sound world. It's an instrument that can be as old or as it is new. Often, it's really new to people, even though it's really old, because they don't know what it's going to sound like. And interestingly enough from a social point of view, it isn't associated with a specific class, and it's history is patchy. It is actually a very European instrument but most people can't even place it geographically – it's culturally and temporally neutral. It's also really hard to notate for, whereas it's ideal for improvisation. Perhaps it makes sense then as my improvising instrument, because what a lot of improvising is about is not having these categorizations. With the grand piano or the violin, for example, there is all that historical baggage. The hurdy-gurdy doesn't have that – it's a free spirit. [40]

In fact, I'm not in control at all. First of all, I intentionally avoid having a stable system. And with this unstable system I try to make weird sounds. In fact, I don't know: before playing, I try to imagine how it will sound, but in reality, it's pretty random. How do I organize all this? How do I make music? Sometimes I have to take risks. For example, I sometimes play a cymbal, or even the snare drum, without using a stand. So it's unstable, but with that I can make weird, interesting sounds, and that's enough for me. I need that. [41]

Heuristics, discovery by accident, come out of an encounter, either with another person, or a technique, or with an object that you put together with other objects. The drums, for example, is bringing objects face to face, causing encounters between objects and this creates an event.

With my instrument, the drums, there are no preoccupations with melody, harmony, tonality or even spectrum so I try to imagine a way of playing that's related to finding pitches or producing continuous sounds, like a piano or an orchestra. [42]

My development is mostly related to the development of my relationship to the instrument. I wanted to answer some very pragmatic questions that I was asking myself. How can I go about things so as not to confine myself to percussion sounds? How can I make them last longer? How should I use objects, play glissandos? I had to struggle violently with the piano to overcome what I perceived as limits. [43]

As a teenager, I started to play with all sorts of objects, to produce sounds and to record them with a very simple multitrack technique. I bought a cheap reel-to-reel recorder and made tape loops, using all sorts of sounds, mixing field recordings I made, sounds produced by objects or instruments I gathered. At the same time, I also played occasionally at rock sessions and that's why I had a drum kit. I also had an inside piano. From the beginning, I've put the drum set together as an assembly of quite different objects: the resonators, the cymbals and the additional objects. A drum set is always a combination of different instruments.

Playing with musicians who play electroacoustic or electronic instruments, my percussion playing has been influenced by these instruments. I've always been interested in playing with people who play electronic instruments, maybe because it also helps me to find material which are beyond traditional percussion playing – which I'm not concerned about as such anyway. In these situations, I'm forced to find new solutions. But an acoustic sound is always distinct from an electronic sound, and I'm interested in the tension between electronic and acoustic sounds or hand-generated and machine-generated repetitions or loops. [44]

When I say that the drums resemble synthesizers, it's because synthesizers are made of parts that you can connect or disconnect as you like. With the big difference that, in a set of drums, any two different drums aren't connected and mixed like in a synthesizer. They're truly separated, and the movement from one drum to the other represents a real journey. And then once you've succeeded in changing your vision in this respect. ... If you see each drum as a territory or a universe, you have to dig deeper into this terrain. [41]

I hate the 'classical' sound of the saxophone, well ... I mean mine ... . I'm interested in these new techniques – like putting a bottle in the bell – because they give me another sound. I feel that there's a very broad sound opportunity that I want to explore to the fullest. I don't want to play the saxophone in a 'classical' way because the sounds don't surprise me. So, I prefer to go more deeply into a technique that can offer me something else. I want to try to continue to 'discover' new techniques. I never want to stop. [45]

I've worked on the tension of the strings a lot: I released the tension in the strings and I chose strings with heavy gauges. ... In fact, I've carried out research from within the concept of the guitar but not around it.

I consider the amplifier as a second part of the electric guitar. The *détournement* takes place in the aberration of the equipment, of the traditional set-up. It's not about modifying the traditional set-up, but of making it adopt unexpected behaviours.

Today, I have a particular affinity with the guitar. I've spent a lot of time on it so my body has been transformed by this practice. The guitar really belongs to me. Take up another instrument? Intellectually, I've got nothing against the idea, but I can't get excited about it. Staying with the same instrument means constantly being faced with what you've learnt, and thus trying to strip back what you've learnt. [46]

I don't feel like an instrumentalist, in the sense that for me it's not an end in itself to discover new things on the instrument. [47]

The computer allows me to play samples, voices or the sound of a machine – this changes over time – and also guitar chords that I cannot play when playing with a prepared guitar. I also use a mixing board, which I loop back on itself and contact microphones. I want to be able to react immediately with all this equipment. [48]

11

Solo improvisation

When I play solo, my instrument is the Other. Of course, there's a human relationship with the audience, but that's not a relationship that's direct.

When you play solo, it's a composition. I know what piece I'm going to play. Before, there were four parts, now there are three, usually continuous. I know what I'm going to do and I improvise within each part. But I've already defined the direction I'm going to take. I start with particular objects, instruments. Then, the route I take is improvised. To use a nice turn of phrase, I might say that it's about living every moment, not playing my own clichés, taking risks. [41]

Sometimes I feel like I want to do solos, which is a new idea for me. Now I always find myself thinking that there is another musician there with me – and the thought of this other person being there inspires me. [18]

I wish I could say there was no difference between playing solo and playing with other people, but that's not actually borne out by experience. I can't listen in the same way when I have a musician beside me. [25]

I love to play on my own. I might say that when I play on my own, I'm also playing with other people: being on your own already means being with a lot of people – even if it's actually a very different thing. In fact, I like both. And I think I need both. I'd like to do more solo concerts to see what I can do, what my music is when I'm on my own. I quite like the idea of sauntering in unprepared, putting my instrument down and doing exactly what I do at home. [02]

I think if you're playing a solo concert you're really being a composer. Certainly once you've done it a few times and you've got a history of some kinds of ideas. [14]

When I play solo, I definitely follow a structure. It's almost pre-programmed. I mean, I scan pre-identified areas, modules that no longer really count as improvisation in the sense of jumping into the void and waiting for the magic to happen.

When I play solo, it's obvious: when I'm done with going back over one small plot, a little section, I don't persist with it. I don't establish continuity. There's then an intention to move to another section, another little area in the garden. I change row. I move into another row, another flowerbed.

Of course the garden also includes minefields and death camps. ... Everything that makes up reality is there ... .

I start with pre-identified, known material. But I should really try to depart from it because I sense the danger of being confined. [20]

When I play solo, there's nevertheless something that's still for me specific to improvisation: suddenly, I find myself in a very particular state of flux and trance and things come up that I don't have time to check or control. And that opens doors. It's not systematic. Rather it's a kind of continuous discourse in which kinds of truths suddenly appear, very important stuff that jumps out at you. Actually I put myself into that state in order to have that stuff jump out at me and surprise me, and to try to see what's hiding behind it. [38]

When you play solo, you've got all the space, the acoustic space, the artistic space. It's all yours. But also you have to do all the work, so the two things balance out in some ways. All the space – but all the responsibility too. My feeling about playing solo is that, once you start, if you have something, you can go where it goes, you can follow. And if you don't have something, you must find something of your own; so even if you have a five-minute solo to begin with, or a thirty-second solo, there must be, if you're an improviser, one thing that you can do alone. And once you start to do that thing, you see where it goes. You follow that track and then you have a path through, which is always useful in the group context as well. [16]

I didn't really have a live dimension to my music until about ten years ago, but at some point I felt that I couldn't work in the studio in isolation any longer and that I needed somehow to translate my sonic concepts to the live domain. I didn't really know how to do that initially but over time I developed different kinds of techniques that allowed me some fluidity in presenting essentially electroacoustic music or studio music within live contexts. From that I started to become more interested in aleatoric music and music with a greater element of chance, and so I developed systems around that. But at the end of the day, in solo performance, you're in control of everything, more or less, and I felt that although I could do great solo performances – based on the reactions I get – and entertain, give the audience what they want, field recordings, electronics, spatialization, and so on, it didn't give me any satisfaction at all. I didn't like doing it and I've stopped doing solo recordings and solo performances for the moment. [22]

When you play solo, there aren't actually all that many questions. I don't ask myself questions. I take a very firm stance. Overall, I know the material that's there that I'm interested in. In any case, still today, I don't have a great desire to move on to something else. I plough the same furrow. Not necessarily the same thing but the same process, a continuous process. The process consists in generating an autonomous system of sound. Which is to say that I set a sound in motion that feeds itself. I don't think about music that much. Rather I think sound, matter, but above all I base myself on the principle of process generation. At first it's unstable, because before there's any organic stability in the to-ing and fro-ing between the instrument and the body, there's a certain instability. But once it's working, it happens by itself or almost. I only have to listen and 'take' what comes up that I'm more or less able to control. 'Taking', for me, is when I decrypt parameters or phenomena that stabilize inside the sound. And I try to maintain them. From there on, it's very physical. It's not all that technical. Let's say it's 'organo-technical' or 'technico-organic'. It's pretty inexplicable actually. It's not all that deliberate in my head. What I mean is that I'm not able to say: 'If I do that, I'll get that.' I know that I can generate a 'system' or a 'process' and that within that, something will either happen or not.

I need something continuous if I'm going to free up my thoughts because as soon as there's silence, it gets much harder. You enter a full/empty thing, so you have to occupy time in a certain way. By occupying this time continuously and concentrating on high pitches, it becomes a little like a meditation. Well almost.

Initially, I did it to empty my thoughts. … My goal was to stop doing my head in over improvisation, stop being mentally active all the time. And that's difficult when you are not in something that self-generates.

In fact, there are several parameters you can reduce: you can reduce finger activity – I was tired of the fingers, it felt like I was back playing the piano – and reduce the idea of phrasing, that is, mental activity. I like the idea of phrasing, but for me it takes you into another mental space when you're playing. There's something very intellectual actually or very literary with phrasing.

What I do is very simple. It's almost nothing in fact, and this almost nothing has opened a much wider field than what I could do by taking very musical, 'instrumental' let's say, decisions. It opens an acoustic field.

For me it's minimal, not in terms of the sound matter, but in the intention. I mean my intention is strictly minimal: how do I do as little as possible, do just one thing!

This allows me to stop having to choose and ask myself questions such as 'Why that rather than that' or 'Where am I going?' I don't see the point of doing a solo if you don't do something totally extreme! I mean a sonic proposition other than what you would do if you were playing with other people, something that is specific to solo playing, to the fact that you're all alone … with yourself. You need something that covers that … .

I produce duration, but my relationship to it is transformed. I change particular parameters, but I don't necessarily eliminate them. I'm not out of time, but I change my relationship to it. In order to do so, I had to eliminate a certain mental relationship, because we are the ones who construct time. I had to find a way of not being intellectually or mentally caught up in time, of producing duration and holding it. Silence isn't easy to handle as far as I'm concerned in the sense that it's still artificial for me. There are plenty of people who work in silence as a continuity. But for me, duration cancels pitch. I'm not interested in the pitch and I don't hear it anymore. That's not what I listen to. It's what's going on inside. It's just a support for me, just something to lean on. It's like the diaphragm. There's the diaphragm and the pitch, two forces, pulling against each other, allowing me to settle on an idea of what I want. And within that I try to see what sort of events are going to come up.

It's increased sensitivity. It's an altered state, but not a duality. [26]

12

The concert situation, the audience, the published recordings

Perhaps we should make music on our own. Why have an audience? It's crazy. I make a living doing this sort of music – I'm one of the few people, I think. [18]

Maybe it isn't so interesting for people to listen to anyone! [06A]

I think that I always play this music for someone's ears, even if they're imaginary. I'm not necessarily aware of it all the time, but from the moment the sound is there, my ears hear it – and I wish other ears did too. I don't know why, but I also think that this music, improvised music, only fully exists during a concert. Quite simply because playing with other people already means playing in front of other people. You compress a moment, you enter a bubble of intensity. It's a music that reaches towards the ears. [02]

I play concerts in my head. This happens to me quite often. I'm at home, I sit down and I play a concert, I hear it. I love this kind of work. [19]

The need to play in public may not be a societal need but rather something that's part of human nature, a need for vibration, contact, energy feedback, something really telluric and totally primitive, a need that seems to me much more basic than culture, the need for relationships, for an exchange of energy. That's all that art is. I may be taking a naive perspective, but it seems to me there's a generosity in performing in public, this need for a generous act, a pure act of giving and receiving, and this is where there's a parallel with religions … it's terrible! [15]

When it works satisfactorily, the relationship with the audience really allows you to push the envelope, to go further. I have sometimes consciously accentuated silences knowing that the perception of the audience could withstand longer durations than mine. In fact, I noticed a long time ago that you often have to give more than seems necessary for the audience to receive what you're playing. If there's no audience, I can't play. I hate playing in the studio where it's mainly your level of skill that counts. The audience helps me a lot and at the same time it bothers me that I need it. [43]

I know why I like playing the saxophone – but why people might be interested in listening to what I play I don't know. I'm delighted that they are. But I do wonder why. And I think it's wholly, completely personal; it must be. And subjective. [05B]

You set up expectations and then you challenge those expectations. You set up boundaries – then you break them. You are breaking expectations or working with them. The audience's expectations or the listeners' are part of the context that you're in and giving them what you think they expect – or to challenge that perception – it is also one of the parameters. [05A]

I'd rather play in private because it seems like, if I have a conversation with someone, I'd rather not have a bunch of people listening. As soon as you have an audience I think there's an odd kind of obligation to have some kind of relationship with them. When there's an audience there's some loose obligation to be doing something for them. Not necessarily entertainment but there's some kind of audience/performer relationship. Of course it's very interesting and it's another thing, but I'm more interested at the moment in the group relationship, in the musical thing. But you know my mind changes about that. Sometimes I really want to play concerts and sometimes I don't want to play at all. [05B]

Making somebody feel happy while playing my sort of music is an incredibly fulfilling thing for me. Finding people who are on that similar sort of wavelength about improvised music or about a certain conception of life is really excellent. And one of the only ways of doing it is by throwing a lot of stuff up against a lot of people and then seeing what comes back. And you make new relationships and things through this. I surprised myself by talking about the social placing of what I did, almost a socially progressive thing … . I overplayed that … that's one element of things. Playing to an audience and playing privately are … of equal significance, I think. They're not the same at all, but they are equally important. I couldn't say that the placing of music in a social context is the more important context, for example. One's private relationship to music is necessary for this sort of music; your own private relationship to this aesthetic and what you do. If you take that side of things lightly the results are bad. [05A]

In concerts, it's completely different than when I play at home. [41]

I always find it difficult to be really focused when there is no audience – even if it's being recorded – and I suppose it's far easier to be more focused in a live concert situation where people are there listening to you. There is more of an urgency in a concert, I suppose. I also approach a session with a more experimental approach, where you can try different things out, and not have such a logical, focused music-making approach. Maybe it's just all my classical training, but it has always been 'the concert is the end result' and maybe my problems are a hangover from that. It really fucks you up playing classical music!

Even when I think I'm divorcing myself emotionally from what I'm doing, I can't escape the fact that I'm there doing it. But that's something that interests me too, not being obviously emotional on the stage. [06A]

My agenda is not to convey emotion and give it to the audience, just to do what I do in that moment. [06B]

There's nothing I hate more than art that patronizes an audience. And I think the whole funding system is restrictive because the people that give money to the arts and artists hand out money to those who they think can communicate with the audience. They think: 'Oh, that artist's doing avant-garde stuff but at least he's putting in some rhythms.' That's lowest common denominator art, it's Tony Blair art, it's middle-of-the-road art. The scene in the UK has been kept back by this idea that we need to sell art to the people, that we mustn't make it difficult for them to understand. [04B]

One has sort of an educated guess about what someone in the audience or fellow musicians might think. [09A]

When things are working well, you're in tune with the whole thing. Even if you're not sure about what you're physically doing, sometimes, it works. In some respects, the most rewarding performances are the ones where you've been very focused and you just enjoyed that experience of being in the middle, right on top of the sound, right in it – when it just flows through you and you don't really do anything, you're just there and it seems to happen. Whether it's meaningful for the audience, you could never tell and it's not worth asking the question really; you're not there to please them, because you don't know what they want, so how could you please them?

When we improvise like we do, it sets up a certain kind of atmosphere, there's a certain kind of psycho-social tension there, so if you take that and put us in front of an audience, it changes things. There is another important ingredient – the audience – so it's a richer, tenser kind of environment in which to work. I don't think the audience is necessary for good improvisation, but I think in performance one tends to be more alert, more aware, because there's that tension.

I think there's a ritual element to a concert. You share, you're in a very privileged position on one level, but I think a performance goes through a sort of catharsis, a good one does in any case, a point when there's the feeling of some kind of transformation. If an audience member comes up to you and says he or she felt refreshed by it, isn't that enough? [07]

I think all performances are different. I think it depends on the deal that's struck before the performance as well as the conditions of the performance – the audience, the sound system and the general atmosphere as well. The concerts I think about most fondly are the ones people tell me were the worst – because they took me somewhere I never expected to go. I have different criteria to a lot of people in terms of measuring what works or what doesn't work, and so when people are entertained, they're lost in the music and feel somehow entertained, I feel like a failure because I don't want to entertain them. I want to make them angry or upset or make it a very difficult listening experience: to work with certain gestures and structures or flows that actually feel difficult and strange and hard for them.

On the one hand, I say that I never think about the audience. I don't know who they are, why they're there, what history or knowledge they bring to the concert. But at the same time, why am I performing in front of an audience if I don't care about them? I can do this at home, in front of a mirror or something! So a big part of me has to take that into consideration, whether I want to acknowledge it or not. If I want to be truthful to myself, I have to recognize that, in some ways, I'm an entertainer and I'm there to provide these people with some kind of value for their money. They come with certain expectations, and I don't particularly want to feel that they've been exploited or cheated. So there are certain things that probably unconsciously affect the choices I make in a concert, and I think in some ways it would be arrogant not to take that into consideration.

I think the audience in some ways does inform what you're likely to do, but you can never tell exactly what they're going to think either. [22]

Being concerned with the process can be a way of really being very generous to the audience. You're not trying to seduce the listeners with anything, you're just making the process very apparent and taking them with you – and that's a very vulnerable position for a musician to be in. [04A]

I try to play the same in concerts as when there's no audience. Because I think it's interesting to try to stay in that state. It's the benchmark. But I don't think I manage it.

Listeners construct their own listening. I don't want to guide their listening. I want to push them to find a unique way of listening. To be intrigued and wonder how to listen to this music. Whether formulated or not.

I try to make sure that the listeners leave with something. Being aware of the fact that there are listeners who are different from me is to play for them, without, for all that, giving them what they're expecting. [47]

Concerts are like a continuation of daily work, but I maintain a very clear separation. I have the impression that at home I'm just practising exercises. It really is work. There's nothing at stake. I continue to work on things that have been identified, but I only try to open them up and develop them in concerts, taking them elsewhere. [20]

You have to symbolically let the audience into the music. You're playing for the audience and you have to give them ways in, physically and emotionally and mentally. It has to be presented. That isn't to say that it has to please them. I think the function for me – a great, useful function of the audience – is just to bring discipline to what I'm doing. Otherwise you can stop and start in a rather undisciplined way, according to the way you feel. When the audience is there, you have to work beyond the way you feel to the responsibility you have to the idea that the music represents. So you have to be on your best behaviour, as it were. I don't know anybody who really plays seriously without an audience. Unless they're recording and listening back – which is also an audience of a kind, a symbolic audience. I think it's important, it gives the music shape. [16]

I wish my music wasn't for specialists, that people who do not know this kind of music had fun listening to it, but this is a wish more than anything else. [29]

Sometimes the audience, the atmosphere, the sound system or some sounds from the outside really influence me. If the audience never stops talking, I might play more quietly. Or extremely loud. If the audience is concentrating hard, the music is completely different; we can focus on each sound. Or if I hear a bird far away, my next sound might be very different. [33]

I don't like it when I leave the audience out. I don't want to offend them.

Improvisers are egotistical. They have the intelligence, the power and the ability to produce stronger things, but they don't do it. They get caught in little details of this or that sound. They spend hours trying to find an object or a technique to achieve this or that sound. I believe that's egotistical because it's not really caring about the audience. Musicians alienate themselves. [31]

When I play with someone for the first time, I prefer to play in private, without an audience, so as to be able to take more risks. I hear a sound and I try to play one, without knowing if it'll work. You do something and you watch for the reaction. You have to do that in order to find out. The form may end up being a disaster, but you learn a lot. With someone I know well, I can do the same in a concert. I know I can do something 'wild', be completely outside of the form, use completely alien sounds, like samples of spoken sentences, without the other person giving up or collapsing. [48]

Sometimes I play to audiences that are out of the improvisation bubble, which is uncomfortable, but I try it in order to attempt to step outside the self-referential niche of contemporary music. If I lose the audience's attention, I might stop and talk to them about what I'm doing, what I'm trying to do and what I'm thinking about, and then go back to performing.

The audience is very important to me. And I want to create this kind of triangle between myself, the other players and the audience. Improvisation is wonderful for doing that – if it's working, and at the right time in the right place. So I think it is a sort of social network. In composition, the composer is the main controller, which makes the performers needy, and in any case they are often nervous about improvising and are not prepared or able to give the time. Given the right ecosystem, anarchy can work so well, and I think improvising is a little bit like that. [40]

I have no intention of creating, making music that's difficult to receive, that's provocative. ... Of course, no doubt it is, but that's natural for me. It's not a postulate. I'm happy when I'm in front of an audience and I hear incredible sounds. It doesn't influence what I'm doing at all when no one in the audience is really listening.

If there's one thing that I'm not interested in, it's reacting to the audience. But obviously, if there's a huge buzz in the audience, I do enjoy it. But I don't see it as musical information and I don't integrate it into my music. It's not a musical phenomenon, not a sound phenomenon that I integrate. It's psychological. It puts me in a state of fragility maybe, but I think I'm pretty much detached from it ... .

I think it's more the improvisation situation that calls what I'm doing into question than the situation itself. What I mean is that whether I was playing in the street over there or in a concert, it would be the improvisation situation I'd be interested in, not the background noise, the psychology or factoring in that I couldn't be heard properly. ... I'm sensitive to the psychology. I'm not immune to it, but it's not something to which I attach much importance. I don't know how to put it. [39]

To my mind, it also depends on your perception of the audience. If you've got an audience that likes our kind of music, you'll be more inclined to just go and improvise without giving any particular thought to it.

That's true. I remember the concert we played in a museum, which was effectively part of a series of chamber music concerts: we knew we'd be playing to a sort of chamber music audience. They were all – well, we're virtually middle-aged now as well! – but at the time, for these middle-aged people in suits, we thought we'd do a bit of structure. And they seemed to like it, actually!

You might end up with a situation where – and thankfully this doesn't happen very often – there's a general consensus among the band that the whole performance hasn't been very successful for one reason or another. There may have been technical mishaps but, at the end of the concert, you have two or three people coming up to you and saying: 'Oh, that was absolutely fantastic.' I never really know how to react to that. [11]

I trust that something that makes me feel that strongly would also translate to an audience. Yeah, I believe in that. [30]

If too many people dig what you're doing, you'd better look at what you're doing. Because you may not be doing what you think you're doing. [34]

Playing live is interesting when the debris also appears. The process has to be seen, not in its mastery, but in its real-time experimentation. [26]

I wouldn't worry about the concert being theatrical. If it is, so what? The idea of it being prepared as theatre is one thing, the idea of it being theatre incidentally is quite another.

I don't think there is anything wrong with the visual side of it; in fact, it may actually enhance things, humanize the relationships or make people realize that there are human beings involved. That's not a bad thing. [07]

Being on stage is unnatural anyway. … Oddly, when I've decided everything in advance, I feel more like I'm in some performance thing, almost in the sporting sense, because I feel a lot of distance with what I'm doing. I almost sense an additional layer of mental representation. [25]

The performance doesn't consist of the audio only. So I am aware of the visual element that I have when I play. The way you look in the mirror and you see yourself. I have an awareness that people might perceive me in some way but, also, I don't want to just get up and do it. It's a performance, there are lights and those lights generate a privilege; the stage is elevated so people can see. You can try and ignore that relationship or you can try and do something with it. Or not play on the stage. So I'm aware of those considerations. It's a recent thing, playing with sunglasses, but it makes it more special somehow. It affects my perception of what's going on. I love it!

The CD is a product which you might find interesting. But the essence of the performance is definitely watching people improvise. The performance happens before your eyes, really far away from the CD. The CD contains some aspects of the performance but it's something quite different. [09B]

I started to improvise with an instrument – in my case the computer – but at some point I didn't want to be restrained by the limitations of this form of improvisation. So basically I started to improvise with all the elements that constitute the concert, to see improvisation more as a situation and to try to push the limits of it. The historical and social construction of the concert doesn't need to be respected. Of course, by doing this, you are creating a stereotype of yourself and you are given a role. But if you manage to make the moment denser without anybody knowing how to articulate it or categorize it, that's hopefully a way of cutting through this stereotype, even if it only lasts a few seconds.

The concert allows me to get somewhere where everyday life might not allow me to get. Maybe this is a theatrical aspect. But doing this in various situations helps me understand the normal framework of the concert.

With my very limited and rudimentary means, I'm trying to explore the limitations of the concert, our different understandings of what a concert is. I don't know what music is but I want to explore the boundaries of the framework that limits your freedom, your scope of action. [24]

I think that stage presence, considered as visual pollution within sound, should be treated as an oddity: What's the body even for? Or at least, as a tension ratio with the audience which moves from the visible to the sonic. It should be possible to use stage presence as a tool to process duration in itself. [39]

When I'm listening to music, I've got this quite particular arrangement that I stare at with my eyes. My eyes are half-focused, and it's like I've got the speakers, then a table or a large cactus and a big depth of field and, like we have in this room here, a view across the street through the neighbours' window, and through their back window, over their garden – it really goes on and on. And my appreciation of the music is somehow deeper when I'm staring at this view. It's like saying: 'If someone has their eyes closed, they're going to get maximum appreciation of the sounds' whereas for me, that's more of a distraction than if I'm just looking at this shitty view. So then, I suppose that amounts to saying: 'What can you do?' You can't really shut down your eyes at a concert. Even the picture in your brain might overwhelm. I think some visual element can heighten your enjoyment of the music. I'm sure someone has written a big book about this. Look at how many people loved Maurice Ravel's 'Boléro', when the Olympic gold medal-winning ice skaters Torvill and Dean skated to the music – the piece went to number one, I think, and people went out of their fucking minds about that piece of music. But I'm serious – there was this amazing ice-skating – no, seriously – and I think lots of people really fell in love with that music because it had this big package holiday-type feel, and those special purple costumes. Turning the lights off completely is quite amazing; it's really exciting and quite different to closing your eyes. Some people think there's a problem with improvisation: they slag it off because they say it's all men, in their fifties, badly dressed, with beards. So it has to be faced, I think, that people will have their eyes open when there's music. All these things are really important: the visual aspect, how it interlinks. I think the word 'neutral' is relevant – for example, those people who say: 'Oh, I'm just neutral, I just get up there and do music.' As if that were possible anyway. It's never that simple. If you have Luciano Pavarotti coming onstage in beachwear, that's going to be really profound. Like when you do a concert in the same clothes you wear to work – if Pavarotti does that, that's going to have a really big impact.

I do think about what I'm going to wear for a concert – but you could easily see me in a café wearing the same thing. What I try to do is an atrophied *Gesamtkunstwerk*. It depends though, doesn't it? Sometimes I can sit pretty steadily on that drum stool too. [09A]

I think improvisation has real value live but that there's a big issue with recordings of improvised music. I think that what gives value to improvisation is live performance. It's as much in the eyes as the ears. The tension between the gesture and the sound produced by this gesture is captivating, between the horizon of possibilities and what only the body makes possible. With recordings, you obviously lose this dimension and you just have a document, a truncated trace … something that has the value … of a document, no more, no less. Anyway, I'm not saying that there aren't some very good recordings of improvised music, but I am saying that it doesn't make for, or very rarely, good records as finished objects, designed to be reproduced through loudspeakers. [25]

In fact, even if it's a high-quality recording, I think it's difficult to recapture, in playback, what happened during the concert: the energy put into it, the relationship with the audience. This is difficult stuff to define that isn't just to do with the sound and therefore doesn't make it onto the recording. [43]

Even if you close your eyes, the difference between a recording and a concert is obvious. When you listen to a recording, the experience is already over. But when you attend an improvisation session, you feel as if anything can happen. [46]

I think that a way of listening can make it onto the recording. I listen to what I've recorded in several ways. I may listen to it from a formal point of view. It can be interesting to see what form is produced even though you haven't necessarily focused on it. Or I listen to it from a sound recording point of view, from a purely sonic point of view, from a more rhythmic point of view, or even from a harmonic point of view. At the same time, I try to figure out if the listening mode you were in when you played it can be heard. I find that very interesting.

The memory of the state I was in partly influences what I hear. What I'm interested in is trying not to have the same listening posture when I listen back to the recording as when I was playing. But that's something I find very difficult. [47]

Recorded improvised music is interesting. Doesn't the fantasy of being a composer come into it somewhere? [37]

It's acceptable for me to say that if something is successful for fifteen minutes you fade it out at that point – if you're thinking about someone listening to the CD over and over.
You finish up with a lot of stuff on tape – a lot of it is good and some of it is bad. Why put the bad stuff on the CD? And if you've got a piece that's good except that it ended twice, why not cut off after the first ending? [11]

At a certain point, you may say to yourself: 'I've been making music for years and I don't have anything down on paper. What's going on here? It's totally ephemeral. Sure, I've published some recordings but hey, they're just kind of skeletons that are hanging around … .' [19]

13

Some political issues

There are power relations everywhere, and a collective improvisation is no exception. One can see all kinds of power relations in a collective improvisation. The problem is that, among improvisers, these relations are mostly seen as something negative. Many musicians believe that they must achieve a kind of balance of forces when they play together. This balance is impossible to achieve: power relations are unbalanced by nature. The attempt to approach balance is always a direct affront to music. If there was a balance, the music would be lifeless – there wouldn't be any reason to start playing. One is driven to play by the imbalance, and what follows are attempts to affirm it and to make the whole even more unequal.

When I speak about power relations in a collective improvisation, I'm not talking about a fight among musicians. On the contrary, once there is a fight, the stronger forces have already lost. This is important to mention because there's a lot of confusion about the matter. Once someone told me, after an improvisation, that I was being too dominant. How can someone possibly be 'too' dominant? You're never dominant enough! Improvised music's dynamics tend to defend the weaker elements whereas it is the stronger ones that should be defended from the weak! [31]

I don't think I'm an interpreter in the classical music sense. I wasn't born to be a soldier. Being an interpreter is like being on a mission, serving a text, a hierarchy, something that's above you. [39]

When I first discovered improvisation, I was interested in the social aspect of it because I was having problems doing the thing I really wanted to do, which was to invent music. At that point, for a while, the idea of having new models of society, of not having a hierarchy within the group, not having a soloist, of making music collectively did interest me. And then I saw how improvisers actually really behave in practice, and I realized that all that was a myth, they are just as selfish – or as selfless – as other people. [28]

The music needs to do things and have relevance in other spheres. So you can focus, yeah, on sounds but then I have to come back and look at other things in the world. And that can be really uncomfortable. I feel awkward and uncomfortable about what I do. I don't feel supremely confident or relaxed – it's a dilemma. I'm more proud of some of the music I've made than others, some concerts. I've felt that I'm doing the right thing, like it was more worthy. I get real mixed feelings. [09A]

When we started in the 1960s, there was a conscious decision to remove ourselves from the conventions of the times in which we lived. And once you get into that position you begin to find out more about it, have a view on it, you begin to take up a relative stance about why you like this music as opposed to that music, why you like pop music rather than cool music, why the East Coast rather than the West Coast. ... All those things that go through your head, they're all part of you formulating your own aesthetics – which I still think is bound up in your view of the world. Why are you looking for one specific thing rather than something else? Because it's somehow supportive of a world in which you would rather be, it's utopian in that sense and evolves out of that. At some point, we had to get out of the models within which we were playing, which were largely rhythm based, or tonally based. We basically threw out both of those things. For a drummer, one of the difficult things, for example, is how to play long sounds – that was an interesting personal exploration. In the end, I find it really hard to distinguish between aesthetic reasons and social ones. They do seem to go hand in hand.

When I listen to certain configurations of music, they suggest certain things to me and sometimes the associations of a certain piece of music will enhance or destroy things for me. A very simple example: Samuel Barber's *Adagio for Strings* is a very long, melancholic, beautiful and long piece for strings. It has a meaning, even if you can't easily define it. But three years ago *The Daily Telegraph*, which is a right-wing newspaper, used that music for its television advertisements, and it completely destroyed the music for me. So I know that music has a meaning because, if they can destroy what I felt for it, by doing what they did to the music, it signifies something. What it signifies is difficult to work out, obviously, and I will confound you even more by suggesting to you what the purpose of improvisation actually is: the purpose of improvisation is to discover the purpose of improvisation. I know it's facile but, in the end, it's all about finding out, without reaching any real conclusions. In a way, the meaning is in the finding out. I do think in the end you attach specific things to the sounds and maybe you can't write about them – I mean you can't say X = Z in terms of absolute quality and quantity. Well, quality you can, but not quantity perhaps. Maybe it is all by association, I mean for example, what do you think about Beethoven's 'Ode to Joy', which they used as the new European anthem?

A sound is not just a sound. Think about what can happen with sounds; think about the use made of sound as a means of oppressing people. It can be used to deafen people; it can be used to make you feel liberated, actually physically different. Sounds can have a physical effect on the way you feel, so there is no neutrality in that, there is a definite human relationship with the sound, it's not just a sound. And as musicians we have a choice about the sounds we use and how we use them.

On a more general level, I fear that if we don't decide what the meaning of our music is someone else will decide for us, and that's not a good thing. So maybe I'm suggesting – and I'm not sure of my thoughts on this, for obvious reasons – that when we make our music, we're actually suggesting, proposing a certain way of life, a certain attitude to the world. I think this ranges from the way we deal with the physicality of our world, our green politics if you like, through to our more intimate politics. I think it's in there somehow, and if it isn't then why are we doing it? Are we simply interested in sound for sound's sake? I'm sure people think that, but I don't believe it. I think in the end, there is more to it than that – but I can't prove it. … You can't, you can only prove it with your commitment to what you do, and you could be fooling yourself, of course. We are all likely to be fooled by rhetoric, aren't we? But I don't think that's reason enough for us not to search for a meaning in what we do. The meaning is important, but precisely what the meaning is, I haven't found out yet. I'm still working on it! [07]

Too quickly and erroneously, improvisation is often considered to be linked to a quest for freedom, to a political music that corresponds to what it was at one time, coming from free jazz in North America and adapted in Europe during the 1960s. But that doesn't really mean anything anymore. There are a lot of musicians who improvise, not in assertion of anything but by default. Even for me, musical improvisation was by default. It wasn't to assert anything. I didn't even know that it was called improvisation. However, improvisation, this way of making music, has its own production, distribution and promotion network. There are specialized venues, festivals, record labels, radio shows and magazines. And this network is a really underground network, which works in opposition to economic diktats and tries to survive as it can, which for me is a strictly political choice. For me, there has always been, from the beginning, the idea that you cannot only be a musician. It's not possible. You also have to be involved in the economics of this music.

I'm talking about the organization of stuff around music. The idea of showing that there's a way of organizing things differently. But the music itself, apart from that, I think it's made up of sounds. It's not political. For me, sounds are neither white nor black. But you don't listen to music outside of a context. So it's the context that's political. [36]

I decided I was always going to work in a normal sort of job to enable me to do improvised music as an art form. I didn't really want to go to subsidizing bodies and national arts organizations because I felt that they compromise your goals and what you're doing. I felt that very strongly. So I thought: 'Self-funding through your own leftover money is the only way to do this.' [05A]

My music doesn't need to have nothing to do with money. I'm not under any obligation to produce something that I can sell as a commodity because I've got a job. I'd go as far as to say that if you're a professional musician and if your livelihood comes from the product that you sell then there are things that you can't do. You cannot risk making yourself incapable of selling the product in the future, whereas we can literally do what we like because we don't have to worry about that. It's difficult to say without sounding sanctimonious or as if I'm preaching – and I really don't wish to – but there is a difference. Personally, I wouldn't want my relationship with music to be financial, I wouldn't want that. [05B]

I guess it's also mentality – I never thought I could make my living from music, it wasn't an option, which is quite sad actually. In Australia, it's not possible, so, what do you do? At one point in history, music was so vital to a community that it was needed to preserve stories, and people needed music in times of crisis to digest situations. Musicians had a key function. When did it change so that a young girl in Australia, with a love of music and an interest in learning and performing, can't choose that life unless she's in an orchestra or is a pop musician? [30]

I don't want to go professional, be serious and have a career. I don't believe in that. I'm not at all interested in that. [48]

My question is this: Do you hear a difference between women improvisers and men? Is there a difference? There shouldn't be a difference. [10]

For me communication with women is easier. Criticism, for example, is simpler. When you try to understand and talk about things together to make things better, I have a better experience with women. Although, I just worked with men and everything went well, it was open. But in general, men are on the defensive. But that can be the case with women too. [29]

My sex is different to most of the people I play with, but it's not something I think about when I'm making music. If I step outside it, I do believe that women and men communicate differently and that this translates into music. I don't think women play differently to men but I think, energy-wise, women are different to men. But it's very difficult to give an example of that. It can be subtle discrimination – where maybe there are five men on stage and they give me more space because I'm a woman when maybe that doesn't serve the music. Or I feel like I'm being treated differently and that makes me play differently. Most of the time, I just miss having women around! A room or stage full of men doesn't feel natural.

People ask me a lot: 'Why don't more women play improvised music?' The truth of it is that I can't answer for the women who don't play, because I am one of the rare women players. I know why I'm drawn to it – and that rarely has anything to do with my sex. I've never let being a woman stop me from doing something, and I've never felt that I've had more or less opportunities because I am a woman doing this music. I've only been in one situation where a curator has asked me to be involved in a programme because he needed 'more chicks' – that was a bummer. I hope that when I'm invited to play, it's because of the sounds I create not because I represent a 'minority group'. [30]

14

How I came to play this music

I needed to make this music. There was no question about it. I already had the beginnings of noise-like impulses before: put the electric bass on the floor, hit it and all that – but always with a strong sense of guilt! I went to listen to a lot of improvised noise music concerts, and it immediately seemed obvious to me. Something inside just clicked.

At first it goes very quickly. When you start improvising, by removing the barriers, it goes very quickly. There's even a state of grace the first year I would say. [01]

I started with the electric guitar. The first tune I liked was 'Europa' by Carlos Santana. I listened to David Bowie, British rock, then hard rock, American rock. Afterwards, I started listening to things like Henry Cow and Fred Frith. I wasn't interested in rock anymore. I took one or two jazz lessons, but I'm not a 'jazzist'. Then I started to study percussion at a *conservatoire*. Actually I was attracted to Latin music. So I wanted to do Latin percussion, congas, timbales and so on. But there was nobody who could teach me that kind of percussion in Le Mans. So I took classes with a classical percussion teacher, I mean contemporary, and I started at the *conservatoire* the year after. I never played Latin percussion in the end … . [02]

The first thing that drew me to the music I make was just going through day-to-day activities and hearing some specific sonic element that felt to me like something I'd never heard before because it was so banal. So when I perform, it's that surprise that I want to present. It's the excitement at hearing something extraordinary that we've all been missing up to that point. It definitely has to do with surprise and discovery and context.

I was listening to rock and punk, then industrial, and started to get more and more interested in what I didn't know – concrete sound, used in composition. I started with Einstürzende Neubauten and then I remember a point when I thought I'd really like to find something that's like this, that has this particular element or that uses sound in this particular way. And every time I thought that I would be able to find it somewhere if I looked hard enough, everything I wanted already existed, and I remember being completely bowled over by that thought: 'This is fucking amazing, everything that I want to hear, somebody is making it for me.' [03]

I think you bring to the music whatever experience you've got. And if you haven't had experience playing other music, I'm not sure that's a problem. [04A]

At some point, I became bored of having to play a certain style simply because it was expected of me. [04B]

I tend not to want to feel connected to the old masters. The whole school has a very sort of academic feel to it, even when it's non-academic in its overall reality. I think I feel closer to the contents of my pockets and my growing up in Ulster in a war-type situation – these are much more important to me than the improvised music tradition in England. The first time I heard improvised music I knew I wasn't going to play anything else. It was one of those life-changing events that struck so deeply. I felt that it gives you an incredible depth. You can look at every aspect of life and connect it all up. There are so many facets and it's so rich. It's not like any other. Those whole sort of life affirming things, being positive, going towards the future and making good things, not decrying stuff because they're bad things from the past but just going ahead and improving things – these are more important conceptions to me.

I had a couple of piano lessons when I was young. But I didn't like it at all. I didn't like the whole side of being taught music. I love music but I didn't like that whole aspect, it didn't seem very pleasant. There were a few embarrassing things along the way but then I came back to music again and bought a guitar. [05A]

Improvised music seemed the most natural music to play really, always.

I love jazz. But I'm more interested in the spirit of it, the kind of essence, not the way they were playing but what they were trying to do. Thinking along those lines, I became much more interested in trying to play the music that I wanted to play and not trying to play like other people. [05B]

I don't want to play the obvious way or what I perceive is expected of me, otherwise I get bored. [06A]

In classical music I have to think so much about technique and how to produce a sound. That has been a problem in the past, because the technical side sometimes takes over my instinct for creating music. That's why I like improvising. I started improvising because it was up to me, without having to worry if I was out of tune, or if I was coming in in the wrong place or making a noise when I shouldn't be making a noise, no pages to turn – all those things that can be a barrier sometimes. [10]

We actually started off doing compositions, some text pieces, Stockhausen text pieces. And we actually wrote some text pieces for the group in the early days. [11]

I think I became a singer because my mother and father were singers. My mother was a soprano and my father was a bass, my uncle was a tenor. There was lots of singing in the family, and I was always interested in those sounds. One of my first memories is having to go to hospital, when I was around three years old. I had pneumonia or whooping cough and the nurse had this horrible voice and I hated her. Both my parents had very beautiful, soft voices. [18]

Why do I improvise? I think it's because I loved playing clarinet when I was a kid. I played it all the time. But sometimes music books bored me. I liked them but … . So I always improvised, as well, playing along with the radio, or some records, but especially with the radio. I put radio channels on and I played along with what was on, anything and everything. That's what formed my listening I think. [19]

I started as a writer and a poet and then, in my early twenties, quite a few composers started becoming interested in my textual work. So, first of all, I worked a bit with some composers and then I started to improvise a little bit with some of them. Then I started to meet musicians who were improvisers and initially it was just fascinating for me because I didn't have a specifically musical background.

The great thing about the group Machine for Making Sense was that it was just chaos; it was a beautiful chaotic system. We'd all be using different assumptions and codes at the same time, so it was like a multi-pronged thing. It was fascinating because you would sort of know what was going on but in fact you didn't, you'd say: 'That was interesting, wasn't it?' and afterwards you'd talk about it and find out that all these things had occurred that you were only half cognisant of.

The first time it was absolutely dreadful. On every level, it was just horrendous. We searched like crazy, thinking there must be some interesting conceptual thing to this disaster, but there wasn't. We were all completely devastated. We liked each other so much, and we liked each other's work so much. And yet that was one of the best experiences in a way, because it wasn't easily apparent how we could come together. We really had to work at it, not in some analytical or prescriptive sort of way, just play together, just work together, just listen to each other, just talk together. And finally we managed to find some sort of trajectory where the chaos found ways of reinventing and recombining. So sometimes, when I work with improvisers and you say: 'Wow, that was great', in the back of my mind I think: 'Was it? Or was it just predictable, was it something that's already happened, was it safe, was it easy?' [21]

The move to Europe was less about leaving Australia and more about coming to Berlin – there are many musicians that inspire me in Australia, the country itself also. I think a lot of my music is connected to my being from Australia. I don't feel like I play like a European or an American, for example. I didn't come to Europe and feel as though my music 'fitted' in this environment.

I see my music visually and I see that the landscape and the soundscape of Australia have been major influences – literally, because I spent all this time mimicking the birds, the farm machinery, the rain, for a residency project in the outback in 2004. This has very much remained in my music. Also attitude-wise, I grew up on the edge of the earth – I feel like I come from very far away and even though I've been living here in Berlin for two years, I feel very much like a foreigner and someone from somewhere very far away, very isolated. [30]

It was funny because in Argentina, nobody was really playing improvised music. All the information we had back then came from CDs that we had to buy on the internet. And there wasn't much internet either – YouTube didn't exist. So the only contact we had with this music was the albums. We played for years before we actually saw an improvised music concert. If you lived in Europe and you went to a concert, you could realize right away what was it about. Only having the records was very different. [31]

My first instrument was a homemade oscillator. My second instrument was a tape recorder. I made some collages. Then I bought a guitar. Then turntables and tape machines. [33]

You learn to do by doing the thing you want to do. It's a process of doing, eliminating, being honest with yourself, being very severe with yourself. You can't be an artist 'like somebody else'.

Once I know how to do something, I don't like to keep doing it. No matter what you do, though, part of everything you've done is still there. I never wanted a 'style'. I wanted to be able to crack the nut of a musical idea. [34]

I improvise because that's what I'm best at doing. I've learnt over the course of many years – I don't know why but improvising produces the richest contribution to my musical output even though I do it less than before. [40]

I was interested in football: it's like a kind of microcosm of English society, a collective, communitarian society. Strangely, it's its social aspect that interested me. But also the sport, with the ball and the goal. Its relationship with music is space. I had a lot of incredible experiences with football. Football is an intellectual sport. You have to plan ahead, anticipate and that's what interests me. It's the same thing: it's not about reacting, but about going together towards the goal, the whole team. It also requires a kind of mental and intellectual flexibility. It's not the same thing as music, but there are commonalities. As to how I came to make music ... when I was little, I hated music. But one day, I asked myself why so many people loved music and I listened to a lot of music, all kinds of music, starting with classical music. [41]

I would have liked to know what it's like to be able to appropriate the music of Bach, Beethoven or Mozart, technically and in a mature way on an instrument. [42]

I played a lot of classical music when I was young. Then I needed to escape and I played jazz. Not mainly because I had listened to it and liked it, but to meet different musicians, release myself from sheet music, the tradition of salon piano, no doubt to improvise a little too. Improvisation came to me gradually. At that time I wanted to escape jazz, which, in fact, was not part of my culture. Little by little, I freed myself as I met new musicians. Without really realizing it, I went towards the sort of improvised music that I felt was mine. What I mean is, this music was me.

There were significant encounters, especially the meeting with Michel Doneda, where I had the wonderful feeling of being in the moment for the first time, not knowing how long I had been playing, not knowing where I was in time. ... It was a very powerful experience, a great shock. I had never experienced that before. I don't know if that was what I was looking for, but in any case I had found something that suited me perfectly. Today, it's more difficult to find this same type of sensation of course, if only because of the greater mastery acquired over the years. [43]

I didn't become a musician by choice, but as the culmination of natural evolution. When I first blew into an alto saxophone, it was a revelation. I liked the sound a lot. It was very natural, like an extension of my own voice. I started to practice it regularly. [45]

Initially, there was a kind of fascination for vibrating strings. At my mother's godmother's house, there were clothes lines at the end of the garden. I was fascinated by these lines, these four lines suspended in the air. I pulled at them and made them vibrate. And that completely fascinated me. Then, at home, I played with elastic bands, bits of twine that I tightened between the furniture and that I plucked. And I noticed that depending on the tension, you didn't really get the same pitch. At some point, I realized that people before me had already had this fascination and had made an object that you could have a lot of fun with in that way – the guitar – and I thought it was fantastic. There was no need to tinker around; something already existed that had been designed for that. [46]

I started music very young, when I was three or four, and I wanted to become a flamenco guitarist. But unfortunately, I grew up in a small German town, and since I was very small, skinny and very shy, the teachers at the music school told me that I could not play the guitar, that the instrument was too big for me – apparently there was no child's guitar – and that, anyway, flamenco was for the Spanish and not for girls. And they told me to play the flute. Then, when I was eleven, they told me that I was old enough to play the guitar. My teacher told me that he would teach me flamenco later, in four or five years. But then, five years later, I realized that he was utterly incapable of teaching that music to me. He was a jazz musician and he knew absolutely nothing about flamenco. For my part, I composed little pacifist or anti-nuclear songs. Then, as my teacher told me that jazz was very difficult, I decided to study classical guitar. A little later, I started to improvise on guitar, alone, and other people found it a bit strange. And since I was also studying the violin, I started playing the guitar with a bow. Among other things I played to accompany the abstract paintings that I was doing at the time. And I thought I was the only person doing weird stuff like that until I moved to Berlin where I discovered that other people were doing stuff like that too. To free myself from the reflexes I had in my fingers because of classical music – my fingers were playing patterns or chords I didn't like on their own – I tried a lot of things, like swapping the strings, playing the guitar like a cello and so on. Later, I also added the computer to replace the old four-track tape recorder I was using. [48]

Unquestionably, *musique concrète* has greatly influenced what I do. [01]

The tradition of improvised music that has most influenced me is the one that comes from the group AMM, a tradition that has more to do with process, more to do with listening – though not necessarily with obvious call and response or dialogue and obvious interaction – more to do with doing things together instead of throwing things back and forth. [05B]

I listen to many different kinds of music and read many kinds of books, philosophy, musicology, aesthetics. So I have many influences from all over the world. [08A]

I'm very influenced by comics and films and not only Japanese. And I'm very influenced by the musicians around me. I do a lot of concerts with Japanese improvisers. I can't deny the fact that I'm Japanese. It's a fact. Sometimes I listen to improvised music and I feel it's European. But I can't explain why. The influence of comics comes in as a way of breaking the meaning. In Japan, the comics culture is mostly broken. I prefer that, and the way they have of looking at things from a distance. It's more like an intention. Sometimes, a joke is stronger than a long silence, more powerful. I like powerful jokes. [08B]

I'm very interested in quantum physics and mechanics. ... I'm not such a romantic that I would write a piece called 'Quarks' – I don't want to make it obvious – but the interest in all these fields of thinking is there. They influence my thinking, and that goes into the way I handle music. So if somebody asks me, do you think this influences your music? I would say straightaway: 'Yes' – but I don't know how. [27]

In the past I always tried not to show in my work any Argentinian trait I could have. I strongly dislike the Argentinian stereotype. And I also felt that music had to come from another place: a kind of exteriority that has nothing to do with the place you come from. On top of this, I've always felt like a foreigner in Argentina. I lived in Buenos Aires my whole life, until I was thirty, and I never got used to how things work over there. However, nowadays I'm more open to play with some Argentinian typical traits or characteristics. I came to understand that one has to start from his/her own experience. It's something very simple but for some reason I refused to do that in the past. I still feel rejection – but I no longer reject it. [31]

When I was thirteen years old, maybe, free jazz and new rock opened my mind. When I was around sixteen years old, I listened to Derek Bailey, and this was really difficult to understand and I asked lots of questions. I didn't like or dislike it, I thought it was really interesting. It was a time when I asked myself a lot of questions. [33]

How I listen to music, the music I listen to, some hidden gardens

As a listener, I don't really have any expectations, defined stuff that I like, that I don't like, that I want to hear, that I don't want to hear. I think I like to let myself be surprised. So I listen in a fairly new and naive way.

If there's something happening from beginning to end, I don't think I ask myself about its musicality, balance, timbre, innovation, style, talent … . When the music is alive you don't have to ask yourself questions. But sometimes, I also like things to make me ask questions. 'I like it' or 'I don't like it' is a bit limited. Why shouldn't something I don't like not be music as well? I remember the first time I saw Jean-Louis Costes in Paris, at Établissements Phonographiques de l'Est. My head exploded. I was at the back of the room and I was afraid to leave. I wanted to leave and I was afraid to leave. There was a kind of danger in it and, for me, this performance was too much. … 'It's too much', I really had that phrase in mind. It went beyond everything, all the aesthetic limits that I had in mind. There was something … and it completely overwhelmed me, but I stayed, I was totally fascinated. It was really a very good experience. There was something very powerful, which opened up a possibility of expression that I'm not capable of but that beforehand, I wouldn't necessarily have accepted. This kind of experience transforms listening. To hear someone with a totally dirty sound yelling into a microphone: just in terms of the sound, there was a proposition there that I didn't at all like but that suddenly created an opening in terms of being able to play with a really disgusting sound … . [02]

Toys are no worse than a grand piano. You know, it's funny, how some things start to become not funny. I have a friend who went to see an improvisation concert. This friend never goes to improvised concerts and as soon as the guitar player started playing – I don't think he was trying to be funny – my friend started bursting out laughing and had to leave the room. He started laughing and realized that he was the only one laughing. He told me: 'I thought it was a joke.' But then he realized that it wasn't a joke and thought: 'Uh-oh, better get the fuck out of the room and pull myself together.' And that's interesting. Maybe if he got into that music he'd end up not laughing. Or someone else, if they saw somebody climb inside a grand piano, might be flabbergasted and think it was outrageous and absurd. It depends on you. [09A]

I think there's a stupidity in asserting at all costs that it's improvised, not composed music. Because I feel like it's an excuse. You're apologizing, or already preparing for criticism. It's like when I see the words 'recorded without effects, without overdubs, without electronics'. I find that completely stupid. There was also a time when you'd see 'without using samplers'. What I really like about listening to a record is the ear's virginity, not knowing what you're putting on. What's written on the cover is interesting, but you read it afterwards. Before that, there's the virginity. And in that virginity, whether the music is made through improvisation or not doesn't matter when you first listen to it.

I remember listening to a record and I thought it was crazy. I thought I had listened to some improvisation that sounded like composed music. I said to myself: 'What incredible precision!' Then I saw them in concert and they were all actually reading a score. The piece had been totally composed. And then, knowing that it had been composed, it seemed incredibly stupid. I thought it was very poor.

In absolute terms, it's very easy to say that it's just sound and you don't care, but actually there's a big difference in the way you listen to it. [36]

Improvisations, improvised musical pieces, shouldn't be listened to as improvisation. I don't listen to improvisation as improvisation. [37]

There's a kind of osmosis, I don't know how to put it: I hear the interior through the sound.. Improvisers or jazz musicians: I hear what they're feeling through the music. When I play with improvisers, I'm in the flow and I can't hear it. But when I'm listening, I hear it. [41]

I ask myself a question which I've never been able to answer: if I didn't make this music, would I go and listen to it at concerts? I'm not so sure. [43]

Among other things, I like listening to folk music, world music or European folk, lots of different stuff.

It seems to me that you're bombarded with information all day long, and it's very pleasurable then to put on a bit of music or listen to whatever it might be. But you get home and you don't feel like listening to anything; you need a bit of headspace. [04A]

I have to say, it's very rare for me to put on a CD and really listen to it. It tends to be when we're preparing meals at home. I listen much more closely to live gigs. [04B]

The thing that I've listened to most is James Blood Ulmer's LP *Revealing*. I've played that so many times – I think it's fantastic. But I don't really listen to very much music, recorded music. Because there's too much music, there's too much. I'm not going to waste time listening to music, I want to play it! [05A]

I don't really listen to improvised music at home. Although all the music I listen to has improvisation as a part of it. Sometimes I listen to AMM or Michel Doneda, but also to Stevie Wonder, Donald Byrd, Don Caballero, hip hop, Slayer, gamelan music, Herbie Nichols, Igor Stravinsky ... Music. [05B]

At the moment I'm listening to blues – Magic Sam from Chicago, for example, and Son House. It's because I was just there and bought some CDs. [06A]

I listen to other music, for example, Scott Walker, The Who, medieval music and Sixties Kitsch Lounge. [06B]

I prefer to listen to music live. I've got lots of CDs, but I don't listen to them that often. I like various kinds of classical music, and jazz, but I don't like it on all the time. Again, I prefer to listen to it live. I think there's something else going on which is much more interesting live. It's part of the ritual, which is a part of the indefinable meaning of the music: being there, you get a different sense of what it's all about as opposed to a CD. It has a different meaning. [07]

I like contemporary music – John Cage, Morton Feldman – American experimental music, but also experimental music from other countries, Iannis Xenakis and other kinds of music, black music, soul music from the 1960s and the 1970s, Marvin Gaye, Curtis Mayfield, James Brown. I like dance music, club music, minimal techno. [08A]

There are musicians who don't listen to music? I listen to many CDs because, in Japan, concerts are expensive. Recently my favourite music has been Hawaiian music. There are some similarities between Hawaiian and improvised music. I especially like Hawaiian music from the 1920s and 1930s. At that time, Hawaiian musicians were very experimental because each musician had his own tuning. That's very interesting to me. But I also listen to pop music from the 1970s and the 1980s, Japanese pop music and classical music. I like guitar music, especially from old recordings. When I was a student at university, I listened to jazz music a lot but not so much recently. I don't know why. [08B]

I've been listening to a lot to King Crimson and prog rock recently. Lots of different things, all the Wandelweiser stuff and whatever I'm working on. If I'm working with an orchestra, I listen to the piece, as preparation. At one point, I went through a real Miles Davis period and then John Coltrane and so on. [10]

There was a phase when I listened to loads of our own music. Just because there was so much of it that had been piling up. I decided: 'That's it, I'm not going to listen to anything else, I'll just absorb myself', which is quite a heavy thing to do in a way. It's all on the same sort of level, in some sense. I just sort of absorbed myself in playing our own stuff and was quite happy doing that. It's nice to have new pieces to listen to. That's one of the reasons for doing it, I think. [11]

What I listen to at home can include listening to improvised music and many different kinds of music too. It changes all the time. I mean last year I did a tour with Gerry Hemingway in America, and he brought along a lot of CDs for the car and I really got into some of this old Kentucky Mountain singing, people like Roscoe Holcomb who are very very rough, guys who've worked in the mountains, in the mines all their lives, kind of singing a strange mixture of things that come from the Baptist Church and Celtic folk tradition and some influences from country blues but all mixed up at some point in the early years of the twentieth century. It was a music they never thought would be recorded. It was done at parties. It was sometimes done at the church. I had a period when I was finding those CDs and looking into that. I've been listening to some of the early rebetiko from Greece, this kind of music, by Greek exiles, returned around the 1920s and 1930s from Turkey and further east and was sung with a lot of that kind of influence from the Middle East. In these songs they're all drug addicts and criminals. The songs are about 'I will slit your brother's throat if you look at my woman again'.

I had to leave jazz. Not only as a playing thing – not that I was playing much more than student jazz. I also had to leave it as a listening thing for many years. But in the last five years, maybe, I've really come back to it and listen to it a lot.

Country blues was the first kind of music that really got me. That kind of pre-war country blues when I was a schoolboy. I suppose it was the tail end of the 'British blues boom', as it was known. There was a radio programme on Sunday nights that played people like Charlie Patton and all those people. That was the first time I thought: 'Ah, this is really something.' [14]

I listen to very different stuff. Sometimes rock. I have periods where I listen to Led Zeppelin all the time. [15]

I have a fantastic stereo system and that's a big change for me. I listen to a lot of jazz records and CDs. I sometimes buy CDs and I get given a lot too. There are so many CDs in the house that I can't listen to them all. I listen a lot to my own compositions and recordings too. I also listen to electronic compositions or pieces of *musique concrète* – a lot of different things. It all sounds really great on my new hi-fi system and that makes a change – I'm enjoying music much more. I think everybody should have a decent system! [17]

Recently I've been getting into John Coltrane records from the 1960s and there's one that I missed, which I didn't have at the time. Coltrane and Elvin Jones – I've just rediscovered them. Those two together are magic. I come from a jazz background so I always thought there was a certain sexiness about the music. I don't like a lot of the dry improvising that sounds like breathy noises: 'Psst' and so on. You know what I mean. I think Coltrane left a few questions, like: 'OK, where can we take this music?' [18]

I listen to a lot of music, I like to listen to music, that's for sure.

I have two favourite records that I've been listening to for a very long time, and that I play along to. The first one is a recording by David Byrne and Brian Eno called *My Life in the Bush of Ghosts*, which dates back to the 1980s. It's a very good record, and it fuels my clarinet playing. I play along to it. I've worked with this record a lot, imitating the sounds with the clarinet. For example, I might only play the bass drum, or the snare, or the bass, or the guitar. ... And then there's *Bitches Brew* by Miles Davis. And I play along to that too. There's also a Klaxon Gueule record that I listen to quite often. And a Russian group from the

1980s, kind of an industrial metal group. Everything is played. They don't use any machines but lots of sensors, springs, metal plates and so on. [19]

I don't listen to rock, or almost any popular music. I listen to recordings that are in my area of improvised music. Often I only listen to them once and then they get put up on the shelf. I don't have enough time, I'm behind, there are loads of … but it nourishes me.

For two or three years, I've been listening to Morton Feldman like crazy. It's related to the night, anxiety and insomnia. I hardly ever listen to Feldman during the day. It's so far from my practice that I probably project the last of my romanticism, my ideal of an almost unachievable beauty, onto it. I also listen to more classical stuff, which mostly revolves around string quartets, Bartók, Shostakovich. And then I have periods that are a little more Messiaen, Xenakis.

There's also a lot of listening to the music that I'm working on, recordings of my own concerts. [20]

I really love dancing to bad disco music. Or to Motown records, Pointer Sisters, Michael Jackson. … But whenever I listen to contemporary music, I have to listen very seriously; I can't do anything else at the same time. And I haven't got enough time to listen as much as I want to. But I hear a lot of live music, improvised or composed contemporary music. One concert a week, maybe, sometimes three. I do listen to a bit of baroque and classical music also. I like Purcell and Rameau, for example, or Beethoven's symphonies, or Bach's *Goldberg Variations*. [21]

I listen to a lot of music. Because I teach I have to research all kinds of music, so I like 1960s fuzz guitar. Davie Allan and the Arrows are a favourite – I love the use of texture and noise in that particular music. A lot of the Folkways Records field recordings from the 1950s and 1960s, from around the world, South America and Bali, for example. I was listening to those recordings with ideas of space and geography in mind, how the recordings themselves suggest a particular sense of space and place. I listen to the classical twentieth-century works, my listening is all over the place – but I think that's healthy. Rock is 85 per cent of my influences and excitement. Music comes from rock. [22]

I listen to Wandelweiser radio when I work at the computer. I often turn it on and it's fantastic – the best music to work with because it's there and it doesn't disturb you. It's a wonderful atmosphere. I know most of the pieces they play on the station very well, but they aren't sing-along pieces. That's actually what I listen to. Or sometimes I have to listen to things which I don't want to. CDs? In the car sometimes. Old Miles Davis, *Kind of Blue*, or Chet Baker, or classical music. But only while driving. And not loud. [27]

I don't listen to music as much as I should. Listening purely for pleasure is something I don't do nearly enough. I never seem to have time to do it, but it's also partly because I enjoy music most when I'm not intending to listen to it. I just happen to hear it and then it catches me. If I sit down and try to listen to something, it can get a bit too self-conscious. But I love the internet because you have access to all this music, even if it's just samples of music. I'm rediscovering popular music. I didn't listen to it when I was a teenager. One of the reasons I didn't was that I knew that I should, therefore I didn't want to. I knew it was the thing teenagers were supposed to do and it seemed such a cliché. Now, with a little distance, I'm rediscovering it. I also enjoy listening to Bach, sometimes, and early music like the music of John Dunstable. I don't listen to a lot of improvised music on record. I was interested in Gérard Grisey a while ago but I didn't really follow it up. I listen to a lot out of curiosity. For a lot of people, music is seen as something you listen to for pleasure. For me, it's a lot more to do with curiosity. I think for a while I fell into the trap of reading about music more than I listened to it. That's not the case anymore. [28]

I listen to French *chanson*. In 2005, I listened to *chanson* for a month. At one time I listened to *Grease*, the musical with John Travolta and Olivia Newton-John. I also listen to Bach. When I listen to improvisation, it's work rather. I also listen to Ethiopian music. Jazz too sometimes. After my classical studies, I played jazz. I like Thelonious Monk and Miles Davis. And I really like some current pop music, like Gnarls Barclay. [29]

I listen to music almost all day. I listen to old records, the radio, my favourite playlists on my computer. A lot of musicians give me CDs, and I listen to those while I work. My ideal listening situation is to put on a whole record and sit down with a cup of tea – but that doesn't happen so often.

I go through phases. At the moment I'm listening to Black Sabbath and Grace Jones on repeat … not sure why. I copied a triple disc set of Pierre Schaeffer that now shows up regularly on the random setting in my iTunes between The Decemberists, TV on the Radio and Anthony Pateras and Robin Fox's new album.

Around my apartment, I hear violinists come to the floor above me to test out the new instruments made by my neighbour, opera singers come to practice with the pianist in the apartment opposite; there's a funk trumpeter four floors up – I love listening to them practise all. And then there's a veritable bird sanctuary in my garden in the warmer months.

I realized that I often need to have something playing on the stereo, because if it's not I have something playing in my head – which can drive me crazy. I have a jukebox in my head. My memory for lyrics and melodies is scary.

I have a lot of recordings of my projects that I have to psych myself up to listen to. I go to see so much live improvised music that I don't feel so drawn to listening to improvised music on CD. [30]

I no longer listen to music. Or if I do, it's just a few things – mostly old, traditional folk music recordings from different countries. My record collection stayed in Argentina, so I haven't had it with me for three years now. I have some music on my computer, but I don't even have a system at home to play it on. I wouldn't listen to it anyway. [31]

I don't listen to music very often when I'm at home. I really like to go to concerts. At home, I mostly prefer to have no music at all. [32]

A few years ago I was kind of a 'hard listener'; I listened to lots of CDs. But not so much anymore. I don't like to listen to music through headphones. I need some air between the speakers and my ears. These last few years, I've been listening to more live music than recorded music. When I do listen to recordings, I listen to old music, 1940s, 1950s and 1960s jazz and free jazz, Ornette Coleman or Eric Dolphy, 1950s or 1960s Japanese pop music. And I still listen to Derek Bailey, solo mainly, or with Evan Parker or Jamie Muir. I always listen to the same music. [33]

I don't listen much to improvised music at home, but I do listen quite a lot to live music. And I listen to electroacoustic music. At the moment, I'm listening to Nigerian pop music, and there are some people I often come back to, like Roscoe Mitchell. When I listen to something, I listen to the same thing 300 times, completely obsessively. [35A]

I go to a lot of concerts and see a lot of improvised music. I always listen to hip hop, it's the first music I was ever into as a kid and I always check out what's happening. I also listen to a lot of 1970s soul music and heavy funk. Some Curtis

Mayfield records are great, *Sweet Exorcist* for example. I have a pile of records that I find really engaging like *The 21st Century Hard-y-Guide-y Man* by Keiji Haino. And I listen to a lot of jazz and electroacoustic music. Live contemporary music too. [35B]

I listen to everything. Most of the time, it's music that I don't know how to play. I bought a Betty Davis record, or I might listen to Curtis Mayfield, or I might listen to AC/DC with my son, or punk, everything … . [36]

I've spent a lot of time not listening to music – I had reached a state of saturation. I used to go to see dance shows instead. Now, I'm listening to a lot of it. I'm listening to everything.

At Christmas, it's more Elizabethan songs. It's a bit of a cliché, but last year that was what I was listening to! In winter, it's more classical music. And contemporary music, a bit all the time. [37]

I listen to a lot of music, live and on record. Everything: electroacoustic music, a lot of classical music from all periods, a lot of jazz, free jazz, pop, rock, world music, shaman songs, Brazilian music and so on. [38]

I listen to a lot of electroacoustic music. It's the music I love most, which I'm most interested in. I don't listen to improvisation much. And I listen to a lot of contemporary music in concert. Not much improvisation. And I listen to pop, music that industrialized mass culture calls popular. [39]

I love to hear music live, I rarely listen to much music at home but if I do, I listen to something incredibly intensely. That's partly because when I'm at home, I'm often composing or improvising so imagining or making music myself and can only deal with nature sounds and relative silence. [40]

I don't listen to a lot of music but I like to listen to sounds, all kinds of sounds. I confess: I often listen to a very banal CD of a Japanese band. I sing and play drums along with it. I practise with it. For the last three or four years. I just love it. I always listen to that band to practise and sing. [41]

I try to go to concerts and I regret that I can't go to more. At home, I listen more to electronic music than to improvised music. I do listen to the records other musicians give to me, but most of the time only once, because as I play this music myself, listening closely to it is not so far away from playing it. It needs a lot of energy, then, which I need for my own activity as a musician. I have the feeling that to be a fan of this kind of music is already to be halfway towards being a musician yourself. Because by listening to this music you become part of the process. I don't think you can listen to this music as background music. You are either ready to take part in the process or not. [44]

Outside of concerts, I don't listen to a lot of music. I'm not attracted by record culture. On the other hand, at home, I often play at the same time as I listen to CDs. [45]

I listen to a lot of very different things, a lot of jazz, the Notre Dame school, a lot of contemporary music (Xenakis, Cage, Feldman, Stockhausen, Tenney, etc.), a lot of traditional music. I do listen to rock, but rarely. Captain Beefheart or David Bowie for example, but not today's pop at all. [47]

I don't listen to a lot of music at home. Sometimes I listen to baroque music, a hip-hop record by DJ Screw, a cantata by Bach entitled *Ach wie flüchtig, ach wie nichtig* that I find very beautiful and that I consider to be pop music. [48]

I like playing the guitar, very badly, in a very melodic rhythmical way – not chords but fingerpicking, Spanish classical. I don't play songs, I basically improvise, move my fingers around. It's enjoyable – but don't tell anyone! [04A]

As a violinist, I don't play any other kind of music. I have no interest in playing any other kind of music. With electronics, I was part of the London underground house scene in the late 1980s and early 1990s and I bought samplers and a TR-909 drum machine and I did techno breakbeat stuff.

I played trombone for a while. I fancy having an electric guitar too. I like the idea of sitting on the sofa in the front room, in front of the television, and picking something out on the guitar. But I think, for me, it would be electric. So if I had the spare cash I'd definitely go out and buy a Fender Stratocaster copy, a good quality one. I'd definitely be up for that. As a teenager, I had a friend who had a guitar and a bass guitar, and we'd take it in turns to jam. I've played bass guitar in bands over the years too. [04B]

I've studied lots of different types of music, the mechanics of music, but I haven't publicly played any music other than improvised music since I made the change. At home I play electric blues music, folk music, Irish music and a bit of piano. I've also got a violin – my grandfather was an Irish folk violinist. I play lots of things, everything. And that informs my improvisation. [05A]

I used to play other types of music but I don't anymore. But I do listen. I could secretly sit in my room and feebly imitate bebop, but I'd rather listen to Charlie Parker do it brilliantly. [05B]

I really detest classical music. I am into contemporary classical music but, you know, the romantic harp repertoire is really awful. It's not interesting. I also play the drums, but not often. I do it when I'm drunk. [06A]

I only function in experimental music; I don't play any other forms of music. [06B]

I don't do any other music, I don't have a secret life, not in music anyway. When I was younger I did try to play the alto saxophone, but I got sick of having to practise in the wardrobe so I wouldn't annoy the neighbours and I gave up after a while. I'm not really a musician at all in some way – I'm just a noise maker, a drummer! [07]

When I was four years old I told my mother: 'I want to play violin.' I don't know why. At university I played double bass in a brass band. At high school I played cello. At junior high school I played clarinet. Nowadays I only play the violin: rock music, ethnic music, Indian music and improvised music. At home I practise my instrument. [08A]

When I was young, my mother let me study the piano, but when I was a teenager I told my mother that I wanted to learn guitar.
Actually, I don't play only improvised music. I have some sort of easy listening groups, and I compose different kinds of music, like country music. I have different ways of making music, but recently, I've been unable to think they're separate. Of course, it's not the same music, but I'm unable to think they have different values. For example, the way I touch the instrument is the same. Yes, I can say it's similar playing country music and improvised music – but in a different way. [08B]

I just stick with improvising. I've got lots of writing, but my music isn't all there yet. It's not what I want it to be. [09A]

I write songs. The words and the music. On the guitar. I played them in public once. Kind of. Just once. [09B]

I play with a pop band. There's a singer, an acoustic guitar, an electric bass, two backing singers, drums and me on the violin. I play my acoustic violin with a pickup.

I used to play the tenor horn. I started on the cornet then the tenor horn and then the baritone. I used to play with a brass band when I was much younger. I do like brass band music, actually. I also used to sing, mainly Welsh folk singing. [10]

I can't see myself doing the same music all my life at all. In fact I'm not interested in that. Even if I really respect the people who do the same thing all their lives ... I don't want to dedicate my life to a cause. I don't see what cause I would want to dedicate my life to, except my life. My life can't only go in one direction. [12]

I used to play the piano, and I found it a very lonely experience. When I went to university I really wanted to play with other people, and it seemed very hard to do on piano. But I play a bit of piano at home. I also used to play keyboards in some avant-rock groups when I was young. [14]

I just play the saxophone. I mess around with other things sometimes but not seriously. [16]

I used to play piano. I whistle sometimes! Maybe I should sing in the future! [17]

I sometimes play a little bit of trumpet again, after a few bottles of wine – but my lip isn't so good. [18]

I've always played a lot of styles at the same time. I played in a classical orchestra in the city where I was born. I played with the brass band. I did pop stuff. I played at church because I have a Catholic education. ... I think that's the way I function. If I only play one type of music, I get bored.

I sing. I sing a lot at home. I improvise, anything, from morning till night. I also play bass. I'm not very good at it but I love it. I have an acoustic bass and sometimes, in the evening, I play it a bit. [19]

I would have liked to play the cello or *sarangi* ... but ... . [20]

I bought a banjo when I was forty years old, but it's a tough instrument. I've performed with it a few times – and this is the one instrument that gets people really mad. When you're bad on banjo it's really really bad. I like it though – some of my favourite performances have been with the banjo. I do prepared banjo – I play it but I don't like the feeling of it, playing strings, it feels stupid, so I put things in it. I'm still working on it. There'll be an outcome one day which might surprise you! It's my dream to tour Europe with my banjo. I don't play tunes on the banjo, let's put it that way. It's a texture that I'm after. I never learned an instrument. I was opposed to it as a teenager. Distortion, more or less: in the 1970s, that was my entry into music. I knew the music I didn't like, but I was looking for the music I liked. It was through distortion that I found it and from there it opened up into different styles of music. [22]

I used to play the piano, but I gave up after having a teacher who was so much into self-expression that I became so self-conscious that I couldn't really play anymore. If I ever have the time, I might play the serpent because I like the way it's related to the voice. [28]

At home, I sometimes play the trumpet. [29]

I used to play the saxophone. I play accordion secretly, just on my own, but not very well. [32]

Last year I bought a very cheap toy saxophone and tried to play it. At home I really like to play a lot of different instruments, strange percussion instruments, keyboards. [33]

I used to play trombone, and I'm thinking of getting another trombone. [35A]

I play synthesizer at home and record solo Moog for hours. [35B]

I would like to play everything, sing, play the piano. I don't play any other music, but I would like to do baroque or folk singing ... . [37]

In private, I play bass guitar. Sometimes I even practice a little bit. It's a nice instrument and totally different from drums. [44]

I improvise with the voice by myself at home, more often than with the saxophone actually. But I'll never do it in public! I would have liked to be a classical singer, I loved the opera before – less now. [45]

I have an electric bass guitar that has only two strings left, and I play it from time to time at home along to Johnny Cash records or stuff like that. I tried to play the double bass a bit. I did classical piano for five or six years. I have a *shehnai*, but I don't know if I'll do anything with it yet. ... I also compose, instrumental music, often for improvisers. I find it an interesting way to meet other musicians, often more interesting than improvised ad hoc meetings. I compose pieces that ask the musicians to make choices, but I also have to work with the musicians because they're open instrumentation pieces. It's interesting, because I do the compositional work on my own. That's what I like about it. I learn a lot about myself by trying to compose music. [47]

At home, I sing a few songs accompanying myself on the guitar. When I was a teenager, during a school trip to East Berlin, I bought a French Renaissance songbook because it was very cheap. It has very sad love songs in it, in minor keys, with descending melodies, and I like them very much. I sing them to cheer me up! [48]

16

Miscellaneous

It's incredibly exciting to play music. I've been looking forward to playing today for ages – what better way to spend the summer? [05B]

If one day it became mainstream, it'd soon need younger musicians to come to kick our asses, spit on us and destroy everything, to move on to something else or offer an alternative to it, resell Celine Dion CDs under the table, stuff like that. [36]

This interview reminds me of being interrogated by the police! [09A]

It depends whether you believe what musicians say or not! And whether or not they actually do what they say or not! And, of course, there may be a big difference between what I say and what I do … . [07]

List of the musicians interviewed

[01]	Thomas Charmetant	2003	Le Ronchois
[02]	Pascal Battus	2003	Bagnolet
[03]	Patrick McGinley	2003	London
[04A]	Matt Davis	2003	London
[04B]	Phil Durrant	2003	London
[05A]	Ross Lambert	2003	London
[05B]	Seymour Wright	2003	London
[06A]	Rhodri Davies	2003	London
[06B]	Mark Wastell	2003	London
[07]	Eddie Prévost	2003	Matching Tye
[08A]	Kazushige Kinoshita	2003	London
[08B]	Taku Unami	2003	London
[09A]	Tim Goldie	2003	Paris
[09B]	Mattin	2003	Paris
[10]	Angharad Davies	2003	Paris
[11]	Morphogenesis [Adam Bohman, Clive Graham, Clive Hall, Michael Prime]	2003	Montreuil
[12]	Frédérick Galiay	2003	Paris
[13]	Quentin Dubost	2003	Paris
[14]	John Butcher	2004	Parthenay
[15]	Ninh Lê Quan	2004	Parthenay
[16]	Evan Parker	2004	Parthenay
[17]	Axel Dörner	2005	Nantes
[18]	Phil Minton	2005	Nantes
[19]	Xavier Charles	2006	Secondigny
[20]	Daunik Lazro	2006	Mulhouse
[21]	Amanda Stewart	2006	Paris
[22]	Philip Samartzis	2007	Paris
[23]	Taku Unami [second interview]	2009	Glasgow
[24]	Mattin [second interview]	2009	Madrid
[25]	Marc Baron	2009	Paris-Genève
[26]	Stéphane Rives	2009	Neuchâtel-Paris
[27]	Radu Malfatti	2009	Glasgow
[28]	Robin Hayward	2009	Berlin
[29]	Andrea Neumann	2009	Berlin
[30]	Clare Cooper	2009	Berlin
[31]	Diego Chamy	2009	Berlin
[32]	Klaus Filip	2009	Iaroslavl
[33]	Otomo Yoshihide	2009	Nickelsdorf

[34]	Bill Dixon	2009	Lisbon
[35A]	Will Guthrie	2009	Paris
[35B]	Clayton Thomas	2009	Paris
[36]	Jérôme Noetinger	2010	Paris
[37]	Olivier Benoit	2010	Paris
[38]	Frédéric Blondy	2010	Paris
[39]	Loïc Blairon	2010	Paris
[40]	Stevie Wishart	2010	Brussels
[41]	Seijiro Murayama	2010	Paris
[42]	Edward Perraud	2010	Poitiers
[43]	Sophie Agnel	2010	Montreuil
[44]	Burkhard Beins	2010	Paris
[45]	Christine Abdelnour	2010	Paris
[46]	Jean-Sébastien Mariage	2010	Paris
[47]	Pierre-Antoine Badaroux	2010	Paris
[48]	Annette Krebs	2011	Paris

The musicians identified by the same number but with a different letter were interviewed together.

The interview with Kevin Drumm was lost. We apologize.

An ear for discord: Improvise, they say

By Bertrand Denzler (BD) and Jean-Luc Guionnet (JLG)

JLG: There was more or less a consensus in the choice of the musicians. We interviewed people who are part of the 'improvised music milieu'. We didn't put any effort into theorizing about whether they're improvisers or not. We never really asked ourselves that question.

BD: Among the musicians that we met, some call themselves improvisers, sometimes seeming to think that improvisation has intrinsic virtues. Others, on the contrary, have doubts about the word and prefer to say that they don't improvise. They no longer want to use the word 'improvisation' when they talk about what they do, either for historical reasons, not wanting to be associated with the movement known as 'improvised music', or because they feel that this term is loaded with too many stylistic or political clichés, too many preconceived ideas about what their music should be like, which might distort how their potential listeners listen to them. Some of them even go so far as no longer wanting to use the word 'music' anymore. But we knew from the start that these two terms – 'improvisation' and 'music' – were delicate terms to handle.

JLG: The purpose, if there was one, was not to answer that question. We did not question those boundaries or the self-designation by musicians of themselves as improviser or not. We took the musicians wherever they happened to be, wherever they found themselves, whether voluntarily or not. We questioned the practice of improvisation by aiming to get to 'the heart of the action' as quickly as possible. In the end, these interviews probably don't help define the territory of improvisation, but they may contribute to taking the meaning of the word further, a meaning that depends on these practices. We might, for example, consider two possible entries into the subject: (i) a reflection on the term 'non-idiomatic' and (ii) an examination of the following pairing: making music in order to improvise / improvising in order to make music.

* * *

JLG: Most of the musicians interviewed do not use the term 'non-idiomatic' but call it something else: 'being in the sound', 'have playing modes', 'have uncodified sounds' or 'not connoted sounds'. But, these judgements are made according to the vague but purportedly defined territory of non-idiomatic improvisation. This is quite common in their discourse.

BD: It's almost as if there were a kind of dream or fantasy of abstraction, a desire or a need to escape from what is known, from identifiable styles or genres, from the history of music, in order to be totally contemporary, ethnically, geographically, culturally or socially unidentifiable, and in the purest possible state of abstraction, in order to get closer to a kind of ideal of contemporaneity and universality. It's as if there were a kind of dream of universality through abstraction – and not via a local culture – of an art form that is at once primitive, eternal, contemporary and universal.

JLG: The problem is that this is too ambiguous. Rather than a motivating force, the non-idiomatic remains a key notion in the practice of this music, provided it amounts to a questioning within the process. Because as soon this notion is applied to the result, it's over. 'Not codifying' then becomes a tool used to eliminate sounds, to mark out one's playing field, which ultimately gives a caricature of what an idiom might be, a very simplified idiom – even if the idea of a music that is culturally and historically elusive has something exciting about it!

BD: The ideal of the absolute non-idiomatic is unattainable, but it can be important to keep it in mind, especially for groups of improvisers who have been working together for a long time and who, from the outside, may be defined by the musical result they produce – the idiom they have built together. When they play together, it is no doubt important that they do not forget to constantly question their own idiom in the light of this ideal of non-idiomatic improvised music.

JLG: But do we actually hear all this that often in the music and in the interviews of the musicians we met? Perhaps some misunderstanding occurs right at the start. Because there's some ambiguity here: Why should 'being in the non-idiomatic' equate to 'being in the sound'? There's a mix-up. It's as if 'being in the sound' were to imply a kind of phenomenology of listening that, of itself, produced a 'natural music' that spoke to everyone. There's a kind of naturalistic ideal, even if the word itself is not used either, as if it were a 'natural music', coming directly out of listening.

BD: Some musicians also seem to speak of a music that is good in and of itself, as if they implied that not judging the aesthetic result, or being able to do 'what they want', or to play collective music necessarily produced a music that was morally superior to music that functions differently or incorporates other considerations. Sometimes, you also get the feeling that they're talking about their music as if it were 'the music of the body', a music that embodies 'spontaneity'. This fantasy of a 'natural' music, music that is both primitive and eternal, non-cultural, pure, sometimes evokes the idea that 'nature is good in and of itself and culture is bad in and of itself'. But for other musicians, the non-idiomatic fantasy corresponds rather to the fantasy of an absolute culture.

JLG: Perhaps, but the border is blurry. You could also criticize the notion of non-idiomatic improvisation because of its imperialist aspect. You could say that it resembles the art market or liberalism, that, as it is the only universal music that relates to everyone, it's a bit like money, a bit like a system that everyone must be able to integrate into, a universal symbolic system, and even a currency of exchange. By the way it's no coincidence that the notion is used in Europe, Japan and the United States but not much elsewhere. This would therefore mean that non-idiomatic improvisation is a sign of deculturation. But we can continue to defend the notion of the non-idiomatic by viewing it as a force for questioning, even if it is not the only one. And even, conversely, as a force for reculturation, after the loss. Because, despite everything, it has always been a powerful force for questioning.

When Derek Bailey uses the term, he sometimes speaks of a multiplication of idioms. Everyone has their own idiom. Everyone is looking for an idiom that becomes more and more specific, that is individual and personal. So, we end up with a 'multi-polyglotism', something he calls non-idiomatic. At other times, however, he talks about it as a kind of task to be accomplished in order to find common ground and be able to play with anyone.

BD: Maybe non-idiomatic improvisation is simply an idea that is supposed to incite us to create musical thinking?

JLG: If you think about other arts, the non-idiomatic represents a point of entry which, more than a subjective desire for expression or even invention, at some point corresponds to the collapse of the hierarchies that exist in the music that we listen to. Hierarchy at all levels. Hierarchy, in the broad sense, of the roles assigned to this or that sound, to this or that system of relationship between sounds, between the people who are playing, composing … . Ultimately, the non-idiomatic is a point of entry for the invention of other hierarchies. It's a symbolic system that collapses and is more or less replaced by another, but that operates by means of an unravelling, a little like abstraction in painting. The unravelling process makes music.

BD: This isn't often true in terms of the musical result. But we continuously reach towards it, and we continuously fail. Perhaps the non-idiomatic is therefore an ongoing attempt to operate this process of unravelling, an attempt that, without ever achieving the desired result, nevertheless alters the music that is being made.

JLG: The process of unravelling doesn't last. It just serves to open the way to taking power in a different way.

BD: In order to rise to this non-idiomatic challenge, a constant motion, a sort of cyclical dynamic is needed between this unravelling and the new systems that are put into place.

JLG: It's an engine and an exhausting one for those who try to fuel it. You load your sounds. Because, today, this process of unravelling has been reversed. There has been a change in gear. From unravelling as previously understood, namely recourse to sensation or perception, or the supposed qualities of sound, or acoustic models – such elements have existed in all modern music until recently – there has, on the contrary, been a shift to the production of loaded or even overloaded sounds: when a sound is made, it is loaded with all the words that are associated with, all that can be known about, this sound, including the most aberrant things, taking on everything that is present and all the similarities that can be called upon – a task that is as equally impossible as the first! Trying to be conscious and knowing why this sound is going to have such-and-such or such-and-such a function in the music, even if, in doing so, I have every chance of getting it wrong, such is the number of possible interpretations, even telling myself that if there is any such thing as music, it takes place within this margin of error. Or, at least, that by loading the sounds, I may manage to feed the music. One would have to imagine that, once in a musical setting, or simply an artistic setting, a kind of monstrous funnel is connected above each sound vibration, no matter how small, a funnel which, filled to the brim with meanings, connotations, loaded in many ways, continuously pours its contents into the flow of listening, and that we must make do with this and do more than this: see this funnel as the thing in which the music is made.

BD: Taken in this way, the non-idiomatic isn't an attempt to create abstraction or purity but an attempt to distil all existing potential, all possible associations. Instead of escaping interpretation, it is seen as the will to reach towards a multiplicity, if not an infinity of possible interpretations, connotations, codings and idioms.

JLG: And that this is an integral part of your sound, that you don't reject all this and even go against your own tendencies in this respect. But this is probably only possible if you have unloaded the sounds beforehand. In sculpture, for example, it is thanks to the purification operated, inter alia, by minimalism that an openness can exist towards all imaginable connotations of a matter, of a form – and sculptors use this. … There's a virtuosity of connotations, which are multiplied by the physical qualities, and we can no longer separate them from each other. Derek Bailey, for example, does this. The history of the guitar is constantly there in his playing. These are intended connotations, which he plays with in the music.

BD: This might be associated with a kind of postmodernism.

JLG: Not postmodernism because we're not playing with idioms, we remain within a non-idiomatic logic. We're not looking at the music from a distance. Our playing does not draw on an aerial view of music or the history of music. For unknown reasons, at a certain moment you want to make a particular sound and it comes out. And that's where you load it with all possible connotations. You're not playing a sampler of all the idioms in the world, as if they were available at will, and you don't have any knowledge to demonstrate through music. You can only load the sounds if you have unloaded them beforehand.

* * *

BD: In addition to non-idiomatic improvisation, we talked about the pairing: making music in order to improvise / improvising in order to make music.

JLG: In music, the traditional position, that of the 'musician', is to say that we improvise to make music. This means that improvisation is one technique among others for making music – this is sometimes also called instant composition. Then there's the performative aspect, which is present in improvised music and which makes music one situation among others that makes improvisation possible. After all these interviews, I've come to the conclusion that a kind of peephole makes it possible to go from one to the other, a peephole, or a passageway, that you might call 'strategy'. Like other notions such as causality, idiocy, hierarchy, emergence or emergent properties, chance or even nature, strategy is, for me, one of a series of blind points in the discourse of musicians. I'm allowing myself to name them, even if the chosen terms can of course give rise to endless debate, because I'm convinced that they designate a series of very real locations within the practice of musical improvisation, besides the name given to them – hidden places perhaps?

Strategy therefore: on the one hand, it's a model – in the mathematical or physical sense of the term – a compositional or playing model. Strategy is then modelled to produce the forms that are given to a sound. For example, a sound is moved from one point to another, while trying to set traps for the listening experience, as if there were a sort of battle going on between physical conditions and the ideal listener's attention, or your average listener, a battle that also exists in composition and that is taken as an aural model. This is what you might call 'formal strategy'. On the other hand, there's something we might call 'real strategy'. In other words, a strategy that actually takes place in the course of making the music, which has an effective impact on the course of things. … All this means that there's a tension between the two, and that this tension acts in real time. One key then is this notion of strategy, present on both sides, on one side as a formal model (improvisation as one technique among others to make music) and on the other as a reality (music as one technique among others allowing improvisation). When we reread our interviews with the musicians, we can see that they are continuously moving from one to the other, very rapidly, and that you can no longer say whether they resort to strategies for reasons of form or to surprise themselves and/or each other.

But there are two families of strategies. There is the strategy of one football team against another, and then there is also the strategy used by a group of mountain climbers or a crew on a boat, where it's a question of survival. In improvised music, you can artificially put yourself under difficult conditions. Then it's a question of survival or not. The challenge is not to win or to seize power but to come out alive, or not, at the end of the concert: as a musician, to come out the other end … or not. There's a powerful link between aesthetics and strategy. It's a question of survival. You can of course deploy a football match strategy in music: trying to play the longest silences, or the loudest sounds, the fastest and so on. Personally, this is not what I'm looking for in this strategy business, and, in particular, this idea of strategy cannot serve the role of peephole between playing music in order to improvise and improvising to make music.

BD: Without using the vocabulary of strategy, you might say that there are two never-ending loops: 'I improvise in order to make music in order to improvise' or 'I make music in order to improvise in order to make music'. Many musicians seem to experience these two loops. You might say that there's a very rapid to-ing and fro-ing between the two elements of the two loops. But this back and forth movement is so fast that it can also be seen as a single loop that has no beginning or end and, in the end as simultaneous, as a state in which it becomes very difficult to separate the fact of making music in order to improvise and the fact of improvising in order to make music. Which means that musicians can be seen as doing both at the same time, continuously, with all intermediate states obviously remaining possible. This would imply that this music is not experimental in the sense that we often understand the word. It's not about trying something out to see what it gives, musically or from a human perspective, nor to experience freedom or spontaneity or collective composition, but rather about fully living out this experience, which has no other purpose other than itself, consisting of doing both at the same time, putting both these issues on the table and taking them seriously: I do everything to 'truly' improvise (according to my own criteria) *and* to make aesthetically satisfactory music (according to my own criteria), without compromising on either of these two requirements.

JLG: Coming back to the question of strategy. On the one hand, from the perspective of form, there's an additional level of representation: you represent this or that strategy. For example, you represent the whispering of the wind or, as with Debussy, a tennis match. Ultimately, there's some kind of representation of music, a representation of what music is supposed to be. On the other hand, strategy truly is present. It's there!

And if I can come back to your example again: improvisation, which is regularly fed back into the loop, serves, with each loop, as a filter, to eliminate the image we have of what music should be, an image that is trashed with each new loop. I improvise in order to make music in order to improvise in order to make music in order to improvise ... the trash can fills up!

BD: Except that the loop is so complex and rapid that everything is constantly put into the trash and it overflows. Perhaps it's an illusion, a kind of state into which improvisers consciously put themselves.

JLG: Yes, it's all about belief. And there's also a link with the non-idiomatic here, which also means 'without representation'. However, it's not about taking the word 'representation' in the sense of opposing the figurative to the non-figurative. It's rather that the status of the representation is not the same. On the one hand, you imitate a mental form, on the other you create a form you have no preconceived image of – even if, immediately afterwards, you do.

BD: From the outside, a listener who doesn't listen in the same way as the musicians who are playing do could analyse what they hear and say, for example, that such-and-such a musician always plays a particular pitch, speed, texture, dynamic or attack in the same way, while, for the improviser, the sound did not exist before. It's not a finished material at first. As an improviser, rather than choosing from ready-made objects in order to place them in a landscape, it's as if you were constantly inventing, or rather reinventing, everything. You manage to believe that you're constantly inventing sounds and forms that did not exist before.

JLG: Forms that did not exist in terms of the status of representation as such. You have to include this in the circuit. The loop issue that we described definitely has to be part of the musical analysis.

BD: In order to be able to experience something that is close to what musicians who are improvising experience, analysis is not enough: the listener has to enter the same mental space as them, share it and think with them, believe in what he or she might normally consider to be an illusion. Listeners can probably have a similar experience to that of improvisational musicians. And this would mean that concerts only work for believers, like a religious ceremony. Believers experience this: thinking in real time with the musician – even if they get it wrong.

JLG: By going to concerts regularly, attention is brought to bear on the work rather than the music.

BD: However, it seems that many improvisers tend towards a state where there's no longer any difference between the two, where the 'quality' of the improvisation and the music can no longer be judged separately, and that they're trying to create a music the intention of which is so clear that it becomes satisfying for listeners who don't distinguish between the two.

* * *

BD: In our interviews, we try to find out how the decision-making processes of the musicians interviewed operate when they are actually in the situation of improvising. We try to get musicians to say what we would see if we 'zoomed in on their brains' while they were improvising.

JLG: At first, when we ask them how they make their decisions, most musicians hardly ever talk to us about interpersonal issues. As the interviews progressed, this question became more and more interesting. In many cases, the focus of conversation changed: at the beginning of the interview, the musician only talked about purely musical issues, but under the pressure of the questioning, they ended up admitting that they also make decisions due to reasons to do with their relationships with other musicians, to surprise or shock someone or, on the contrary, to conform. They talk to us about situations in which they intend to do something before giving it up so as not to upset others, in order to remain within the agreed aesthetics of the group.

The fact of talking about interpersonal issues might be viewed as evoking a theory in which the group is considered as a small egalitarian society. But we can also see these issues in a less idealized way and envisage the stage as a test tube into which three or four individuals are placed, with sound as a pretext, in order to observe how a society constructs itself, with all the problems that that implies, and how the sound produced bears the trace of this process. According to this vision, the sound produced is the signature of a purely human, almost historical process: birth, death, war, revolution, changes in power and so on. Thinking about it like this helps to better understand what we do. This is one of the essential parameters for the analysis of improvisation.

BD: Is music, then, a pretext that produces a 'musical object' that may have a certain autonomy, but that can only be understood if you manage to decode it in this way?

JLG: The music is not a pretext for having experiences. When I talk about the signature, I mean that the music *is* this interpersonal process. It's pure music! Because it is purely that and, conversely, it seems to me that many compositions try to imitate this and give a sweetened image of it. Why sweetened? Because, as was the case with strategy, these compositions are a representation of these societies – up to the symphony orchestra, which is a sort of dictatorial republic – while improvisers must always get everything back on track, every time, even if it seems as if they're constructing stuff from odds and ends, or sometimes, as is the risk, giving power to a fool.

BD: However, it would seem to be very difficult to draw the line between 'I make decisions based on purely musical criteria', according to an expected musical result, and 'I make decisions to influence others or to provoke something'. Because the two are interdependent. When I take a musical decision, even if I think I'm doing so in a 'purely musical' way, even if I describe this decision using words that define musical parameters (pitch, dynamics, duration, etc.), the decision will, consciously or not, influence others. In the same way, if I make a decision to 'manipulate' others, to arouse psychological, emotional or sensory reactions in them – for example, by playing a sound that I know others do not like or that causes them problems – I give the music a form that can only be obtained through improvisation. One might think that these two things are related in this music. This would mean that the aesthetic objective of improvised music is therefore to make music that takes unpredictable rather than unforeseen forms (forms which no one can predict, regardless of what musicians have planned), 'uncomposable', non-representable forms, that improvised music alone can produce. This would make improvised music a music that is, *a priori*, 'unthinkable', but not necessarily a music that has never been heard.

JLG: Yes, but all that is very subtle and highly complex. Billions of pieces of information are passing by, whether they are controlled or not. That's why I've been talking about a human society: liking or disliking or posing problems are all only a figure of speech. From a formal point of view, this further multiplies the plurality or ambiguity of the status of a given sound, an element that is already present in composition. When you improvise, a sound can definitely have more the status of a sign than the status of a sound, and vice versa. Sounds are ambiguous and we play on this ambiguity. Here, there's a big difference between composed and improvised music, a difference that has already been mentioned regarding strategy. A sign-sound in the course of an improvisation has (or doesn't have, depending!) a real impact on what's happening. If the sign assumes, as it should, its representational role, its impact, in contrast to what happens in the context of written music, does not need to be represented: the impact simply occurs. Take the example of silence: a silence in improvised music cannot be compared to a silence in composed music, and even less so to a silence in electroacoustic music. As a matter of fact, in the case of electroacoustic music, there aren't really any silences, since there is always a medium. In composed music, silence is expected. The listener isn't really waiting for anything (all is well!), whereas in improvised music, we are suspended, in the (exaggerated?) power of the person who is playing (perhaps all is not well).

BD: This is a good example, but here too, we cannot separate things completely, because in some improvised music concerts you sometimes hear silences that are not charged with this tension and which are as obvious as those in composed music. And in composed music, performers sometimes make us believe that their silences are loaded with all possible possibilities, and there's a tension, an indeterminacy as intense as in improvised music, even when we know the work by heart. Maybe it doesn't only depend on the musician but also on the listener. If the listener is thinking musically, or believes they are thinking musically at the same time as the person playing it, the silence can probably, in any music, contain the tension of something that is being created in the here and now, in real time, which did not exist before. In the discourse of the improvisers we interviewed, this point of convergence between all the ways of making music comes up regularly: they often speak to us of those moments when there is no longer any opposition between improvisation and composition, between musical decisions and interpersonal decisions, where all this merges into one, where these questions disappear, where it all sort of becomes self-evident.

JLG: However, some improvisers also truly hold up the ideal of posing problems, without ever being in aesthetic contemplation.

BD: Of course, but whether it is sought out or not, it seems that this is something that is experienced. And it may be that this brings up interesting questions. When the musicians talk to us about it, it's as if they are describing moments when the group of improvisers really manages to develop collective musical thinking that is in the process of being made – whether they adorn it with intrinsic virtues (collective thinking is necessarily better than individual thinking) or they distrust it, even fight it (collective thinking is necessarily consensual, freedom-killing, standardizing, etc.) – it being understood that these two positions can of course coexist in the same person.

In the end, it's as if everything that our interviewees told us about improvisation and music were true, even the contradictions. One of the possible ways into this universe would therefore appear to be to agree to put oneself in a highly complex, unstable and shifting system, in which everything is always true, in which clear boundaries cannot be drawn and in which the musicians are constantly involved in many interlocking ways of functioning, at different levels and degrees depending on the situation, using all kinds of mental 'engines' that, even when they are opposed, operate at the same time, or even together, to enable the collective group process.

JLG: Yes, but it is sometimes useful to exaggerate positions a bit to see how far one can go. As for silences, effecting a maximum differentiation of all possible silences makes it possible to create the greatest possible space. In relation to decision-making, there are also huge differences between practices and instruments, between the voice, wind instruments, the piano, electronics and so on. These differences need to be taken seriously because they involve very different conceptions of the status of choice. If you take the voice for example, the body itself is the medium and everything is accessible at any time, without any intermediary. And when I play the organ, for example, everything is in front of me and I can hesitate between notes for as long as I want, at the same time as playing, because I do not necessarily need to do anything in order to play. This poses the problem of choosing from a menu or of not being guided by a menu at all. This is problematic, given the fact that I think that one of the challenges of improvisation is to question what freedom is, or to test that particular notion.

You often hear that when there's choice, you're free. But, for me, it's the opposite: when there's choice, you're no longer free at all because you have the choice between possibilities that have already been thought out in advance. Which brings us to the question: What can you do to avoid having to choose from the menu when you play an instrument that lends itself to menu choices? This is where internal strategies come into play. Some musicians want to work with a menu and others do not. However, choice doesn't mean that you're free, and having choice doesn't necessarily make for improvisation. And by the way, there are many compositions in which performers can choose from a reservoir of sounds. Improvisers can position themselves within a non-choice system and say to themselves that when choice does reappear that it must be that they have previously made a (strategic?) mistake. At that moment, they can, for example, choose to wait in order to allow this choice opportunity to pass. It's a good strategy regarding oneself to force oneself to find a way to avoid the alternative and get to the heart of things. But the opposite is also defensible!

This issue arises in the practice of improvisation and is worth exploring. It is partly related to the tools used, and it would be very interesting to see what might come out of linking the use of instruments in improvisation with certain philosophies, such as that of Gilbert Simondon, regarding the tool and the technical object. A saxophone is a technical object, an almost transcendental concentrate, a projection of possible actions into matter, a utilitarian and symbolic representation of the human spirit. Sometimes, it would be much more practical if the tool were transformed, but it is maintained as it is for symbolic or other reasons!

BD: However, it is also possible to imagine vocalists with a clear vision of their possible collection of finished sounds and organists who manage to see their instrument differently and put themselves in a state of non-knowing, by, for example, looking for situations where they do not have time to think in terms of choice.

JLG: In speaking of the relationship between choice and freedom, it may be emphasized that improvisation is a human activity that makes it possible to ask that particular question in a rather violent way. To say that having choice is not freedom poses huge problems for some people. … Where pragmatic philosophy has taken on the status of common sense, it is almost impossible to gain traction for this idea. And yet freedom belongs to whoever it is who draws up the menu. When I go to a restaurant and choose between dish A and dish B, freedom, or at least an additional piece of freedom, resides with whoever has done the cooking, not the person who chooses between A and B.

What matters are the internal strategies that we put into action in order to do whatever it is we're doing, whatever that might be. Making 'weird sounds', for example, among other functions, amounts to making sounds that we do not really control and that, as a result, lead us by the end of the nose as much as we lead them. There is a kind of to-ing and fro-ing between the result and the action, which means that we no longer have the time to think about choice and that we have other things to do, that we surf on time. With all the tools that we now possess, including IT tools, improvisers invent ways to 'cause sound' that puts the unexpected into the circuit without making it aleatory. In contemporary music, composers often use aleatoricism, but this is not the case here. Improvisers put themselves at the limits of technical capabilities, or they loop a mixer by pushing it to places where it can tend towards silence or the opposite. The same thing goes for instruments. Once you manage to master this (because people do!), you start again from scratch. Therefore it's an endless process.

BD: There comes a time when you realize that you can put yourself in a position of non-choice, even with instruments, sounds and people you know very well. This experience is just a means of 'reinventing' things with anything, with something you are not at all familiar with or with something you know very well.

JLG: Experiencing the absence of a menu brings you back to the menu, but to a meta-menu that can lead to the idea that sometimes one good decision is better than a multitude of small decisions. With all this in mind, taking this whole issue on board, you can end up saying to yourself: 'I have the choice of making this sound for this or that reason and I'm going to stick with this choice.' Having constraining strategies to make things happen becomes possible once again, and even desirable. But that presupposes, I think, having undergone this whole process.

BD: One possible solution is perhaps to make the decision, each time, to demarcate a more or less stable space, with sometimes porous borders, making choices in advance concerning, for example, the instrument you're going to play or the musicians you're going to play with, and once you're in this space, to manage to believe that it is indeed the only one that exists, that that is the world and that there aren't any choices left. I use the word 'space' because it seems to me that the imaginary world of improvisers who are improvising is more akin to a space than a duration. Then it becomes a question of keeping this space alive by every means possible and imaginable, with form, for example, being just one means among others and not an end in itself. This space is definable *a priori* and *a posteriori*. But when you are in it, that's where you 'live your life' as a musician (or as part of the audience). You cannot see this space from the outside. Indeed there is no outside. This space includes all possibilities. There's room for all the complex and contradictory processes that we have described, and the question of choice disappears. You don't have any choice. You have to keep this space alive, with the others, with everything that you are, by agreeing to risk failure. If you want to avoid falling into the void, you don't have time to hesitate between several possibilities. You have to know what has to be done at every moment, down to the nearest millimetre, so that this space continues to exist, whatever it looks like and even if it keeps changing, if only subtly.

This text was first published in French in *L'expérience de l'expérimentation* by Matthieu Saladin (editor), Les Presses du Réel, 2015.

Thanks to Matthieu Saladin.

Diagrams

These diagrams by the editors allow a thematization of some of the topics addressed by the musicians interviewed and put these topics in tension.

They are based on words used, sometimes implicitly, by the musicians.

They offer avenues for reflection and listening, and possible tools which may help one to better understand what is going on during a musical improvisation.

Diagram 1

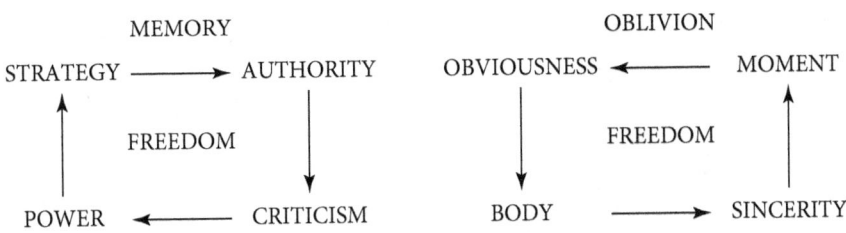

Diagram 2

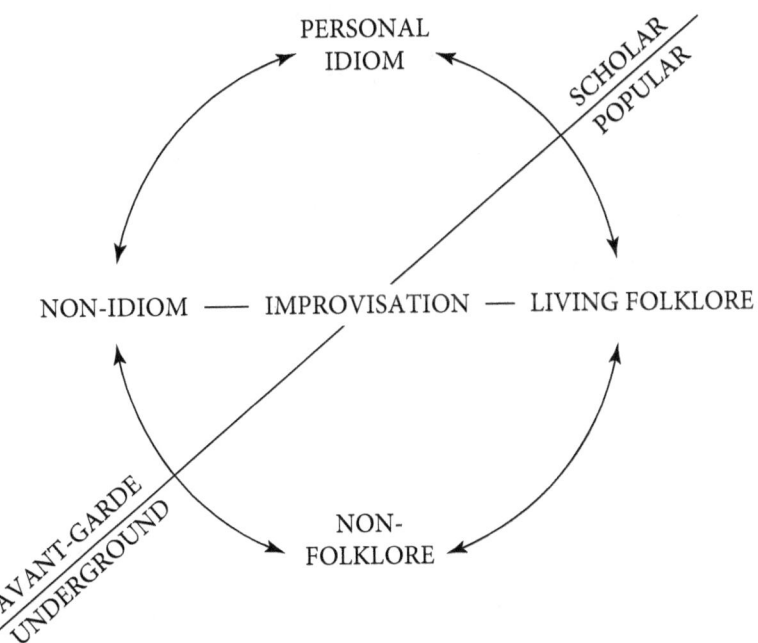

Diagram 3

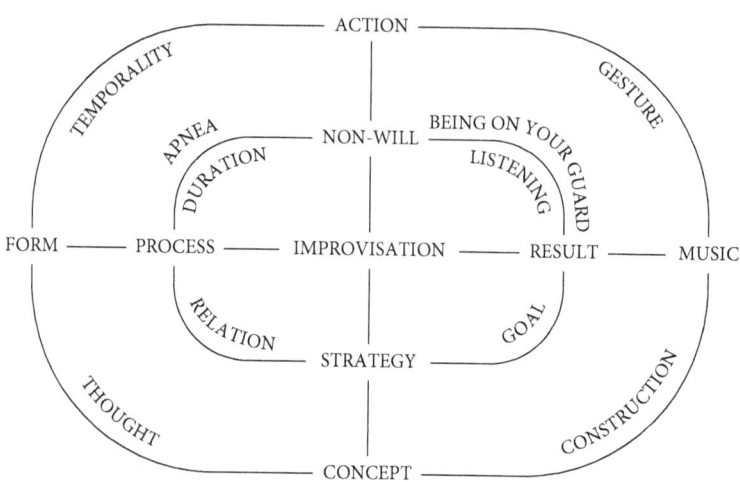

Diagram 4

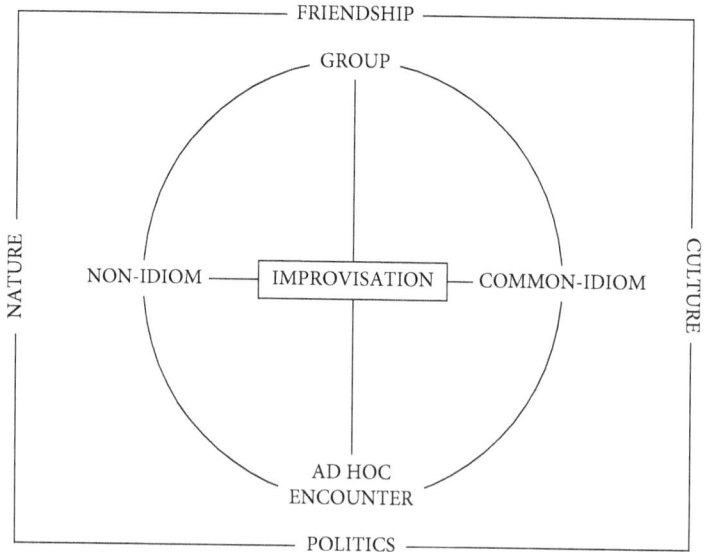

Diagram 5

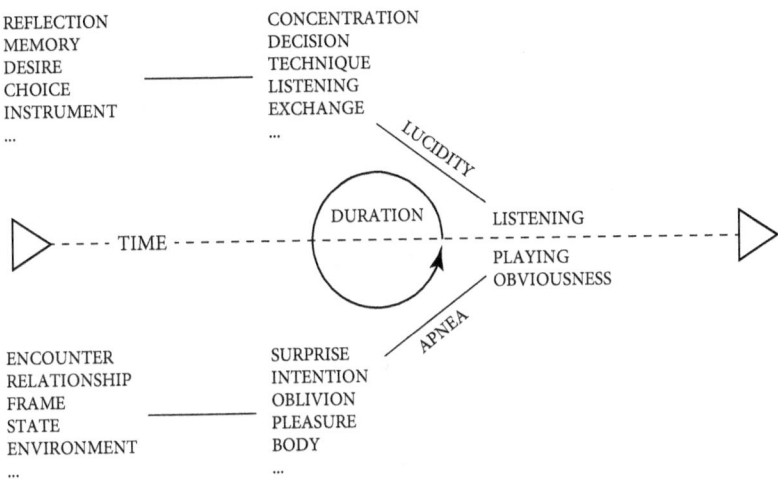

Diagram 6

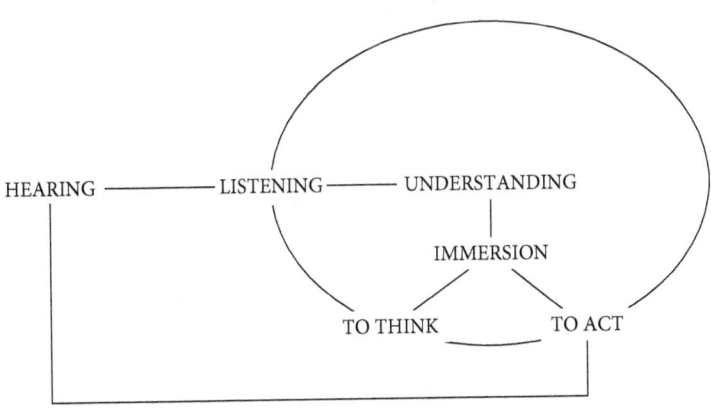

Diagram 7

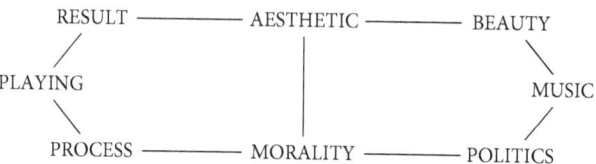

Diagram 8

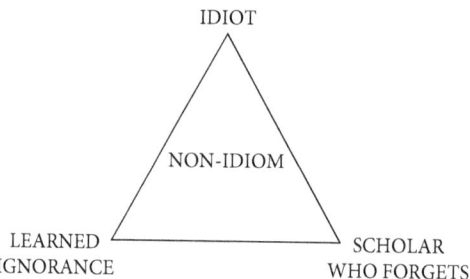

Diagram 9

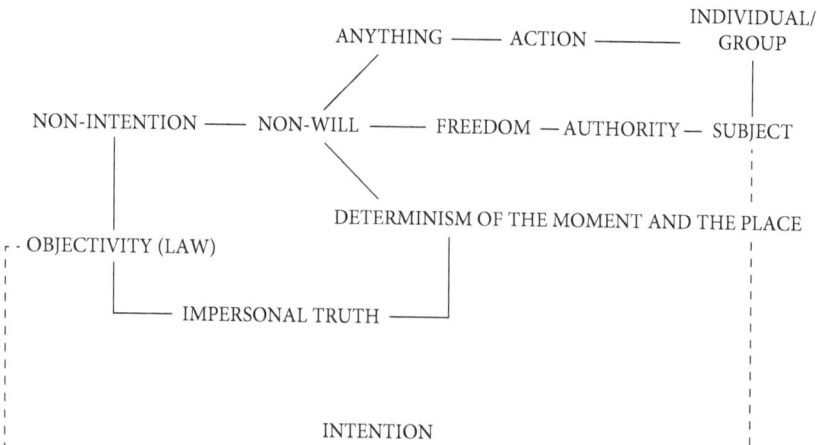

Diagram 10

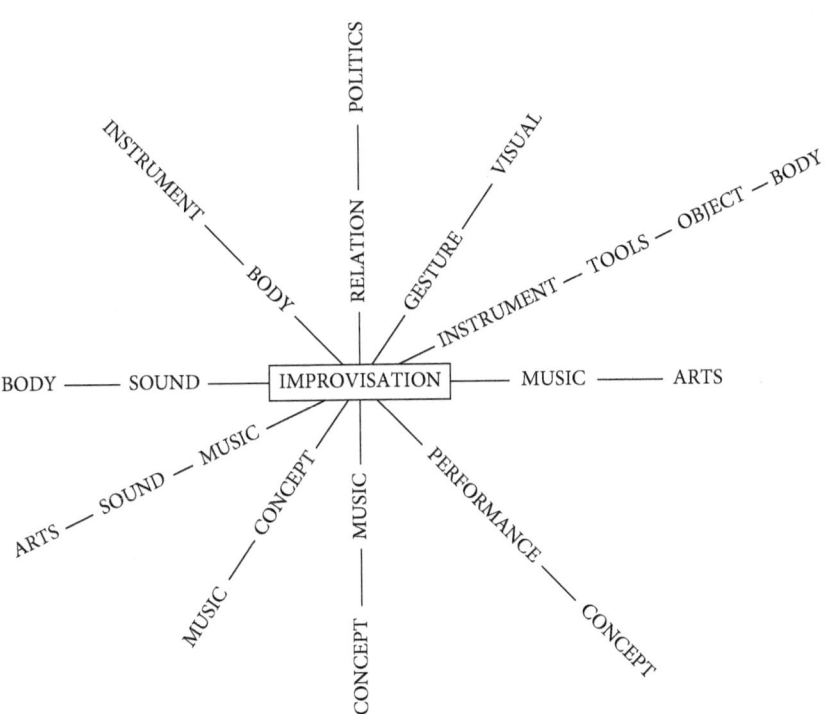

www.ingramcontent.com/pod-product-compliance
Lightning Source LLC
Chambersburg PA
CBHW052041300426
44117CB00012B/1913